kylie
confidential

'Style is your own interpretation of what you are
and what you project to others.'

KYLIE MINOGUE,
July 1998

author's acknowledgements

Thanks to everyone who has helped me with this book and made it such fun to do. They include Paul Marcolin, Peter Holt, Jane Oddy, Spencer Bright, Alison Jane Reid, Rick Sky, Frank Thorne and Cassandra Hooper. Some people wanted to remain anonymous because of the very small world nature of the record business and I have respected their wishes. I hope they enjoy the book.

Doug Booth was an enormous help in Melbourne and Lizzie Clachan did invaluable research in London. I would also like to mention the many excellent websites devoted to all things Kylie – particularly Limbo and Confide – which were of great interest to me.

At Michael O'Mara Books my thanks to Michael O'Mara for commissioning the book, my editor Karen Dolan for her encouragement and sharp memory, Gabrielle Mander, Toby Buchan, Rhian McKay, Judith Palmer, Bryony Evens and Camille Debruyne. Thanks are also due to Diana Briscoe for compiling the discography.

At Simon & Schuster my thanks to Jonathan Atkins for his commitment to the book, my editor Rumana Haider for her enthusiasm and good humour and David Mann for his stunning cover design. I am indebted to Adrian Morris for Kylie's fascinating birth chart which begins this book.

I am also grateful to Zoë Lawrence for helping with the manuscript and keeping me sane.

kylie
confidential

SEAN SMITH

POCKET
BOOKS

This paperback edition first published by Pocket Books, 2003
An imprint of Simon & Schuster UK Ltd
A Viacom Company

1 3 5 7 9 10 8 6 4 2

Simon & Schuster UK Ltd
Africa House
64-78 Kingsway
London WC2B 6AH

www.simonsays.co.uk

Simon & Schuster Australia
Sydney

A CIP catalogue record for this book is available from the British Library

ISBN 0-7434-6801-5

Printed and bound in Great Britain by
Bookmarque, Croydon, Surrey.

photograph acknowledgements

Page 1: Richard Young/Rex Features; page 2: (*top*) The *Sun*/Rex Features, (*left*) Richard Young/Rex
Features, (*bottom*) London Features International; page 3: Richard Stonehouse/Camera Press
London; page 4: (*top*) The *Sun*/Rex Features, (*left*) Rex Features, (*bottom*) London Features
International; page 5: Rex Features; page 6: (*upper*) © allaction.co.uk, (*lower*) S.I.N/Corbis UK Ltd;
page 7: (*upper*) Edward Hirst/Rex Features, (*lower*) Brian Rasic/Rex Features; page 8: (*top*)
Sygma/Corbis UK Ltd, (*top right*) Julian Makey/Rex Features, (*centre left*) Photo B.D.V/Corbis UK
Ltd, (*bottom*) Theodore Wood/Camera Press London; page 9: Hellestad Rune Sygma/Corbis UK
Ltd; page 10: Dallas Kilponen/The *Sun Herald*/Fairfax Photo Library; page 11: Peter Carrette/Rex
Features; page 12: Mark Shenley/Camera Press London; page 13: Nikos/Rex Features; page 14:
Brian Rasic/Rex Features; page 15: (*top*) Rex Features, (*bottom*) Mark Shenley/Camera Press
London; page 16: (*top*) Dan Merson/Camera Press London, (*bottom*) David Fisher-DF/London
Features International; page 17: Fairfax Photo Library; page 18: Brendan Beirne/Rex Features;
page 19: (*main image*) Photo B.D.V/Corbis UK Ltd, (*inset*) Rex Features; page 20: (*top*) Richard
Young/Rex Features, (*bottom*) Bigpicturesphoto.com; page 21: Richard Young/Rex Features; page
22: Richard Young/Rex Features; page 23: (*top*) SIPA/Rex Features, (*bottom*) Stewart Mark/Camera
Press London; page 24: William Conran/Camera Press London; page 25: (*top left*) Stephane
Cardinale/Imapress/Camera Press London, (*top right*) Bigpicturesphoto.com, (*bottom*) Shamim Ferd
Sygma/Corbis UK Ltd; page 26: Javed Jafferji/Camera Press London; page 27: (*top*) PA Photos,
(*bottom*) Sygma/Corbis UK Ltd; page 28: (*top*) Richard Young/Rex Features, (*bottom*) PA Photos;
page 29: Bigpicturesphoto.com; page 30: Hellestad Rune Sygma/Corbis UK Ltd; page 31: (*top*)
Bigpicturesphoto.com, (*left*) Bigpicturesphoto.com, (*bottom*) Bigpicturesphoto.com; page 32:
Richard Young/Rex Features.

With grateful thanks to Zooid Pictures Limited and the individual agencies listed above.

contents

introduction

Let me declare an interest. Kylie Minogue is terrific. I cannot believe that the girl I first wrote about when she was performing the Stock, Aitken and Waterman songbook has just been voted Number 2 in a poll of the greatest women in music history. My first task in compiling this portrait of Kylie was to take a step back from the general Minogue euphoria and try and work out how it happened: how on earth has Kylie journeyed from curly topped figure of fun, churning out ersatz tunes for a teeny disco market to superstar icon with astonishing appeal across a whole spectrum of ages? Has it happened by accident or by design, with talent or with luck? The more investigation I conducted into Kylie's rich life the more I realised I was attempting a very difficult jigsaw puzzle.

From friends and relations and people I bumped into in the coffee shop I compiled a list of the ten most asked questions about Kylie – the one's that will never be answered in a friendly fanzine style interview. It's not a huge, definitive poll. They are in no particular order of importance but I used them as a guide to make sure I found out what everyone wanted to know about her and could subsequently include in **Kylie Confidential**.

What is the secret of her survival in the notoriously fickle world of pop?

The biggest weapon in Kylie's celebrity armoury is her understanding of the importance of 'image'. Even the very greatest like Elvis and The Beatles began with a carefully presented image: Elvis was the dangerous 'white' rock and roll star at a time when all the cutting edge talent was black; The Beatles were lovable mop-tops from Liverpool. The Rolling Stones have managed to stretch a bad boy image to last nearly 40 years.

Kylie exploited her image from the very early days of Stock, Aitken and Waterman. She revealed, 'I changed my image so much because that's all I had control over.' Kylie was not allowed much musical clout then but she could choose what she wore in a video. The importance of changing image, especially for a female artist, is that it prevents the public from becoming bored. Madonna is brilliant at this but Kylie can match her. Kylie's gold hot pants which launched her bottom on a gasping world in the Spinning Around video have become one of the legends of pop – a masterstroke.

From that point on, with the help of her style guru William Baker, Kylie has become a fashion icon. In September 2002 she was voted 'Woman of the Year' in the Elle Style Awards which is about as good as it gets for a female celebrity. Kylie cannot afford to stand still. The white 'scene of crime' suit she wore for the video of 'Can't Get You Out Of My Head' was sensational but she cannot wear it again. She will need a whole new wardrobe for her next album.

Can Kylie sing?

Compared with some of the tuneless wonders in the charts today Kylie is practically Maria Callas. She has had to work at it. Right from the start of 'The Loco-Motion' in Australia Kylie has never been anything less than the complete professional – everyone who has worked with her has been impressed with that quality. For her first demo Kylie was nursed through the song line by line. That was the only time – now she enjoys a reputation as a bit of a one-take wonder. Pete Waterman observed, 'We would literally only get an hour to work with her, but we always got things done.' A Kylie vocal is instantly recognisable which is half the battle for a singer.

How tall is Kylie?

Kylie is a hair over 5ft tall, the same height as her mother Carol. She has had to suffer all the barbs about her height even though she is the same size as Geri Halliwell. She is in perfect proportion but like a computer image scaled down to 75 per cent size. Fortunately for Kylie the camera does not know how big or small you are. She fills the frame and the camera has always loved her.

Why does Kylie have such bad luck with men?

Poor Kylie. She really has to put up with a great deal of unflattering scrutiny of her relationships and her love life. However, none of her relationships ever seem to last more than about two years. She has declared love for three men over the years: Michael Hutchence, Stephane Sednaoui and most recently James Gooding. A different sort of celebrity woman (the Liz Taylor syndrome) might well have married all three and be three times divorced. In September 2002 the papers even carried reports that Gooding and Kylie had 'married' in a secret ceremony on Bali. The less romantic reality was that they had already been split for some time. By the end of the month Gooding had been cast as some sort of villain for apparently ditching his two-timing girlfriend. The general consensus was that Kylie could do much better than a male model with a roving eye.

It just goes to show how much we regard Kylie as a sister, to be protected from one and all.

It was suggested to me during my investigations that Kylie had a bit of a commitment problem – almost to the extent of being phobic about it. But many people, especially celebrities, drift from one relationship to the next. Robbie Williams is considered Jack the Lad moving from girl to girl but he is only five years younger than Kylie. It's a male/female thing. Kylie has stood accused of being defined by the men in her life but no man she has ever been out with could seriously be said to have been more famous than she. The men are being defined by Kylie – not the other way round. And that includes Michael Hutchence – nonsensically perceived as her corrupter.

How much cosmetic surgery has Kylie had?

This is a favourite girl question. No celebrity is ever going to admit to anything other than beauty achieved by entirely natural means. It is always put down to revolutionary diet, yoga, natural skin products from the Amazon jungle or going to the gym six hours a day. It is never attributed to skilful wielding of a surgeon's knife, sucking out of unwanted fat by a machine, injections or the introduction of silicone implants. And lawyers are always watching!

Kylie looks incredible for 34 so the botox/collagen spotting brigade have been keeping close watch. Kylie, however, was very upset at the suggestions in the UK press following the Brit awards last February that her famous bottom had been surgically enhanced. That was below the belt! Incidentally, the fixation with Kylie's rear is getting out of hand. Her waxwork at Madame Tussaud's has suffered serious erosion because of people fondling her bottom. Kylie herself is fed up with people gawping at it on the street.

Is Kylie good in bed?

She is fantastic although, alas, I only have that third-hand. Kylie has never been the 'girl-next-door'. It was one of the first myths I was able to dispel. The girl next door was Charlene Mitchell, her character from Neighbours. Paul Marcolin who had a sexual encounter with Kylie when she was sweet sixteen recalled that she knew exactly how to please a man. He just shut his eyes and let her get on with it. Michael Hutchence, a rock singer with the reputation of a huge sexual appetite, described Kylie as the best f*** in the world. The lady herself once gave herself a performance mark of seven out of ten, eight on especially good occasions. The reason she did not mark herself higher? She believes there should always be room for improvement.

Do Kylie and Dannii really hate each other?

This is another key myth in the Kylie story. There have always been rumours that the two girls are sworn enemies but, according to the people I spoke to who knew them both, it is completely untrue. There has always been rivalry there dating back to when they were both little girl 'wannabes'. Dannii was the more famous youngster and Kylie was often introduced as 'Dannii's elder sister' which must have spurred her ambition.

The Minogue girls did once give a show-stopping performance of 'Sisters Are Doing It For Themselves' and the track would be a certain number one but it is not likely to happen anytime soon. Kylie has always been very careful not to become some sort of double act with Dannii. It would be very easy to fall in to that trap so, although they both live in London, they are rarely seen out together preferring to talk on the phone and meet up at their homes.

They were due to release their last singles on the same day, October 28th. But Kylie decided to hold back 'Come Into MY World' for a week or two.

Will Kylie ever marry and have children?

In 1989 Kylie said she wanted a church wedding and three children – two girls and a boy, just like her own parents. At the time she was 21 and she is now 34. She has been asked the question a million times since then as if her adoring public are willing her to settle down. She has had to deny she was going to marry James Gooding in early 2002. Her sister Dannii maintains that Kylie is still a young woman and not worried about the ticking of her biological clock. Today's reality is that Kylie may well have children but not get married. There have been whispers that she is going to find time in 2003 to have a baby. Her anatomy is being closely watched for any signs of a baby bump. We will only know when Kylie chooses to tell us.

She must be very rich so why does she still bother?

Being a star is a job for life. All the paraphernalia that goes with being a grade A superstar is like the most powerful of drugs. It is addictive and Kylie is hooked. She has huge drive and motivation and an inner steel. She has always possessed those qualities and is prepared to push herself both mentally and physically to the very limits of her brittle self. Just a couple of weeks after stories appeared this autumn of a breakdown and a period of rest in Australia she was back smiling for the cameras at Heathrow and then off to Paris to fulfil an engagement at a motor show. Kylie has spent the last couple of years – arguably the most successful in her career – teetering on the edge of tears of exhaustion.

Kylie has been a millionairess practically since her teens and, thanks to her father Ron, is very astute where money is concerned. Her fortune is at least £12 million and rising. It may be double that. 'Kylie Minogue Limited' as I like to call it, is her business and, as such, is a long term commitment. She was named the 29th most powerful person in the music business in October 2002 – amazing for the girl who made tea for Stock, Aitken and Waterman. Now that she has reached the status of an institution she is not going to give it all up.

What will Kylie be doing when she is 50?

Her star chart (see 'Kylie Predictable') reveals that 40 will in fact be the age when Kylie will reach a crossroads in her life. She has always kept her private and public life separate and, as far as I can tell, her career up until now has always come first. There was a reality jolt at the end of 2001 when her father Ron needed an operation for prostate cancer. Kylie comes across as a bona fide 'the show must go on' star. At the start of her 2002 UK tour she was reported to have bravely taken to the stage despite backstage tears at the break up with James Gooding.

My guess is that Kylie will always be a star and will always be a performer. It's what she knows and what she does. How about headlining a musical on the West End stage or on Broadway? That would be something.

SEAN SMITH, NOVEMBER 2002

Kylie: Born 28 May 1968

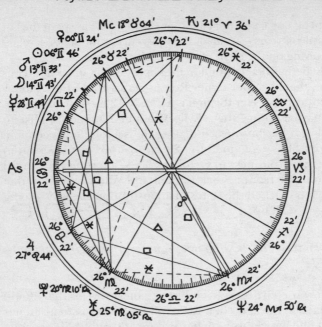

Planet		⊙	☽	☿	♀	♂	♃	♄	♅	♆	♇
SUN	⊙										
MOON	☽	♂									
MERCURY	☿										
VENUS	♀	♂									
MARS	♂	♂	♂								
JUPITER	♃			⚹	□						
SATURN	♄	∠									
URANUS	♅			□	△						
NEPTUNE	♆				☍		□		⚹		
PLUTO	♇		□					⊼	♂		
ASCENDANT	As								□	⚹	△
MIDHEAVEN	Mc									☍	△

kylie
predictable

Kylie is many people rolled into one . . .

Unequivocally, Kylie's chart reveals her to be exceptionally creative and musical. She has three planets forming a T-square with a potential for enormous energy. They are artistic Venus, bountiful Jupiter, and Neptune, ruler of the performing arts. This formation will bring challenges throughout Kylie's life, but if she confronts them, she will have the capacity to fulfil all that she desires.

Personality

Kylie's sun sign is Gemini, the sign of communication and versatility. Ruled by the planet Mercury, Geminis have 'mercurial' minds and an eloquent way with words. They are intelligent and quick-witted but can become impatient when others do not think as fast as they do. They are easily bored, shifting from one task to another without necessarily finishing the first. They live on their nerves, which can often cause unnecessary tension and strain in their day-to-day lives. The worst fault of Geminis is superficiality, but that is offset by their ability to be witty and engaging companions.

Including the Sun, Kylie has an incredible five planets in Gemini, which greatly increases the strength of the sign's qualities. She is a powerful example of a Gemini. With the Moon in Gemini, she will always want to be a free spirit; Mercury's influence gives her the desire to pursue new ideas; Venus intensifies her ability to project her artistic qualities; Mars makes her express her ideas forcefully and, crucially, in a very competitive way. Kylie's ambitious spirit may be the cause of misunderstandings and fallings-out within her working environment.

Her Gemini Sun/Moon combination makes Kylie lively, flirtatious, childlike and thoughtful. But it also makes her moody. The number of planets in Gemini, however, signifies that her head will always rule her heart.

With Cancer as her Ascendant, Kylie can be touchy when things go wrong and is a constant worrier about anything, large or small. Despite her sensitive and caring nature, she can appear very cool and detached and has a powerful desire for privacy. She wants the best of both worlds – not only material rewards in her work but also the comfort of emotional security. She likes to be seen as dependable and trustworthy, but there are other key features in her chart that cause these admirable goals to remain elusive.

Born at the time of a New Moon, Kylie will always have an enthusiasm for new beginnings. The Moon, Venus and Mars all exert a powerful influence on her Sun in the house of hopes and wishes and, as a result, Kylie has the strong feeling that she can achieve anything which, when combined with her high level of motivation, leads to inevitable success. She does, however, have a tendency to gloss over her own imperfections while, at the same time, believing she is the victim of all kinds of imaginary slights.

Kylie's is an original talent, clearly indicated by the square Mercury makes with Uranus, but there is also a disturbing aspect between Venus and Neptune which suggests she has a boundless and dangerous imagination. So much so, in fact, that her vision frequently becomes clouded and, with Jupiter also making a stressful aspect to Neptune, dreams may never be realized. Throughout Kylie's chart there is a fear of competition and the indication that she constantly compares herself to others, leading to feelings of great dissatisfaction. Inevitably her life is full of friction and difficulties.

Kylie should concentrate on her own abilities and examine her life in the context of the progress she has personally made.

Relationships

Kylie has a tendency to be unnerved by close and intimate relationships. Like most Gemini Sun/Moon characters, she believes feelings are a dark uncontrollable force. Unfortunately for her, nebulous Neptune, in a pivotal part of her chart, can cloud her judgement when choosing a partner. She may suspect him of dishonesty or, conversely, she may herself be extremely gullible and easily influenced. Neptune in the area of the chart ruling emotions indicates that her expectations will rarely be fulfilled because she is seeking an ideal man.

Kylie's chart shows there is a confusion over love and aims in life. **She has an enormous need to love, to be loved and be seen as lovable**, but her strong aspirations blur her idea of love. She is desperately anxious to establish a close relationship but she has problems trying to cope with such a thing. She asserts herself so strongly in her career and other aspects of her life to make up for the lack of emotional satisfaction.

Most people born under the sign of Gemini have some difficulty with emotions and may never deal with their personal problems. They have to confront the 'shadow' as the influential psychologist Jung called it. Problems become much worse when emotional anxieties form part of the individual's shadow. Kylie must learn to be more candid in her relationships, to discuss her problems openly and blow away any cloudy thoughts.

Work and Career

Throughout her career Kylie will always have the ability to reinvent herself and make changes and, as a Gemini, this doesn't frighten her. With Uranus, the planet of change, making a sympathetic link with her Cancer Ascendant, she revels in new possibilities and is fascinated by novel, rebellious ideas. There is little chance that she will ever be boring.

Kylie is ambitious for recognition. She can achieve and maintain this through hard work and her innate creative ability. Mercury's influence allows her to display an enquiring mind as well as a receptive one. She will not settle for staying in the same place in her career. Financial security is important, however, enabling Kylie to invest wisely in establishing a home where she can flourish and feel safe.

Kylie needs a trusted adviser to help her. This is essential because of the strong parental influence in her chart. Only by recognizing this will she find success is absolutely secure.

Influences from her Past

Undoubtedly there is a great deal of family influence in Kylie's chart but there are some puzzling contradictions. Traditionally, with the Moon in Gemini, one would assume her mother was a driving force in stimulating development, if an emotionally distant one. Kylie's Sun/Venus conjunction, however, indicates that while Kylie was the apple of her father's eye, her parents played a unified role in her life. There were also times when Kylie would have been blamed for things at home which were not her fault, a fate which often befalls the eldest child. As a result she remains sensitive to criticism as an adult.

A Gemini Moon suggests that **a desire to succeed would have been instilled in Kylie from an early age**, but there would have been little nurturing. This indication is supported by the strong square between stern Saturn and her Ascendant. Home life would have been rather austere with an emphasis on perfect behaviour and an expectation that Kylie would perform tasks and chores without question. Normally, Saturn relates to influences from the father but, in her case, this could represent either parent, whichever one is the more dominant. Kylie would have had enormous respect for her parents but perhaps there was little tenderness at home. The positive effect of this upbringing is that it gave Kylie an indefatigable persistence, regardless of any setback she might experience.

During Kylie's life there have been several instances of great change. The first was in late 1979 through to the early part of 1980 when she was eleven. Uranus, the planet of change, linking up with the powerful Venus/Jupiter/Neptune connection in her chart, would have brought a period of creativity, of stimulating opportunities and the realization of what these chances might lead to in the future. The relative position of these three planets in her chart, however, also highlights the area of her life where she will suffer the greatest setbacks – her shared emotions, psychological makeup and private world. In 1990 and throughout 1991, 'transiting' Neptune made a very stressful aspect to two of the most significant of her natal planets, the Moon and Mars. During this time she would have experienced great psychological confusion, emotional problems and conflicting desires. Her experiences from this period of her life would have had a lasting effect on the way she presented herself to the outside world – her image.

In 1997 and 1998 Kylie would have been experiencing the effects of her first 'Saturn return'. Saturn is the great testing planet and the first time it returns to the same position in the birth chart usually occurs at about the age of twenty-nine. It brings, or should bring, the realization that a substantial part of your life has passed and heralds a desire for change. When, in 2000, the planet subsequently passed over the area of Kylie's chart that governs her career she would have taken stock of her life so far, evaluated her achievements and decided whether she was happy with the path she was pursuing.

It was vital that Kylie learned from the testing times she encountered in 1990 and 1991, cut out the dead wood in her life from 1997 and 1998 and made the correct decision enabling her to move forward in 2000. If she has managed to do all of these three things then she should have prepared herself for anything – almost – the Fates may care to throw at her in the years ahead.

Kylie's Future

Her biggest test will come in 2008 when she reaches the age of forty. It will last for two years. By then she may well have transformed herself yet again into something totally different from the Kylie we know today. Her future happiness can be assured if she places her faith in people she can trust, both in her private life and in her career. She should keep these two areas of her life distinctly separate and not allow one to cloud the other. 'Can't Get You Out Of My Head' is a sentiment better suited to a Kylie song title than the ups and downs of her real life.

ADRIAN MORRIS, 2002

Notes

Ascendant (As) or Rising Sign
Kylie is a Gemini (her sun sign) with Cancer rising. In other words, the **Ascendant** (Cancer) was the sign of the zodiac which was rising on the eastern horizon at the moment of birth. The zodiac is the imaginary 'belt' in the sky made up of the twelve signs encircling the earth.

aspect The configuration of various points on the birth chart in relation to one another. The chart is divided up into 360 degrees and one planet is in '**aspect**' to another when there is a specific number of degrees or angle between them.

conjunction An **aspect** in which two points, such as two **planets**, are close enough for their energies to combine.

Midheaven (Mc) The symbolic astrological point in the sky immediately above where the individual was born. It represents the career, goals and objectives in life.

natal Refers to the position of a **planet** at the time of birth.

opposition An **aspect** of 180 degrees between two points, for example between two **planets**, in a birth chart. It can be inharmonious and challenging.

planets The word **planet** originates from the Greek for 'wander', which explains why both the Sun and the Moon are classified as **planets** in astrology because they are seen to 'wander' across the sky. They are, of course, perceived differently in astronomy where they are identified as merely a star and a moon respectively. The other, more traditional **planets** used in astrology are Mercury, Venus, Mars, Jupiter, Saturn, Uranus, Neptune and Pluto.

Saturn return The period when the planet Saturn returns to its original **natal** position in the birth chart. Taking about 29.46 years to complete an orbit of the Sun we experience a **Saturn return** twice in our lives, once around the age of twenty-nine and the other just before we reach sixty. It indicates a time of change and reassessment.

square An **aspect** of 90 degrees between two points, such as **planets**, in a birth chart. Like the opposition it can be inharmonious and challenging.

T-square When three **planets** form a T-shape, two directly opposite each other and the third at right angles to them. The formation brings challenges throughout life, but once confronted, can produce personal power.

transiting Identifies **planets** that are moving across the sky as opposed to the **planets** whose position is fixed in the birth chart. By considering the interaction between the **transiting planets** and those in the charts, the astrologer can predict certain conditions that are likely to take place.

kylie
motivated

THE CROWD WAS ECSTATIC. Here were some of the cast from their favourite television soap, *Neighbours*, letting their hair down and treating them to a classic song, 'The Loco-Motion' by Little Eva. And out front was Charlene, aka Kylie Minogue, the most popular actress on TV. Her pocket size concealed a pair of powerful lungs and she could really hold a tune. They had already wowed the crowd with 'I Got You Babe'; now someone on stage had said, 'Let's do another song', and they went straight into the sixties' dance hit. The band knew how to play it, and Kylie knew all the words – a legacy, no doubt, of singing it a million times into her hairbrush at home with sister Dannii. It was an impromptu *tour de force*. Or so it seemed. The reality was that Kylie had never heard the song until a short time before and had been practising hard to get it right.

Kylie has often said that much of her career was a 'happy accident'. One of her favourite observations about her success comes from her father Ron, who told her that she was lucky because she always skipped steps one to eight and went straight to numbers nine and ten. 'Miraculously I get away with it,' she confessed. It is a nice story, but its flippancy masks the drive and ambition, and the hours of hard graft she has devoted to learning lines, practising dance steps until her feet are covered in blisters and plasters, and grappling with difficult melodies, so that her performances are never less than completely polished.

So strong was Kylie's desire to be a performer that she had paid her own money – part of her fee from her acting breakthrough on *The Henderson Kids* – to record two demos for the executives of *Young Talent Time*. She chose 'Dim All the Lights', a 1979 dance hit by Donna Summer, and 'New Attitude' by Patti LaBelle, reflecting her early interest in black disco music. Donna Summer was the Queen of Disco with 'I Feel Love' and 'Love to Love You Baby' – hardly girl-next-door songs. Coincidentally, Donna was to find a career revival under the guidance of Stock, Aitken and Waterman who would be so instrumental in taking Kylie to the very top. Patti LaBelle had sung the original version of 'Lady Marmalade' in 1975. In 2001 it was a number-one hit for Christina Aguilera, Mya, Pink and Li'l Kim, whose version was recorded for the film *Moulin Rouge*, which featured Kylie in a cameo role as The Green Fairy.

Kylie was seventeen when she did those first recordings and not yet in *Neighbours*. Nothing came from them at first, other than a friendship with one of the producers who heard them. He was called Greg Petherick, one of the forgotten men of the Kylie Minogue story. He never forgot the talent of the girl who, throughout her early career, was usually referred to as 'Dannii Minogue's elder sister,' an unwanted sobriquet that spurred her on to try to match her younger sister's achievements.

The following year saw Kylie firmly established in the cast of *Neighbours*, enjoying a secret relationship with Jason Donovan and, for the first time, emerging from her sister's shadow. Some of her fellow cast members shared her dreams of music stardom – Jason, Guy Pearce (now a successful Hollywood actor) and Craig McLachlan. In that rather macho Aussie way, they decided to form a band, Ramsay Street's answer to INXS. They thought it might be good to have some of the girls along for decoration and occasional vocals, so Kylie became involved. They had absolutely no idea that Kylie would soon leave them stuck in the starting blocks while she ran the whole 100 metres.

The original 'Neighbours Band' consisted of Peter O'Brien (Shane Ramsay), Alan Dale (Jim Robinson) and Paul Keane (Des Clarke). It began as a once-a-week diversion after filming had finished on a Thursday. Greg Petherick would book a downtown rehearsal room for the boys to use for their 'jam session'. He invited Kylie and Jason down to join them. Kylie sat quietly, watching, taking everything in, playing a little tambourine while Jason sang, strummed guitar and did his impersonation of Michael Hutchence. 'It was interesting, to say the least' said Greg. Jason, however, soon got bored. Not so Kylie, who started to sing along a little. Then one week she asked Greg if he could find a song specifically for her to sing with the band. He rummaged around in his record collection and produced 'The Loco-Motion', performed by Little Eva (the stage name of a young black singer from Bellhaven, North Carolina, called Eva Boyd), a bit of a one-hit-wonder. The song was a product of the great song-writing team of Carole King and Gerry Goffin and had been a huge hit in 1964. Kylie loved it instantly. Every week she would practise and everyone agreed it was a show-stopper.

Kylie had joined *Neighbours* in March 1986 and was a big hit with viewers. One of her early story-lines involved the efforts of Scott (Jason Donovan) and Mike (Guy Pearce) to form a band and make a demo. They asked Charlene (Kylie) to sing backing vocals. And with the delicious irony of art imitating life, they played the demo for a record company boss who thought the boys were rubbish, but loved Charlene's singing. In August, her old mentor from *The Henderson Kids*, Alan Hardy, approached her to take part in a special fundraiser for his favourite Australian Rules Football team, Fitzroy, at the Dallas Brooks Hall in Melbourne. He had no idea about 'The Loco-Motion' sessions with Greg and the boys, but he did recall how Kylie was always singing on the set of his show. Kylie and her co-star Nadine Gardner would spend hours together, listening to each other's records and copying the tunes. They proudly announced that when they were older, 'We're going to be singers!' Hardy never forgot the on-set opinion that the two girls had great voices and so he persuaded Kylie to perform the Sonny and Cher standard with local actor John Waters. On the night, he recalled, Kylie was very nervous and shy about performing. But one of the outstanding qualities Kylie possesses is the determination to overcome any nerves to give a great performance – the art of being a star. She was a sensation with an audience which was incredulous that Charlene from *Neighbours* could have such a great voice. Their response gave Kylie confidence. When they started up 'The Loco-Motion' as an encore, she was the star of the show. Within a year, Kylie's version of the song would be the biggest-selling Australian single of the decade.

There is a famous saying in golf: 'the more I practise, the luckier I get.' It could apply to Kylie's career.

★

Kylie was a natural performer from a very early age. Normally, one might take such precociousness with a pinch of salt. It sounds good to think of Kylie and Dannii as suburban Shirley Temples spurring each other on to ever more glorious heights of cuteness. When Kylie was still in pigtails her mother Carol took her to a small annual Festival of Music and Art at a country town called Dandenong, just outside Melbourne. It was a showcase for serious local talent but, as a diversion, there was a piano competition for talented tots. Kylie bounced on stage, played 'Run, Rabbit, Run' and carried off a prize. She gave the judges one of her perkiest smiles and they were completely charmed by her.

Even though Dannii was three years younger than Kylie she was, if anything, even more precocious than her big sister. They had singing and dancing lessons together and learnt to play the piano. Whenever their parents went out for the evening and their grandparents babysat, the two sisters would treat them to impromptu performances of their favourite songs at the time. Usually the choice would be Abba, who were enormously popular in Australia in the mid-seventies. But sometimes they would showcase songs in their parents' collection of records by The Beatles and The Rolling Stones. The mind boggles at the thought of the two little girls belting out 'Satisfaction', but they were on safer ground with the Queen of Australian pop Olivia Newton-John. As Sandy in the film *Grease*, Newton-John prompted a million girls to declare 'You're The One That I Want' into their hairbrushes. Needless to say, Kylie dreamed of one day being just like her heroine Olivia.

Danielle was always the more exuberant of the sisters, a characteristic easily misconstrued as being pushy. A popular misconception is that the two are, and always have been, bitter rivals and do not get on. Their rivalry is what drives them on to match each other's success. These days Dannii is a long way behind Kylie in terms of worldwide popularity but, in many ways, their careers are mirror images of one another – they both made their breakthroughs while young, and both have remained household names throughout their teens and twenties. They are both currently single, with a string of unhappy relationships behind them. They have both set up home in London, thousands of miles away from their family home. They are both all-singing, all-dancing gay icons. They are both in their thirties now and look so alike they could be twins. And a month after Kylie was number one in the UK with 'Can't Get You Out of My Head', Dannii reached number two with 'Who Do You Love Now?', a collaboration with dance act Riva. They were very nearly in direct competition for once over the release of their autumn singles in 2002. The tracks were originally scheduled to be in the shops on the same day. No sooner had the newspapers eagerly reported that there would finally be chart rivalry between the two than Kylie delayed putting out 'Come Into My World', her fourth single release from Fever. It may be that for once Kylie was not certain whether she would come out on top because 'Put The Needle On It' was Dannii's first single since 'Who Do You Love Now?' and therefore appeared a much fresher sound.

Poor Dannii seems always to be half a step behind. But it was not always so. Until Kylie joined *Neighbours*, Dannii was by far the more famous of the two. And Kylie owed her start in showbusiness to her younger sister. Thanks to family connections – their Aunt Suzette was an actress – Dannii was asked to audition at an independent Melbourne production company, called Crawford's, and, in order to keep the peace, their mother Carol decided to take Kylie along as well. They both did well, but Dannii was too young for the part they had in mind, so they cast ten-year-old Kylie. The show was *The Sullivans*, a popular, if dire, soap of the seventies set during World War Two. Kylie played Carla, a Dutch orphan girl, who befriended a group of Australian troops. Mercifully, she was killed off after a few episodes. That did not stop *The Sullivans* being rerun in the late eighties, purely so that a devoted audience could catch Kylie's debut.

Carol Minogue had to soothe Dannii's disappointment but her chance came later when, in the same series, they needed a Kylie lookalike to play the part of Carla in a soldier's dream sequence. After *The Sullivans*, Kylie landed another small part in a series called *Skyways*, which was set in and around an airport. On set she met for the first time a goofy child called Jason Donovan. They played brother and sister, but all Kylie remembers is that he was 'really chubby with a bowl haircut'. The role only required a few weeks' work. *Skyways* was one of those wonderfully naff shoestring dramas. 'We have a plane crash,' recalled Kylie. 'You can see the tissue paper on the plane as they're rocking it. In one scene I am hugging a koala bear. Another character asks me something and you can see that I have absolutely no idea what I'm supposed to do.'

Perhaps unsurprisingly, *The Sullivans* and *Skyways* did not lead to Kylie being the most popular child actress in the land. She started senior school at Camberwell High and could only watch in awe as her sister became one of the most famous children in Australia. Dannii was the number-one star of *Young Talent Time*, one of the most popular shows in Australia. It was a much bigger show in Australia than *Neighbours* ever was, and cynical pop fans in the UK have no idea what a big star Dannii was at the time. One of the girls who danced on the show observed, 'Dannii was so popular. I can't believe Dannii has not made it as big as Kylie. She was always the favourite on *YTT*.'

Dannii's parents, particularly Carol, would always travel with the show when it went on the road. She was a permanent fixture in the audience, proudly watching her daughter perform. Greg Petherick was the floor manager on the show for eight years and knew the Minogue family quite well then. It was a friendship that would serve Kylie well in the future. Dannii even started her own clothing label, something Kylie, a keen dressmaker, had always wanted to do. The Dannii label consisted of her name with two little love hearts above the 'i's. When she, too, became famous, Kylie would often use a love heart next to her name.

While Dannii basked in the fame of *YTT*, Kylie was left to cope with a more mundane existence at school. She was no less ambitious, but there was nothing she could do at this stage to match her sister's success. Instead, she had to grin and bear it when she was introduced as Dannii's elder sister. But, although there has always been a healthy professional rivalry between the two Minogue girls, there is no suggestion that there has ever been a personal rift between them. Kylie has said that she never held Dannii's success against her, even if she found having a famous sister a bit of a strain at school. Paul Marcolin, who knew Kylie when she was sixteen, remembered her telling him how she helped Dannii answer the hundreds of letters she received every week from fans of *YTT*: 'There was no hint of jealousy. The impression I got was that they were great mates and that Kylie was more than willing to help Dannii. She said it quite proudly and I think it was a case of bigger sister helping out. She was quite enthused about it all.'

Kylie also told Marcolin about her 'big breakthrough,' a part in a new television series called *The Henderson Kids*. Once in a lifetime, something 'Hollywood' will happen that will lead to that big break. It happened to Daniel Radcliffe when he sat next to producer David Heyman at the cinema. Heyman was looking for a likely boy to cast in the role of Harry Potter and found him in these unlikely surroundings. Nothing like that ever happened to Kylie Minogue. Like a million other aspiring actors, she had to trudge around to auditions, hoping to catch the casting director's eye. On this occasion, she saw a newspaper advertisement seeking young actors aged between eleven and sixteen for a new television series. Auditions are potentially soul-destroying, but Kylie had an inner self-belief. Her co-star in *The Henderson Kids*, Nadine Garner, observed, 'She had a great sense of herself. There was this air of determination and quiet ambition.'

The Henderson Kids had a substantial budget for an Australian series at the time – Aus $3 million – and was going to be filmed on location in the countryside around Melbourne. If Kylie landed a role, it would mean a summer off school. Now that she was sixteen, she did not need her mother, Carol, to hold her hand at an audition. Instead, she put on one of the dresses she had made at home, did her own make-up and presented herself for consideration to the producer Alan Hardy and the director Chris Langman. Hardy could not believe that she was the same girl who had been in *The Sullivans* four years earlier. She was still very little but, in other ways, was a mature girl for her age. Garner, who was only fourteen, remembered that Kylie was aware of her femininity and was much more worldly than she.

Langman and Hardy decided to take a chance on Kylie. Both were impressed by her naturalness and thought she had the right personality for the part of Char, one of nine roles that required a young actor. Langman admitted that they cast her on a whim more than on any more substantial consideration. They were worried about her high-pitched voice and her tendency to lose her words somewhere in her teeth, but they hoped a voice coach could sort that out. Kylie was more worried by the fact that she had to dye her hair a bright shade of red for the role. Fortunately, she would not be running the daily gauntlet of comments from her classmates, and, every week, would apply a semi-permanent colour to her hair in the shower. By the time filming was finished, she could not wait to return to her natural dark blonde.

The plot of *The Henderson Kids* was hardly *War and Peace*, but it did allow Kylie to improve her acting skills and she worked very hard on the clarity of her speech and her emotional range. She put an enormous amount of energy into her role, something which, even at this early stage of her career, took its toll physically. She would burst into tears if anyone shouted at her on set and Nadine Gardner described her as 'fragile'. Nadine played the lead role of Tamara Henderson who, with her brother Paul, was taken in by their uncle after their mother died in a car crash. Their uncle was a policeman in a country town and the twelve-part series followed their adventures. Kylie's character, Char, lived in the town and became Tamara's best friend. She wore bright orange pants, colourful shirts that clashed horribly and spent most of the time chewing pink bubblegum: 'I'm so sick of this stuff, but it's part of my character,' admitted Kylie, making an early concession to complete professionalism.

Kylie was determined to do well and not pass up this chance by abusing the freedom of being away from home for the first time. When the cast was away on location, Langman was particularly impressed by the professionalism she displayed, despite her youth: 'She was always prepared, always on time, always focused and very much aware of her image and her look.' It is an observation of the 1984 vintage Kylie that could fittingly describe the Kylie Minogue of 2002/2003.

She did not waste the opportunity that *The Henderson Kids* gave her. She immediately starred in a one-off episode of another Crawford's series, *The Zoo Family*. She played Yvonne, an abused child, who was given a temporary home by a zoo caretaker. The episode was entitled 'Yvonne the Terrible' which is exactly what the child was. She lived up to her name by letting all the animals out of their cages and generally wrecking the zoo. At the end of the episode, she had a Damascene moment when she saw a young roo, which had also been a battered infant, return to mother kanga. Kylie impressed everybody. She would soon be seventeen, but convincingly played a very plausible twelve-year-old. Kylie was proving to be as adaptable in her acting career as she would be later as a singer. Gwenda Price, her producer on *The Zoo Family*, was convinced that Kylie would be a 'stayer'.

Kylie had already learnt one of the most important lessons of a show business career – you are only as good as your last role, or your last song, or your last performance. It was a lesson Dannii, too, would have to learn when *Young Talent Time* folded when she was sixteen. There is a world of difference between being the star of *YTT* and just being 'the kid who used to be on that TV show'. After *The Zoo Family*, Kylie was back on the audition trail – this time she beat fifty rivals to the leading female role in a six-part mini series, *Fame and Misfortune*. Kylie had to play a scheming minx, which she managed to do successfully, demonstrating that she was expanding her acting range. But she still hankered after a career as a singer, an ambition sharpened by her energetic sister's continued exposure.

During this period of her career, Kylie's verve and drive were forever being underestimated by people who could not see past a little girl trying to overcome her shyness. Kylie had true grit. She needed it when she went for a meeting with Alan Hardy, who was putting *The Henderson Kids II* into production. He sat her down and gently explained that she was being dropped because her part was being written out of the second series. Kylie was upset, of course, but she did not go home, mope and think that was the end of her bid for fame. Within four months she had grasped an even better opportunity with both hands.

★

Charlene Mitchell was a spitfire with a machine-gun tongue, which she would unleash should any man unwisely try to patronize her by calling her 'love' or, even worse, 'babe'. As we know from Kylie herself, her lack of height may have been a disadvantage on the sports field, but it was a definite plus when it came to playing young, spunky types. Charlene was a tomboy who left school to become a car mechanic, and seemed to spend most of her life in a pair of unflattering overalls that completely disguised the fact that there was a future sex symbol underneath. From such an unpromising situation, Kylie quickly turned Charlene into the most popular girl on Australian television and, more crucially, the most talked-about television character in Britain, where *Neighbours* would prove to be an eighties phenomenon. It would be just the platform she needed to launch her real ambition to be a chart-topping singer. Television exposure gives artists a real edge when it comes to having hit records – even the pub dog in a popular soap would probably have a number one if it released a record.

Neighbours was the brainchild of Reg Watson, head of drama for the Grundy Organization and the man responsible for such kitsch classics as *Prisoner Cell Block H* and *The Young Doctors*. He had also launched the soap *Crossroads* on an unsuspecting British audience before he moved to Australia, so had early experience of wooden sets filled with wooden actors. *Neighbours* was a brilliant idea because it was such a simple one, a story of everyday families and their ordinary lives. Watson had a lot of trouble convincing his bosses that it was not as dull as it sounded: 'When I told them about it, eyebrows were raised and thumbs were turned down. They had doubts about a concept which was simply about communication between parents and their children.'

Neighbours, which was originally to be called *One Way Street*, first hit television screens on Channel Seven in March 1985 when Kylie was just finishing filming *The Henderson Kids*. It was very innocent and non-controversial and seemed ideal daytime soap fodder. Watson was trying to recreate the warm feeling of life in a Brisbane suburb, where he grew up: 'If you were at the beach when it started raining, your neighbour would dash out, take your washing off the line and fold it ready for your return.' Sad things would happen in Ramsay Street, Erinsborough, but very few bad things. Surprisingly, Channel Seven dropped the show after just six months, but rival Channel Ten picked it up almost immediately and began airing it the following January, with a brief to Grundy that there should be a greater emphasis on younger characters. The target audience was teenage schoolgirls. That was the decision which would give Kylie her chance and would ultimately provide her with the fan base for music stardom.

The phenomenal appeal of Charlene Mitchell – she preferred to be called Lenny – proved not only to be Kylie's launch pad to international stardom but also confused the public into thinking that Kylie and Charlene were the same person. It was a classic case of life imitating art. It was Charlene, the classic girl-next-door with a feisty edge, who would be number one with 'The Loco-Motion' and 'I Should Be So Lucky'. It was not the ambitious Melbourne actress Kylie Minogue, a worldly-wise girl with a strong sense of destiny. When everybody gasped at her apparent transformation under the Machiavellian influence of Michael Hutchence, they saw it as Charlene who had so dramatically changed. How dare the dissolute rock star corrupt our girl from Ramsay Street!

Kylie was not Charlene Mitchell at all. She was not a bit like her. But, as she proved at her audition for the part, she could transform herself into Charlene as soon as the cameras rolled. Kylie was one of forty girls who auditioned and, superficially, she had not made much of an effort. She had no make-up on and her hair was a mess, but as talent director Jan Russ recalled, 'The camera loved her.' Kylie read for the part and her Charlene had just the right blend of wholesomeness and attitude – just as Kylie's own pop image would later have.

As always, Kylie was determined to make the best of the opportunity. It was, after all, five days a week of permanent exposure. The one advantage the young stars of *Neighbours* had over other familiar television faces was that promoting them was part of the publicity strategy to force the programme into the consciousness of the nation's youngsters. As a result, Kylie was out in the community right from the start, with personal appearances at shopping malls and youth centres. It is a tactic well-tried and tested in the pop world as a means of raising public awareness. Kylie was completely focused on what she could get out of *Neighbours* and was always the complete professional, even when her singing career took off. One of the show's directors, Andrew Friedman, told author Dino Scatena, 'Even at the height of her career with the music and the publicity, she was always there; always early, always keen and always willing to learn. She was always aware of her work.'

Kylie as the complete professional is a recurring theme, but it would be wrong to say that she was naïve enough to think of *Neighbours* as great art. Former pop columnist

Peter Holt remembered Kylie telling him that she could not wait to get out of the series and move to London. She revealed:

'It opened the showbiz door for me, but I can't wait to get out of it as soon as possible. I never liked soaps whether home-produced or imported and, to be honest, in spite of its success *Neighbours* is a bit rough. It's only the story of three families but everything happens to them! It's all rather implausible and sometimes I have to grit my teeth when I film an unlikely situation. I shudder at the speed it is turned out day after day. The writers are still working on the script when we start filming.

'Of course I am not complaining. *Neighbours* has been marvellous for me. I am just amazed that so many people are attracted to it. The trouble is that it gives a completely distorted view of normal life in Australia.'

Those are hardly the words of a woolly-headed pop poppet. Kylie was completely focused during her time with *Neighbours* and, not for the last time, she demonstrated a willingness to push her body to the limit of its fragile capabilities. As any actor in a soap will testify, it is always a punishing schedule. Her alarm clock would sound an unwelcome hurrah at 5.30am, a quick shower, breakfast on the run, make-up at 6.30am, rehearsals at 7.30am, a fifteen-minute run through, twenty minutes of filming and all that for one minute of the show. It would be an exhausting schedule for an Olympic athlete. And then there was publicity and the recording career she was so desperate to progress.

Kylie had only been in *Neighbours* for five months when she grabbed the chance to sing in public for the first time at Alan Hardy's football benefit. It was a triumph but it was only just a start. Kylie needed to get a record deal and, in order to do that, she needed to cut a demo. Her friend Greg

Petherick knew just the man to help – an engineer called Kaj Dahlstrom who ran a small recording studio in Melbourne. They decided that 'The Loco-Motion' was a good place to start and Dahlstrom laid down a backing track which had a funkier feel than Little Eva's version. There is nothing quite like the thrill of a trip to a studio to make a real record. Kylie was so excited when she made the journey across Melbourne to where the aptly named 'Sing Sing' studios were situated. The only problem was that when she arrived Kylie realized she could not sing in the same key as the backing track, so she had to go away again while Dahlstrom set about changing everything to the higher E Minor key. It took him a week and then Kylie came back. It was all new to her, but she responded well as he nursed her through the song line by line. Many artists – even very famous chart-toppers – have to record their songs line by line because their pitch is not perfect. But this was Kylie's first go and she would soon make sure she was as professional in this sphere as she was in every other aspect of her career. Pete Waterman, who would become her early pop Svengali, observed, 'She'd be exhausted half the time, but when she had to work, her whole personality would transform and she would light up. We would literally only get an hour at a time to work with her, but we always got things done.'

Dahlstrom hawked the demo around various record companies before there was a glimmer of interest from the Melbourne-based Mushroom Records. Michael Gudinski, the company chairman, sent a memo to two executives asking them to listen to the demo because he thought it was 'kinda cute' and might be worth taking a chance on. The crucial selling point for Mushroom was that Kylie had swiftly become one of the most recognizable faces in Australia. By the time they signed her up in the spring of 1987 Kylie, on the eve of her nineteenth birthday, had been voted Most Popular

Australian Actress at the annual Logies, the premier TV awards. The award was voted for by readers of the magazine *TV Week*, so it accurately reflected the strength of Kylie's following in the country. Afterwards, wearing a bright red leather skirt she had made herself, she admitted, 'I wish I had been better prepared. I was so nervous I forgot to thank all the people in the show.' It was a huge accolade for such a relative newcomer and, in her moment of triumph, Kylie had chastised herself for a lack of professionalism.

The executives at Mushroom were very smart where Kylie was concerned. Firstly, they wanted to introduce a sound similar to the one that had been dominating the British charts. They asked Pete Waterman if he could send someone to Melbourne to work with their engineers. Waterman and his partners Mike Stock and Matt Aitken already had an impressive list of UK hits to their name. Waterman agreed to 'loan' them Mike Duffy, a Canadian employee. The managing director of Mushroom had met up with Waterman at MIDEM, the international music trading conference held annually in Cannes, and had told him that they had signed up Kylie Minogue. Amusingly, Pete did not have a clue who she was.

Secondly, Amanda Pelman, who was in charge of Mushroom's promotion, and who was responsible for signing Kylie to the label, realized that the singing Kylie should complement the acting Kylie. There was a ready-made audience of young girls who could identify with the character of Charlene Mitchell and could will her to be successful as a popstar. Pelman wanted a million girls in a million bedrooms to sing 'The Loco-Motion' into their hairbrushes, just as Kylie herself had done when she imagined she was Olivia Newton-John. The character of Charlene was gearing up to the most famous episode of all time in *Neighbours* – her marriage to Scott, played by blonde, surfer-boy heart-throb Jason

Donovan. In the eyes of a spellbound viewing public, the wedding of these two fictional characters would be the biggest event since Prince Charles married Lady Diana Spencer. It is no coincidence that Mushroom were desperate for the first Kylie record to be released in tandem with this episode. This was cold-hearted, dead-eyed opportunism that was practically guaranteed to be a successful strategy. It was no 'happy accident' that Mike Duffy's version of 'The Loco-Motion' was released in mid-July 1987, just two weeks after millions of potential record buyers had watched the 'wedding of the year'.

Mike Duffy had only started work on the track the previous month so it had all been a bit of a rush, but they were able to use Kylie's original vocal from the 'Sing Sing' session. Pete Waterman, who had loved the Little Eva version, had encouraged Duffy to have a go at copying his sound. He conceded, 'It sounded roughly, very roughly, like one of ours.' Waterman gave him his blessing but was astonished a few short weeks later to be woken at 3am by an excited Duffy shouting down the phone that 'The Loco-Motion' was number one. He was so surprised he got up and put on the track. Duffy had sent him a final copy but he had not yet got round to listening to it. He played it through: 'It was rubbish, so I went back to bed.'

'The Loco-Motion' was number one in Australia for seven weeks, the biggest-selling record there of both 1987 and of the entire decade. It was time for Kylie, now with new agent Terry Blamey holding her hand, to step into the international market place. The Stock, Aitken and Waterman era was about to start, the next phase of Kylie's march to world domination, or 'happy accident' as she prefers to call it.

Confidentially: 'My life has always been geared to my career.'

kylie
sexed

T HE TALL, athletic schoolboy footballer was delighted when Kylie scribbled down her telephone number before giving him a little peck on the cheek goodnight. It had been a memorable party. It had been a memorable night. First they had kissed passionately, then she had told him her name was Kylie just before they had made love on a cold, concrete floor. And now the phone number. What a way for him to lose his virginity!

Kylie has always had a rebellious streak. She freely admits that she went through a wild stage as a teenager, smoking, drinking and giving her parents a tough time. A streak of defiance is a key ingredient of her survival. It goes a long way to explaining why she revelled in her relationship with Michael Hutchence, why she ditched Stock,

Aitken and Waterman and why, throughout her astonishing career, she has continued to shock and surprise. When she had found success, she admitted that she had had a 'really good upbringing' and that her parents, Ron and Carol, handled a recalcitrant girl with hormones flying in all directions in the way that most parents would have done: 'I used to think, I'm fourteen or fifteen and I'm old enough to do whatever I want. We used to have terrible fights. Nowadays, I can understand the things they did and I'd probably be the same if I had kids. I thought they were being incredibly unreasonable, and all my friends seemed to have so much more freedom.'

Many of the kids, especially the girls, at Camberwell High School were quite advanced for their age. Kylie used to work in a video store in Burke Road, Camberwell, on Saturday mornings to earn a few dollars to spend on clothes or, more often, the material to run up her own creations on the sewing machine at home. She had a real aptitude for dress-making and her interest in fashion stems from that time. She might well have made a successful career out of fashion if acting, and then singing, had not snared her first. At weekends she would join friends for parties or a night out at the pubs they knew would serve underage drinkers. One in particular was a hundred metres from the police station in the Kew district of Melbourne and, on the occasions when the local constabulary popped in to check IDs, it was always amusing to see the number of girls who would have an urgent need to visit the toilets. Other places to meet boys included the local swimming pools and bowling alley. Kylie has always loved swimming and, unsurprisingly, met one of her first boyfriends, David Wood, at a pool.

Unusually within her circle, the teenage Kylie was into funky, black music, like Donna Summer and especially Prince, her musical hero. Her favourite record, however, was 'Sexual Healing' by Marvin Gaye, one of the most erotic tracks of all time and perennially favourite background music for making love. Kylie clearly has always enjoyed sex. That was the strong impression she gave Paolo Marcolin on the unforgettable night when she became his first lover. She was also, at the age of sixteen years and two months, fully experienced in the ways of pleasing a man.

It was a cool August Friday night in the middle of an Australian winter and Paolo was in high spirits. Earlier he had played in the final match of the schools' football season in the state of Victoria. This was Australian Rules Football, a game that's best described as a combination of soccer and basketball. It can be very physical, although the participants do not wear all the padding and paraphernalia associated with gridiron. You have to be fit, and Paolo had the physique of a young man who took his sport seriously. His parents were first-generation immigrants from Italy and he had the advantage, as far as the young female population of Melbourne was concerned, of a traditional Latin look of dark hair and olive skin. Despite his obvious good looks, Paolo had spent his school years more interested in sport than girls and, as a result, was quite innocent for his age of just eighteen.

Everyone was on a high this particular evening because Marcellin College, his exclusive, Catholic private school in Melbourne's eastern suburbs, had won the match of the season against their arch rivals, Assumption College, and, as a result, were unofficial Victorian grammar school champions. Paolo, an attacking wingman, had played a blinding game, so was more than up for the celebrations planned for that night. It was party time. The venue for the festivities was the home of team-mate Damian Bonser, who lived just a few doors down from Paolo in the relatively new and up-and-coming district of Templestowe, about five miles from Kylie's house. By the time she arrived with a group of schoolfriends, the beer was well and truly flowing. As well as the victorious players, there were supporters and a number of parents. Paulo's mother even popped in for a while to toast his team's success.

Paolo settled himself in a chair in the lounge and was chatting to the boys, drinking beer and generally basking in the glory of their win, when he spotted a girl in an armchair across the other side of the room, surrounded by half a dozen eager boys. She was slender, with blonde curly hair and a winning smile. There were only a very few girls at the party, so she stood out and caught the attention of most of the boys there, especially Paolo: 'There was a lack of female options, so I bit the bullet and just wandered over to where she was and sat on the arm of the chair.' Paolo started listening to the conversation, hoping he would get the chance to say more than two words to the girl, when he was joined by another friend, Nick, who was one of the biggest and loudest guys in the team. Nick was also very inebriated and leaned on Paolo's left shoulder to hold himself upright: 'His weight started to push me down towards the girl,' recalled Paolo. 'I am basically a shy sort of person and not the sort who hits on women. I turned around and looked at her to almost apologize but, before I could say anything, we started kissing. It all happened so spontaneously.' The spark was instantaneous and obvious to the other suitors, who, disgruntled, moved away to try their luck elsewhere.

By this stage it was past 11 o'clock and the parental presence was thinning out. Paolo was feeling self-conscious snogging the girl because his mates would make loud and gormless comments every time they walked past the chair. He suggested they went somewhere more private: 'She agreed without question, so we got up and went outside into the backyard where there was a fire going in an old drum. It wasn't that cold for an August night – perhaps about twelve degrees, but we kept each other warm by kissing and cuddling. There were a few people walking around, but it was quite dark and there wasn't as much comment as there had been in the living room.

'By this stage my hands were wandering a bit and we were getting even hotter by the fire. Out of the blue she said to me, "Do you want to go somewhere even more private?" Of course I agreed. It sounded great to me. We walked down the driveway of the house, around the front and up the other side. She had no idea where she was going, but eventually she took me to the opposite side of the house. There were a few people catching taxis, so we walked round the corner to be out of sight – or so I thought. We started kissing again and I remember that I actually told her my name at this point and she said she was called Kylie. Before that point I hadn't a clue who she was. The next thing I knew her hands had gone down and she had undone my fly, got the old fella out, and dropped to her knees. I thought it was pretty amazing for a sixteen-year-old.'

Paolo found himself in a state of bliss as Kylie went into action: 'She was fantastic and knew exactly what she was doing. I just shut my eyes and let her get on with it.' Alas, his ecstasy was short-lived when he opened his eyes and realized they were in full view of other party guests: 'I don't think they were watching Kylie in action but I'm sure a couple of them would have wondered what was going on in the dark. I felt very conspicuous and more than a little uneasy that we might be spotted.'

Fortunately, he spied a tiny door next to him, grabbed the door handle and was relieved when it opened, so that he could bundle Kylie inside, away from prying eyes. It was not exactly five-star luxury. The room appeared to be a small workshop underneath the front of the house. The first problem was that neither of them could find the light switch and it was very dark inside, with just a small window at the front letting in a chink of light. Neither of the young lovers cared too much, as passion got the better of them. Nor, remembers Paolo, did it matter to Kylie that he had no protection with him. He later discovered, when it came up in conversation, that she was not on the Pill.

That was in the future. For the moment it was important to take off as few clothes as possible because the dingy room was absolutely freezing. Fortunately, Kylie was wearing a skirt, which made things easier, although Paolo had to remove his jeans. They had sex first on the chair: 'I was on top but this wasn't very comfortable so I took hold of her again and we laid on the floor.' Paolo, ever the gentleman, took off his jacket and laid it on the ice-cold floor for Kylie to lie on, before they started again. 'It was freezing but I had enough alcohol in my veins for me not to notice. I was really enjoying myself because Kylie was so nice, but then we heard some voices sniggering outside the door.'

Suddenly passion died in a desperate flurry to get dressed. Too late: 'The door burst open just as Kylie was putting her panties back on and my mate Nick, the same one who had leaned on me in the lounge, walked in: 'He just said, "Oh *here* you are," but I was embarrassed. Fortunately, the darkness hid my red face and I just mumbled, 'Yeah, yeah.' But there was enough light showing through the open door for him to see exactly what we had been up to. Kylie was standing behind me, so I couldn't see whether she was as embarrassed as me. But she followed us outside.' If Paolo had been able properly to see his teenage temptress, he would have noticed how upset she was. He was soon in no doubt: 'All of a sudden she started crying. Real sobs. I just didn't know what to do, so I tried to reach out and reassure her but she just brushed me off. She was wailing: "You've just used me." I assured her that wasn't the case and asked for her phone number. That seemed to cheer her up a bit, because she stopped crying although she was still tearful.'

In his excitement and youthful pride at having had sex for the first time, Paolo let slip exactly what had happened when another team-mate came over to ask what was going on. 'I said, "Don't say anything but I just shagged her."' That was all the encouragement the friend needed to announce the fact at the top of his voice. Paolo was aghast: 'There was a balcony where everybody had gathered, and they all must have heard what my mate said. Kylie didn't appear to react, so perhaps she didn't realize what he had said.'

Back inside the house, Paolo found a pen and a scrap of paper so that Kylie could write down her name and phone number. Shortly afterwards, Kylie's friends shouted out that they were leaving and that she should go with them. She told Paolo that she had to go to work the next morning. Once more, his sporting mates were less than tactful. One asked if he was going to ask Kylie out – to which another blurted out, 'Don't worry, he's already been there.' Kylie must have heard, because she was standing right next to Paolo at the time. But, after a little goodnight kiss, she was gone and Paolo returned to drink beer and talk with his friends.

When he went in to school on the following Monday, Paolo discovered his exploits were still the talk of his set. He thought he had better find out a little more about Kylie. He learned that she went to Camberwell High School and that she was the sister of Dannii Minogue, whom everybody in Australia had heard of at the time because of her starring role in the TV series, *Young Talent Time*. He discreetly asked around and was pleased to discover that none of his friends, or even acquaintances, had enjoyed a sexual encounter with

Kylie. Perhaps she was not what his friends would call an easy lay. Perhaps he was special.

Now that they had had sex, it was time to think about a first date. Playing it cool, Paolo waited until the middle of the week to call up. They chatted briefly and Kylie mentioned that she was a fan of Prince, so he asked her if she fancied going to see his movie *Purple Rain* at the Hoyts Midtown cinema the following weekend. He could not have come up with a more appealing idea, because Prince was Kylie's pop idol and she was dying to see his first film.

Kylie suggested he take the bus from Templestowe to Camberwell Junction and meet her there. They could then take the tram into the city. By Saturday, Paolo was full of anticipation at seeing his first lover for the second time. Kylie was clearly excited, too, because, as soon as she caught sight of him, she ran over and planted a big, exuberant kiss on his lips. They hopped on a tram and spent the thirty-minute journey talking non-stop all about themselves, as people always do on a first date. Kylie told him she had just been hired to appear in a new television series called *The Henderson Kids*, but she was a little worried about it because they wanted to dye her hair bright red. She gave him the impression that she saw the role as her big break. She also told him that she loved helping Dannii reply to the sacks of fan mail she received for *Young Talent Time*. 'Kylie had a nice bubbly personality,' recalled Paolo. 'She was very easy to talk to and get along with.'

It was after they had got off the tram and were walking to the cinema that Paolo had his first misgivings. 'I suddenly noticed how tiny she was. I am close on six foot and she was literally a foot shorter than me. I felt very awkward and self-conscious. People have asked me what it was like and the only way I have been able to put it is that it was like taking out my little sister. She was sixteen, but I realized she looked

February 2002 – Kylie performs at the Brits at London's Earls Court.
She walked away with two awards.

Above and below: Kylie with her sister Dannii, three years her junior – for a time in the early 80's Dannii was the more famous of the two.

Above: With her younger brother Brendan.

With a young admirer at the London launch of *Kylie*, a glossy photographic book celebrating her life and image, October 1999

Above: With her mother, Carol Minogue, and **left**, with Anne Charleston, who played her screen mother, Madge in *Neighbours*.

Opposite: Kylie and Jason sing their 1988 duet, 'Especially For You'. Unknown to the public, they had been engaged in a passionate relationship.

Appearing with Kylie...

Left: With Pete Waterman, who had a huge influence on Kylie's early career.

Below: Elton John, in drag, at the Stonewall Fund Gala at the Royal Albert Hall, London, in October 1995

Below: Nick Cave, with whom she recorded 'Where The Wild Roses Grow'

Opposite: Robbie Williams at the MTV Europe Awards in Stockholm, November 2000. Their duet, 'Kids', reached No.2 in the UK.

Photographed in London arriving for a *Q* magazine awards ceremony

much younger than that because of her size – even though she was so mature for her age in other ways.' Kylie, meanwhile, was happily unaware of her date's growing unease: 'She was saying things like, "I can't wait to introduce you to all my friends." She was being very chatty and I was listening, but at the same time I was thinking, "I'm not sure about this. Do I really want to be with this girl?"'

Paolo has no idea if Kylie was beginning to pick up on his negative vibes at this point, but he was becoming quieter and quieter. They went in to watch the movie together and, just like every other young couple, bought popcorn and enjoyed a little kiss and a cuddle before the film started. There was no groping in the back row! After the movie, they caught the tram back to Camberwell. By this time, Paolo had decided that he did not want to take things any further with Kylie, and set about trying to let her down gently. He used the old excuse that he would have far too much work to do in the coming months, as he had been neglecting his studies to play football, and he had his Year Twelve exams (the Australian equivalent of A-levels in the UK). 'I told her I would not have a great deal of time to socialize, which was actually true. I genuinely didn't have time for a girlfriend, even one as brilliant sexually as Kylie.'

Eventually, poor Kylie got the heavy hint and agreed that this would be their first and last serious date together. 'She had gone from a long-term relationship to a casual fling in half an hour.' The ability to make hard, even painful, decisions is one of Kylie's great strengths, one that has been important to her throughout her life and career. Perhaps this early teenage setback enabled her to identify when it is time to walk away with your dignity intact. Paolo will never know if Kylie was crestfallen or not, as she made the last leg of her journey home by herself from Camberwell Junction. He took a bus which conveniently passed The Harp pub in

Kew where, through the window, he spotted some of his mates drinking. He got off at the next stop to go back and join them until it was chucking-out time.

And that was pretty much it, although he had mentioned that he had a ticket for her to a school social in a couple of weeks' time. It was a typical school disco, where the girls all talk to each other about boys and the lads all talk to each other about sport. Kylie turned up, Paolo gave her the ticket, but as soon as they went inside they split up and spent the evening with their respective friends. If Kylie was hurt by what had happened, she did not let on to him. He was pleased to see that she went home by herself and did not immediately go on to the next likely guy.

The Paolo saga puts to bed much of the myth of Kylie as an innocent girl-next-door. Her behaviour with him was hardly unusual for teenage girls in Melbourne at the time. Paolo himself observed, 'A lot of the girls we all knew at the time were sexually active. Kylie was mature sexually, but we knew of girls of thirteen and fourteen who were having sex with boyfriends. I am not saying they had multiple partners – just with their boyfriends.' Maybe Kylie saw Paolo as boyfriend material. If so, she was quickly disillusioned, because he was not ready for that. Instead, it was an enjoyable fling. And it exposes the lie that Kylie was 'corrupted' by sex Svengali Michael Huchence, as has been portrayed time and time again. She may even have taught *him* a thing or two between the sheets. His ungallant and oft-reported boast that Kylie was the best f*** in the world does not seem quite so incredible. The other intriguing 'first' in the Templestowe knee-trembler was that it was the first time that Kylie took a risk in being discovered *in flagrante*. It would not be the last.

Paolo now prefers to be known as Paul. He still lives in Melbourne, where he is happily married with two children and has a successful career as a graphic designer, after a brief spell as a personal fitness trainer. He saw Kylie once more when he was twenty, and she was the star of *Neighbours*. He was driving home from university and saw her walking down the street before going into the video store she used to work in. He decided against stopping to catch up on old times: 'I don't have any regrets about breaking up with Kylie or missing out on being part of her career, because I just don't think it would have worked.'

Confidentially: 'Do you want to go somewhere even more private?'

kylie
precocious

I T WAS AN INNOCENT QUESTION. The blonde journalist
was chatty and friendly and simply asked Kylie, over a
bowl of pasta, if she had a boyfriend. She was number one
in the UK charts and, naturally, it was one of the first things
her millions of fans would want to know. Kylie 'confessed'
that she had not had a steady boyfriend for more than two
years, in other words for the entire time she had been in
Neighbours. She had conveniently forgotten that for the
majority of that period she had been virtually shacked up
with Jason Donovan.

Kylie is not the first, and certainly will not be the last,
star to manipulate the facts to suit the image that, at any
given moment, she wants to convey. Old-style Hollywood
stars promoted certain images at the behest of studio

bosses who did not want the movie-going public to know that, for example, the hunky leading man was, in fact, gay. At least one female superstar has it written into her recording contract that she cannot reveal her true sexuality. It might well ruin her image. The key to manipulating the public is image. If you change the goalposts of the public's perception, you run the risk of alienating some or many of your fans. The key to manipulating the public is image. Stephen Gately of Boyzone could arguably have fallen into that category. His career has stalled ever since he 'came out' in 1999. He was the cute boy fantasy of every pubescent (and pre-pubescent) girl, but, overnight, became someone they could not have, even in their dreams. Would Will Young have won television's *Pop Idol* contest if he had 'come out' during the competition?

Obviously, Kylie is not gay, far from it, but the principle of cheating the public, in order to promote a carefully conceived image, remains the same. The character of Charlene Mitchell was a curiously asexual girl-next-door, far too nice to be getting steamy over the cocoa every night. Kylie had fancied the now grown-up Jason from the beginning of her involvement in *Neighbours*. He was a quintessential hunk – blond, tanned and muscular – and she enlisted the help of old friend Greg Petherick to act as a go-between to find out if there was any spark of reciprocal interest. She was thrilled to discover there was indeed and, as a thank you for his help, later gave Greg a photograph of herself and her new man on the set. She had handwritten a little message and embellished it with love hearts.

Jason had joined *Neighbours* just before Kylie. He played Scott Robinson, the youngest son of Jim Robinson. The character had been in the show from the start, but played by another actor. When *Neighbours* changed from Channel Seven to Channel Ten, it was decided that Scott would change, too. Enter Jason. Like Kylie, he had been a child actor but he came from more of a show business background. His father is the well-known Australian actor Terry Donovan, who later would play builder Doug Willis in *Neighbours*, and his mother, Sue McIntyre, was a glamorous television newsreader. His parents divorced when he was five and, as a teenager, Jason always remained closer to his father, geographically as well as emotionally. Jason lived at the bottom of Terry's garden in a one-room bungalow, a teenage grunge paradise where he could strum guitar and dream of being Michael Hutchence. Kylie loved hanging out at Jason's place, not having to bother to wear make-up or smart clothes, but just being able to relax, away from the pressure of being a celebrity. It is the lifestyle she still favours today and, when not on show, Kylie is barely recognizable as a singing superstar. She is certainly not a fashion icon when she pops out to buy a loaf of bread or have a cappuccino with her friends.

Gradually, the camera picked up the chemistry between Jason and Kylie. Her character, Charlene, was originally booked for a thirteen-week run but this was quickly extended when the programme's bosses realized that the couple represented a marketing gold mine. The romance between Scott and Charlene 'made' the show.

Jason observed, 'There was just a feeling between us that probably happens once in a million times.' Their first screen kiss was front-page news not just in Australia but also in the UK, where *Neighbours* first went on air in October 1986. It became a phenomenon of British television when artful schedulers decided to show it twice a day. Mothers watched the lunchtime episode while it was nice and peaceful at home, and then the kids would switch on the early evening repeat when they arrived back from school. Kylie and Jason did not appear on British screens until the following summer, but soon were just as popular in the UK as in Australia. They were described as Britain's most idolized teenagers, loved by both young and old.

Meanwhile, the pair had made a decision back home in Melbourne which would have an enormous effect on their future together. They had agreed to a demand from *Neighbours'* bosses to keep their off-screen relationship absolutely secret. Brian Walsh, the Promotions Manager for Channel Ten, warned them that if their romance became public knowledge it would ruin the show, and their own popularity. The view was that, while the audience loved the fictional love affair between Charlene and Scott, they might not be able to handle Kylie and Jason arguing in the supermarket over which brand of cereal to buy. Kylie's decision was almost Faustian in the way it coloured her future life. She was putting her career before her private relationship. She has continued on the same path ever since. She has never abandoned her working commitments for love. She did not do it even for Michael Hutchence, one of the greatest loves of her life. And she has continued to keep parts of her life secret from her adoring fans. This air of mystery remains part of her appeal. Later, in a fairly candid interview, after her duet with Jason 'Especially For You' had been the first number one of 1989 Kylie said, 'Everyone believes we are [together] and I suppose it's quite obvious but no one can be 100 per cent sure, can they? If they knew all about us, where we slept, what we did together, and so on, wouldn't it spoil the mystery?'

With their secret safe, the public continued to lap up the romance between Charlene and Scott. In one memorable episode, Charlene was going to 'give' herself to Scott in a hotel room. Everything was going well, until Scott found out that Lenny was not a virgin. He stormed out leaving her crying on the bed. For that, he received a much applauded punch on the jaw from Lenny. The PR people never missed a trick and a story promptly appeared in the media that Kylie was now known on the set as 'Bruiser' because she had laid Jason out with one punch. A more likely scenario would have been that, had she connected, Kylie would have suffered a broken hand.

And then there was *the* wedding in July 1987. It was episode number 523. Charlene had been unable to persuade her mother to give the seal of approval to her living in sin with Scott, so had decided to marry him. Scott had rolled up on his skateboard, still wearing his school uniform, and proposed. Jason says, 'It was a really nice natural scene. I didn't feel stupid at all. Sometimes you look at a script and you think, "Oh God! I've got to tell her she's the most gorgeous person in the world and that I can't live without her and here I am on this stupid skateboard trying to drag her out from underneath an oily car engine."'

Kylie and Jason were mobbed at a shopping mall in Sydney while they were filming the wedding reception scenes. Somehow, 4,000 fans found out where it was taking place and some ended up in hospital as a result of the mêlée. Unsurprisingly, the following day, the newspapers were full of reports of a 'riot'. Kylie complained that the wedding scene itself was very tiring, and that she had to walk up the aisle some twenty times before everyone was happy – ironically, despite much speculation over the years, she has never been close to being a bride in real life. Once again, the public confused fact and fiction, and Kylie found people coming up to her in the street, congratulating her on her 'marriage'.

That wedding remains one of the most popular moments in the history of soap, and the pinnacle of Kylie's acting career – so far. Charlene and Scott were the most popular couple in Australia, regularly appearing on the cover of *TV Week*. The Australian edition of *Time* magazine was caught up in the hype. They featured Charlene and Scott on the front cover inside a pink heart, with the headline, 'Aussie Soaps Capture The World'. *Time* was trying to make sense of the cult of niceness, in which *Neighbours* played a leading role. It was, the magazine argued, soap as 'social engineering', an antidote to modern melodrama. The characters were the embodiment of comfy armchairs – the unbearable niceness of being.

Even Jason Donovan acknowledged, 'A lot of people get us muddled up with Charlene and Scott, but we're really quite different.' The cult of niceness is one of the constant themes of Kylie's professional life.

The pair appeared together at a charity gala where they sang a duet in public for the first time, a version of 'No One Is To Blame', a hit for Howard Jones in 1985. Sister Dannii also joined Kylie to sing 'Sisters Are Doing It For Themselves', a track which they have, surprisingly, avoided releasing.

Jason was certainly right about the differences between his screen character and real life because when he and Kylie returned home, tired after a day's filming, he would abandon his clean-living, surfer-boy image and dream of being a rock star. In the future he would extol the virtues of cannabis, declaring he would rather walk into a room full of dope smokers than one filled with alcoholics: 'It just puts a smile on your face at the end of the day.'

Some observers believe that the issue of drugs became a divisive element in the relationship between Kylie and Jason. That did not appear to be the case between Kylie and Michael Hutchence, a much more serious drug user, a few years later. It was not, however, the most destructive element for Kylie and Jason. The amount of time they spent apart pursuing their own ambitions was much more critical. As Jason would observe, 'I found it really hard to deal with her fame at the time. I was extremely jealous of Kylie.'

A curious interview with Kylie appeared in *TV Week* in October 1988, in which she admitted how much she missed Jason when she was away from him. She also confessed that she did not live at home all the time. Nobody told Jason about the interview, which seemed very indiscreet of Kylie, so when he appeared on television three days later to plug a record, and denied any relationship with Kylie, he was made to look a complete idiot. Kylie's team denied that she had ever given the interview, in order not to destroy the myth about her and Jason. But, if she did say it, what a sad admission of how she really felt. It certainly did not sit comfortably on the shelf next to the souvenir magazine from the same year, *Kylie and Jason: Just Good Friends*. Within a year, she and Jason had drifted apart. Perhaps the killer punch was when Jason declared that he had not yet experienced true love and was still looking.

For a while, they were happy.

In January 1986, when Kylie auditioned for her role in *Neighbours*, a new board game called 'So You Want To Be A Rockstar' went on sale around Australia. The idea was that each player represented a band and followed its ups and downs from first gig to, hopefully, a number one album. The game was devised by Simon Young, director of business affairs at Mushroom Records, and his friend Terry Blamey, a former drummer, who was the music talent co-ordinator for the TV programme, *Hey, It's Saturday* and also managed a novelty act featuring a former Australian Rules Footballer called Jacko. Blamey had been in bands in the late 1960s but had decided that 'it was more lucrative to be a manager or an agent.' Young and Blamey resolved not to include anything that involved sex and drugs in the board game, but just stuck to the rock and roll.

Blamey explained the philosophy of the game: 'You can lie, but then people can lie back to you. You don't have to tell the truth, you can charge whatever you like, you can give things away free, you can hire them, you can lease them, you can swap them.

'It is as wide open in terms of bargaining as it is in the real world, but it all comes back to you when you are in a less favourable position.

'The winner does extremely well. He ends up with a lot of money and a lot of chart success.'

With exquisite timing, barely six months would pass before Blamey took control of Kylie Minogue's career. They have both done extremely well, ending up with lots of money and chart success – enough to have easily won any board game. Blamey's 20 per cent of all things Kylie has made him a multi-millionaire, but they are still a strong partnership fifteen years later and he remains fiercely protective of his famous client. Blamey was practically part of the family at Mushroom and was in a strong position to take over the reins of Kylie Minogue's career when she needed personal day-to-day handling of her life. Mushroom had taken her to number one with 'The Loco-Motion' but she would need something more than shared responsibility if the next phase of her career – the international years – was to be a success.

Only one person stood between Terry Blamey and his appointment as Kylie's manager – Kylie's father Ron. He was naturally cautious, very shrewd and had maximized all the opportunities for both Kylie and Dannii up until this point. He was most definitely not the sort of man who would be seduced by the glamour of the pop business. His feet were so firmly on the ground, he had lead in his boots. From the very outset, he had set up a limited company, Kaydeebee, to control the finances of his children, and had a reputation for being thrifty. Kay was for Kylie, Dee was for Dannii and Bee stood for their brother Brendan. It was an amusing reminder of when the three children used to squabble over which television programmes they wanted to watch, and so a rota for using the remote control was posted in the kitchen – Monday K, Tuesday D, Wednesday B, and so on. Ron was an accountant by profession; he had been the Director of Finance of Camberwell Council before the success of his daughters meant he could not commit to a full-time job. He went on to work as a consult-ant for three days a week, before finally quitting for good in 1989 to devote himself to the family business. Evidence of his acumen came to light when it was disclosed that he had managed to secure a car valued at Aus $17,000 for just $2,000 as part of a severance package. He also took three months' pay and a long service bonus away with him. The car was sold a few months later to a local dealer for an undisclosed price.

Ron has always had a solid contractual arrangement with Kylie who, as a result, has never had any financial concerns of any kind over the money she has earned. She is not at all mean with money, but has just inherited a natural pru-dence, so that she will always go for the bargain in a supermarket – even today, when she is one of the richest women in entertainment. Like Ron, her mother Carol goes on the payroll when Kylie is on tour. She works backstage helping the dancers, a legacy of her own training as a dancer when she was younger. Although Kylie is very close to her mother, she admits she has always been a daddy's girl. It was, therefore, essential that Terry Blamey pass the

'Ron' test before he could be accepted into the Minogue inner sanctum. Gary Ashley, of Mushroom Records, described Blamey as a 'straight-up guy', and it was this quality that Minogue Senior liked and thought he could work with in the future. The longevity of 'Kylie Minogue Limited', the team behind the public Kylie, is proof of what a mutually beneficial decision that was. While Ron remained in Melbourne in the 1990s, Terry Blamey upped sticks and moved close to Kylie, rather like a sensible elder brother looking after a vulnerable sister. Even today, record company insiders marvel at the way he rules Kylie with a 'rod of iron'. That is not strictly true, but he certainly enjoys a reputation as a hard man with whom to do business.

From the outset, Blamey has sought to maintain the public image and, consequently, the public affection in which Kylie is held. The only time he conspicuously failed in this aim was soon after her breakthrough in the UK, when she was savaged by the British press, a state of affairs which he has never allowed to happen twice. From those early days, he has closely controlled her image and, more importantly, her image changes. Kaydeebee has a stranglehold on the copyright for all her pictures, her music and her merchandise. In effect, Kylie owns all things Kylie. Her bank account swells a little every time you see a picture of her in a magazine. There is likely to be trouble if anybody tries to take an unauthorized picture of Kylie.

After the final concert of her Australian tour in 1991, there was a party at The Freezer nightclub in the Darlinghurst district of Sydney. One freelance photographer was asked to leave his cameras at the door, but sneaked in a small Instamatic and started taking pictures of Kylie with an actor called Marcus Graham. When he left the club, he claimed he was pursued by one of Kylie's minders and a party guest who, he alleged, pinned him up against a wall, took five rolls of film from him and opened up every one of his cameras. It was just at the time Kylie and Michael Hutchence had been in the newspapers after having broken up, so maybe Kylie was particularly touchy about having her picture taken with another man. Terry Blamey, with masterful understatement, said of the incident, 'We didn't want to create a scene.'

In the eleven years since that incident, team 'Kylie Minogue Limited.' has grown so much that a small army is involved every time the public Kylie makes a move. Her father no longer takes a day-to-day interest, but Blamey certainly does. Then there are record company executives and publicity people, her personal assistants, her stylist, hair, make-up and clothes people. The public Kylie is like a grand prix racing car. It is a team effort. She may be the driver, but she would still be in the pits if it were not for the rest of the crew.

Confidentially: 'Jason has his career and I have mine.'

kylie
protected

KYLIE MINOGUE, popular soap actress, and now fledgling pop star, waited patiently, curled up on the sofa. Terry Blamey was there to keep an eye on things. They had enjoyed their week together in London, sightseeing from the top of a tourist bus and getting in line for the Tower of London and Madame Tussaud's. But these outings had just been a pleasant bonus. The real reason they had used up Kylie's short filming break from *Neighbours* in October 1987 was to meet up with Pete Waterman and proceed with the masterplan for international stardom. The only problem was that this was their last day and they had yet to clap eyes on the chart wizard. Instead, they were apparently wasting their last afternoon in London in the reception area of the unpretentious Vine Yard studio complex behind Borough tube station, near London Bridge.

Fortunately, Kylie had no idea of the bedlam behind closed doors. Waterman was not even in London that day. He was relaxing at his mansion in Newton-le-Willows, Merseyside, when his partner Mike Stock rang up to enquire if a small Antipodean rang any bells – a small Antipodean called Kylie Minogue. Waterman had forgotten to mention that he had agreed to a joint venture with Mushroom Records to help Kylie's recording career. He had never even watched *Neighbours,* so the whole thing had gone straight out of his head. 'She's in town,' he told Stock, helpfully, only to be told that she was actually sitting in reception and had to be on her way back to the airport in a few hours: 'She's expecting to do something with us, now!' Without thinking, Waterman replied, 'She should be so lucky.' The rest, as they say, is history. It is a great story, and one that Waterman never tires of telling.

The biggest-selling record of 1988 was written by fax between London and Merseyside in about half an hour – although Stock does not give Waterman much credit for the song. Later in the day, Waterman rang the studio to find out how Kylie's vocal was coming along. Matt Aitken, the other member of the famous Hit Factory triumvirate, came on the line and announced, 'This girl's got a really good voice.' The record done, the Hit Factory promptly forgot all about Kylie Minogue. At this stage, Pete Waterman had never even met the girl who would take over his commercial life. He had yet to hear the record.

Six weeks later, at the PWL (Pete Waterman Limited) Christmas party at the Natural History Museum in London, a record came on that he did not recognize: 'I thought it was fantastic, so I ran over to the DJ and asked him what it was. He said, "It's Kylie Minogue, 'I Should Be So Lucky'."' Waterman turned to Mike Stock and told him the track would be a smash. Waterman, who has an uncanny sense of the commercial, was absolutely right. He was the glue that joined together the songwriting skills of Mike Stock, the musicianship of guitarist, Matt Aitken, and the talent of their singers. Kylie once compared the Hit Factory to a Hollywood Studio – if that's the case, then Pete Waterman is Sam Goldwyn ('I am willing to admit that I may not always be right – but I am never wrong').

Waterman did not fully appreciate just how popular *Neighbours* was becoming in the UK, and how everybody wanted to hear 'Charlene's' record. *Neighbours* was watched regularly by fifteen million viewers a day, which was a considerable potential record-buying market. Waterman confessed that he had absolutely no conception of the 'power of Kylie's presence in the market-place.' It was an intangible power that she has always possessed. There is a little of the chicken and the egg about *Neighbours* and Kylie's pop career. Would *Neighbours* have been an enduring commercial success without 'I Should Be So Lucky', or would Kylie have made it as a singer without *Neighbours*? It is probably a bit of both. The exposure given to the record because it was 'Charlene' was huge – but then, at the time, Stock, Aitken and Waterman could have turned their grannies into stars. In 1987, before Kylie, they had sold thirty-seven million records worldwide.

The BBC was instrumental in the speed with which the nation knew that Kylie had made a record. She may have been number one in Australia, New Zealand and Hong Kong, but that did not mean a thing in Oxford Street. But *The Noel Edmonds Christmas Day Special* sent a film crew out to Australia to film Kylie singing 'I Should Be So Lucky'. This was significant exposure and neatly coincided with *Neighbours* being shown twice daily. In those days, Noel Edmonds was one of the biggest names on British television, so it was a big break for Kylie. The single was finally released on 23 January, 1988. It was the month of the Australian bicentennial celebrations. Kylie was in Sydney as one of the celebrity guest list to meet Prince Charles and Princess Diana. Charles met her first and gave her the tried and tested royal enquiry: 'And what do you do?' Kylie timidly replied that she worked on *Neighbours,* and Charles smilingly told her he would make sure he watched an episode. When it came to speaking to Diana, six feet tall in high heels, and the most famous woman in the world, Kylie was completely tongue-tied. For a minute, she was Minnie Minogue, the little girl from the Melbourne suburbs, and not the performer who was a blink away from international fame. Diana's tragic death in 1997 left a vacancy for the title of the world's most famous style icon: who would have guessed that it would end up being filled by Kylie?

Three weeks after the single was released, Kylie, back home in Melbourne, was awoken by her mother with the news that there was a phone call from England. She was grumpy at first, fearing it was a British journalist after an early morning scoop. Instead, it was the PWL office congratulating her on reaching number one. It would be the first single in a decade to stay at the top of the charts for five weeks. Far from being a 'happy accident', each step in Kylie's proposed world domination was being carefully planned. When she gave interviews about her latest success, she admitted that her future with *Neighbours* was uncertain, even though she still had six months to go on her contract: 'I've done *Neighbours* since I left school. I'd obviously like to do other things. I'd be in London right now if I could, but I have commitments to *Neighbours.*' The reality was that, in eighteen short months, Kylie had outgrown the homespun Aussie soap. When she left the series in June 1988, she was given as a leaving present a mahogany mirror and a framed montage of her magazine covers. Her last episode, when

Charlene drove off to a new life in Queensland, was broadcast in the UK in October when 'Je Ne Sais Pas Pourquoi'
(Pete Waterman's favourite among his Kylie songs) was her
third consecutive top three hit. Kylie had done even better
in Finland, where her first four releases reached number
one – a record.

Kylie was still a teenager. But, at nineteen, she was positively an old lady next to the girl she knocked off the
number one spot, sixteen-year-old Tiffany with 'I Think
We're Alone Now'. Great things were predicted for the
auburn-haired girl from Oklahoma, but she managed just
two more top ten hits and was on the chart scrapheap within
a year. Her demise is a salutary lesson in just how hard it is to
stay at the top in such a fickle business for one year, let alone
for fifteen. Kylie, however, had probably had the best first
year in the singles chart of any female artist ever.

Stock, Aitken and Waterman were unlikely candidates to
have become the British equivalent of Tamla-Motown. They
had met in 1984, when none of their careers was
particularly soaring. Waterman was a brash yet sociable
ex-Mecca Ballroom DJ, Aitken a former cruise-line guitarist
and Stock used to play in a hotel band – hardly pop royalty.
Yet, for a few years, they gelled into the most formidable
hit-making team in the world. According to Mike Stock, the
confident Waterman had told his partners, 'Stick with me,
boys, and I'll show you how to make a hit record.' And he
did. Their roster of stars at the time read like a who's who
of unhip: Samantha Fox, Sinitta, Sonia, Hazell Dean, Mel &
Kim, Rick Astley, Bananarama . . . and the bubble-haired
soap star Kylie Minogue. Their aim was to produce classic
three-minute hit singles. It was not rocket science.
Waterman explained, 'We have taken pop music back to

the people who buy records, not the journalists who preach to people.' They set out to appeal to listeners with 'Woolworth's Ears'.

It is easy to underestimate the craftsmanship of a Stock, Aitken and Waterman record, and just as facile to suggest they all sound the same. They constructed energetic records around one catchy melody. Music author Spencer Bright recalled, 'Like everyone else at the time, I found Stock, Aitken and Waterman pretty gruesome. But you could not deny the hummability of their music, or their skill.'

And the lyrics were canny. They did not seek to save the world in three minutes. Instead they focused on key emotions, which would appeal to the young, impressionable, record-buying public. There are, for instance, an astonishing number of SAW records which have the word 'heart' in the title. Kylie released 'Hand On Your Heart', Jason – 'Too Many Broken Hearts'; Rick Astley – 'Take Me To Your Heart'; Sinitta – 'Cross My Broken Heart'; Sonia – 'Listen To Your Heart'; Dead Or Alive – 'My Heart Goes Bang'; Cliff Richard – 'I Just Don't Have The Heart'. Besides this simplistic approach, anything that might offend was banned, so there was no sex, no bottoms. And no 'baby', which Mike Stock considered the most clichéd word in popular music. The satirical magazine *Punch* devised a spoof Stock, Aitken and Waterman song for their Winter Special in 1989. They called it 'Your Arms Are In My Heart'.

The 1988 bestselling roster for Stock, Aitken and Waterman in the UK reads:

ARTIST	SONG	SALES
1. Kylie Minogue	'I Should Be So Lucky'	672,568
2. Kylie Minogue	'The Loco-Motion'	439,575
3. Kylie Minogue	'Je Ne Sais Pas Pourquoi'	315,201
4. Kylie Minogue	'Got To Be Certain'	278,000

5. Jason Donovan	'Nothing Can Divide Us'	266,194
6. Brother Beyond	'The Harder I Try '	232,000
7. Rick Astley	'Together Forever'	223,112
8. Brother Beyond	'He Ain't No Competition'	202,000
9. Rick Astley	'She Wants To Dance With Me'	182,793
10. Bananarama	'I Want You Back'	175,000

Kylie had already completely eclipsed the competition in the Stock, Aitken and Waterman stable. According to Waterman, Kylie's success was the worst thing that ever happened to him: 'I don't mean that against Kylie, but merely that she was so successful that I had to fall in line with that success. I didn't want my company to become one artist, as much as I loved that artist, as much as now history shows what a wonderful artist she is, and how proud I am of her.'

There is a fashion for instant nostalgia in New Millennium Britain, and the Kylie Minogue of the Stock, Aitken and Waterman era is no exception. As Spencer Bright acknowledged, 'We are less judgmental today of commercial sounds.' At the time, there was a great wave of anti-Kylie feeling with 'I Hate Kylie Minogue' pins and satirical versions of 'I Should Feel So Yucky' and 'I'm a Lucky Ducky'. A great deal of the criticism was fuelled by jealousy, especially as PWL was an independent label formed specifically to make Kylie records, and independents were traditionally the home of more cutting-edge sounds like The Smiths and, later, Oasis. Waterman explained, 'We were pissing people off incredibly because every record we had released dominated the independent chart. Kylie Minogue was number one in the independent chart! That was popular.'

*

For her part Kylie loved the fame, but the criticism hit hard. She is as resilient as her name suggests – Kylie is an old Aboriginal word for Boomerang – but she hated the knocks at SAW: 'They were given such a lot of grief by so many people at the time, and so was I. We were all in it together. Now everyone says "ooh, what great songs."'

Jason Donovan was desperate for a slice of the fame his girlfriend was enjoying. From the moment that Kylie had released a record, there was speculation that 'Scott' would follow suit. He came over with Kylie on one of her recording trips to London, and Pete Waterman took them out for a Chinese meal and asked Kylie whether she wanted him to work with Jason. She said yes, and the deal was done. It is quite telling that this deal was agreed on Kylie's say-so.

Whenever Kylie and Jason were in London at the same time they would stay together but, just as in *Neighbours* and at Mushroom Records, their true relationship was kept secret. By this time, it was one of the worst-kept secrets in show business but, amazingly, nobody printed it, even though pictures of the couple holidaying in Bali had been published. A PWL insider explained, 'It was quite bizarre, because everyone knew. They were always holding hands and kissing in the car.' Contrary to popular belief, it was Jason who had a roving eye, well before Michael Hutchence turned Kylie's head. He was like a kid in a candy store when he first came to London on a promotional tour. The insider observed, 'She [Kylie] was totally into it [their relationship] and I remember him saying that she was really keen and everything. But he was saying "I'm a young man and I just want to enjoy myself while I'm here – and she wants to get more serious." I think that probably caused friction between them. It was inevitable it wasn't going to last.'

Intriguingly, the decision to keep their relationship secret at this time was just as much to protect Jason's career as Kylie's. For two years Jason was the ultimate teen-girl fantasy. He was eligible, and every girl studying for her exams or working behind the counter in a store felt they had a chance of going out with him. Fantasy is what it's all about and, unlike Jason, the more street-wise Kylie has never lost sight of that, whether as girl-next-door or as a wet dream.

The ultimate fantasy coupling of Jason and Kylie was on their number one 'Especially For You', which is either cheesy and cynical or the best love song ever, depending on whether you like fluffy, cuddly toys, or not. This was 'pop noodle' – popular, but not to everyone's taste. 'We didn't want to do it,' said Waterman, fearing it might be considered too tacky. In the end he was persuaded by public pressure, and because Kylie thought it was a good idea. She described the duet merely as an extension of work for her and Jason: 'We'd done everything else together.' Waterman and Matt Aitken flew to Sydney to record the pair's vocals, caught the next flight home, and went straight to the studio to work on the mix in time to turn the track into a Christmas hit. It took only three days, from start to finish.

Professionally, there was nowhere for Jason and Kylie to go together, and soon their private life was rocky. The writing was on the wall at Kylie's twenty-first birthday party in Melbourne. A gleaming white Mercedes transported Kylie and Jason to the trendy Red Eagle Hotel in Albert Park, where a huge crowd of fans and almost as many journalists were waiting to catch a glimpse of their heroine. Kylie, whose fashion sense had been steadily developing, was in a semi-see-through black silk dress and when she clambered out of the front seat, everybody surged forward to wish her a Happy Birthday. Jason was completely forgotten as he scrambled out of the back – so much so, that as soon as someone had escorted Kylie through the door, a bouncer promptly slammed it in poor Jason's face. Kylie had to wait inside the foyer for him to be rescued and restored to her side.

The studio system of The Hit Factory meant that Kylie

was far more involved in post-production than in the actual making of the Kylie sound. One of the famous trio was once reported to have said Kylie could have burped into the mike and it would have been a hit, an arrogant view, which would not have gone down well with 'Kylie Minogue Limited'. But this was a hard-headed, conveyor-belt operation, and the artists could either stay for the bumpy ride or, like Rick Astley, jump ship. For once, there was a 'happy accident' when Rick Astley walked out, leaving them with a song ready to go. The very next day, when Jason walked in, Waterman told him he had found just the song for him and Jason recorded 'Too Many Broken Hearts'.

After the débâcle of her first mauling by the English press, Kylie was never again caught out by the media. Instead, a new corporate Kylie, neatly packaged and always immaculate, was presented to the world. Behind the smiling face, Kylie was feeling the strain but, on the surface, she toed the company line of being the world's most normal girl – as if her star-spangled life had ever been normal. She never courted controversy. She would always say that she was tired, nervous at this or that and always flash a big toothy smile. She was asked if she would like to live overseas and replied, 'I'll always call Australia home,' which did not answer the question. It would not be long before London was her permanent home.

Kylie is a far better actress than she is given credit for and she is a past master at giving nothing away. Former pop columnist Rick Sky placed her at number one in his list of worst interviewees, although he admitted her beauty was some compensation. 'She was incredibly unforthcoming,' he recalled. 'It made me wonder what a nineteen-year-old girl had to hide. She was quite po-faced and everything I asked her about came to a dead end.' In the beginning, Kylie was worried about spilling the beans about Jason, or that she would be questioned about rumours of anorexia. After a while, it just became second nature to give away nothing or, more precisely, exactly as much as she wanted to divulge.

She also had back-up. Andrew Watt, a local Melbourne music journalist, was commissioned by Mushroom to write Kylie's fanzine copy, the soft-focus biography that is oxygen for every star. He was also conveniently placed in press conferences to derail things, should any tough questions be asked about topless photos or weight loss. Watt would put up his hand and ask, most sincerely, 'So Kylie, what's it like working with Pete Waterman?' Soon, Kylie herself became adept at deflecting these questions without her 'plant'.

This did not stop her putting her foot in it every so often. When she was in South Africa in late 1989, the year before Nelson Mandela's 'walk to freedom', she was asked what she thought about the situation in that country. She replied, 'I think they should stop killing the rhinos.' Once said, there was no retracting it, although Kylie denied the report when it appeared, claiming that the journalist obviously had a 'deep hatred for me'. The Kylie of the mid-nineties might have claimed that she was being ironic, but at this time, in the early stages of her relationship with Michael Hutchence, it was not part of her image makeover to come across as a blonde airhead. Having been 'burned', as she herself put it, Kylie vowed never to be caught out in that fashion again.

It has led to some embarrassing exchanges, of which there is no better example than the time she shared an interview for *Select* magazine with Primal Scream front man, Bobby Gillespie. It was the night after the UK General Election in 1992, which the Tory party, under John Major, won.

GILLESPIE: 'What did you think about last night, Kylie?
We were sickened, totally.

KYLIE: I wouldn't wish to express my opinions. I've made
that mistake before [rhinos?] and it was blown totally out
of all proportion, so I vowed not to talk about it. Ever.

INTERVIEWER: What happened then?

KYLIE: I don't even want to get into it, it's like bringing it
up again. I have interest in politics, but not involvement.
My interest is in the environment. [rhinos?]

GILLESPIE: Well, we don't give a shit about the environment
. . . we care about people.

INTERVIEWER: Kylie, much has been made of your SexKylie
makeover . . .

The control that Kylie herself, Terry Blamey and Ron
Minogue exercised over all things Kylie was edging towards
a stranglehold. The most important commodity Kylie had
was not her voice, her face, her hair or even her bottom – it
was her image, of which they were all a part. Nothing could
be allowed to deflect from the strict control of that image,
whether it be her relationship with Jason Donovan or the
subtle changes in her clothes, her videos or her music. 'Better The Devil You Know', 'Shocked' and 'What Do I Have
To Do?' were more sophisticated than her 'Charlene' songs
'I Should Be So Lucky' and 'Got To Be Certain'. Kylie has
often cited the fact that her fan base has 'grown up with
her' as one of the reasons for her enduring appeal.

It was not at all helpful to her changing image that, a
year after she left *Neighbours*, the Grundy production company released a video entitled *Scott and Charlene: A Love
Story*. Kylie rightly considered that she might be typecast as
Charlene if this syrup was stuck on the shelves year after
year. At PWL, they had already noticed that she was beginning to change naturally into a trendier young woman,

wearing clothes that suited her more than the jeans-and-sweater Charlene look. Kylie decided to take her grievance to court, but was allocated a presiding judge who said he had never heard of Kylie Minogue before the case and that he had 'fast-forwarded his way through the video because he wasn't prepared to spend an hour-and-a-half watching it.' The judge found against Kylie, declaring that it was obviously the success of *Neighbours* that had directly launched her career.

To say Kylie was annoyed is an understatement and she certainly voiced an opinion on this issue: 'It's not even *Neighbours*. That's not what I was paid a measly fee of money for [Aus $2000 a week]. . . . I have spent a lot of time getting away from Charlene. I know some people say, "*Neighbours* made you what you are." But it didn't. It's exploitation.'

Kylie was on a five-year contract with PWL and, after just one year she was a millionairess, her fortune carefully invested by her father Ron, who was very tough when dealing with the machinations of the pop world. When Waterman was in Australia recording 'Especially For You', he was cornered by Minogue Senior who demanded that Kylie see some of her hard-earned cash. A startled Waterman had to write out a cheque to Kaydeebee on the spot, for a substantial amount. Part of that money was speedily put down as deposit on an Aus $500,000 dollar house in Melbourne, even though Kylie knew she would scarcely live there, if at all. But, more importantly, she was a very proud artist and, as she grew up, she became more aware of what she considered to be a lack of respect for her contribution. Kylie was growing in confidence. Her debut album became the biggest-selling album of all time by a female artist – enough to turn anyone's head. However, she did not suddenly think she could do better without Stock, Aitken and Waterman. It was a gradual process, over which she agonized, as Jason Donovan remembered: 'Kylie struggled very much with the whole Stock, Aitken Waterman thing. I always wondered, "Why are you doing it? Just get out, if you don't like it – get out."'

The Hit Factory was not a cosy air-kissing organization. This was conveyor-belt business and Kylie Minogue records were continually on the production line. Waterman had great respect for Kylie as a professional, but admitted he never got 'that close' to performers personally: 'We work with artists. We don't work with friends. I always think it is too dangerous to get too close to an artist. You'll always get let down because they will shit on you.' That strong view did not stop Waterman letting Kylie and her mother Carol live in his flat above the studio (he moved into a hotel), while Kylie was recording her first album. Nor did it stop Waterman inviting Kylie to stay at his country mansion, where she was able to indulge her love of horses. At the time, Kylie was being hounded about her new relationship with Michael Hutchence and needed a refuge. One Sunday morning, Kylie's horse shied at a milk lorry and bolted into the distance. Waterman, terrified that his leading artist was in peril, set off in pursuit on his large grey, only to realize that he had totally lost control of the animal in his furious gallop. Far from being the rescuer, he needed rescuing himself. He was thrown off, catching his foot in the stirrup. He was wearing a riding hat, so was fortunate that only his ego was bruised as he was carted along. Suddenly, Kylie appeared from nowhere and stopped his horse from dragging him any further up the road.

The one exception to the 'no mates' working philosophy of SAW was Jason Donovan. Waterman declared, 'He was a mate and he was treated like a mate. We had a genuine affection for the guy.' Jason shared Waterman's passion for cars, and the pair would dash off to Silverstone together to watch the motor racing.

As Kylie gained in confidence, her professional routine with The Hit Factory was no longer what she wanted it to be. She would turn up at the studio and they would play her the backing track, print out the lyrics, and then Mike Stock would go through it, showing her the cues. And she went straight in front of the microphone and did her vocal in one take, or perhaps two. Kylie was frustrated: 'I just wanted to be a bit more involved, and it reached the point where I was not happy any more at being told to go and "have a cup of tea till we call you".'

The problem for Kylie was how to break the chains binding her to PWL. Returning to the Hollywood analogy, Kylie's progression is reminiscent of the young Judy Garland (minus the drugs). The petite Garland was also trapped as a child star, controlled by factories, desperate to throw off the child/woman image which had brought her initial fame. She would also become an icon to a gay community magnetized by her mixture of camp and vulnerability. Kylie threw off the chains in rebellious, aggressive fashion. The blonde wig and micro-skirt of her 'Hutchence era' were a bold statement of intent. This was consolidated by her increased artistic involvement in her videos and the use of producers independent of Stock, Aitken and Waterman.

Kylie had gone to Pete Waterman and told him that she wanted to write with Matt Aitken and Mike Stock. He told her that would not be possible because the three of them worked as a unit. He said she would have to collaborate with someone else. Waterman acknowledged that Kylie was headstrong about her career but also described her as his 'star centre forward'. Perhaps The Hit Factory had underestimated just how strong and just how motivated Kylie actually is. These days, a more confident Kylie will happily admit that her career is the most important thing in her life. The pop business is not a game to her. She is not a little dolly bird passing the time until she gets married.

Mike Stock recognized as early as 1990 that Kylie, with the massive success she had enjoyed in the past two years, would not be satisfied with just coming in and singing. He predicted, 'She'll want to do it all very soon and we won't be involved anymore.' Kylie stayed with Stock, Aitken and Waterman until the end of her contract. When Jason left the stable in 1991, she was the only original remaining artist. Jason saw himself as a grungy Michael Hutchence-type rock star – guitar, tousled hair and jeans, an image a million miles away from the clean-cut pop star that SAW wanted. Jason ended up starring in an Andrew Lloyd Webber musical that had even less street cred than any Stock, Aitken and Waterman collaboration.

Kylie had twenty successive hits on the PWL label, including four number ones. For a while, it seemed like daggers drawn between Kylie and her three mentors. Kylie felt she needed to distance herself from them. But now, she and Waterman are reconciled in a mutual admiration society. Kylie has confessed that she ran a million miles away from the PWL days in her ultimately successful quest to change the public perception of her. These days, she is in 'awe of that time', and the trio's ability to churn out hit after hit. She has even said that she would not rule out working with Pete Waterman again. Ironically, it was the triumvirate themselves who fell out. Stock and Aitken ended up on one side of a legal battle over Kylie's back catalogue and Waterman on the other.

Confidentially: 'I wanted the choice to stay in the studio and not be sent out for a cup of tea.'

kylie
vulnerable

EVERYONE at Stock, Aitken and Waterman's Hit Factory was worried about their most precious asset. Kylie was working herself into the ground. It was a never-ending round of recording sessions, photo shoots, television appearances and the treadmill that accompanies any drive for fame. And it was not just in the UK. Kylie's popularity had exploded in Europe, and she was having to dart backwards and forwards across to the Continent, to fulfil constant demands on her time. She was heading for a nervous breakdown in the fast lane. A company insider explained, 'Kylie was young and very fragile because she was quite a small little thing so it was taking its toll. I don't think she'd say we flogged her to death but, in retrospect, we could maybe have cut down a bit. She was very tired and stressed out and would be like "Do I *have* to do all this?"' She was homesick and lonely, and trying to deal with the gradual disintegration of her relationship with Jason Donovan. Her sister Dannii revealed that Kylie would ring home every day, seeking solace from her family. Kylie herself admitted she could not eat or sleep, and was constantly crying.

It had all become too much for her, and it was time for Terry Blamey to step in. Terry has been a superb manager to Kylie over the years, offering support and an astute business brain to 'Kylie Minogue Limited'. But, more than that, he has always been there for her. He understood that Kylie had had enough and, after consultation with Pete Waterman, whisked her on to a plane back to Australia to spend two months recovering at her parents' home. She did absolutely nothing, except for enjoying long lie-ins, taking her dog, Gabby, for walks, shopping in Chapel Street and meeting old girlfriends for coffee in St Kilda. Pete Waterman, who has always had the greatest respect for Kylie's talent, observed, 'She was a tiny girl and obviously had a huge workload, so she'd be exhausted half the time.'

It was not the first time that stress and exhaustion had plagued Kylie, and it would not be the last. Kylie is not the all-round tough cookie some might think. She has enormous drive and motivation, but sometimes her body lets her down. As long ago as February 1988, when her first UK single 'I Should Be So Lucky' was number one, a British music journalist, Jane Oddy, travelled over to Melbourne to have lunch with seventeen-year-old Kylie, during a break from her gruelling schedule on *Neighbours*. Jane was astonished at how exhausted Kylie looked: 'She was tired out and so thin.' Kylie told Jane about the effect her punishing schedule was having on her. 'I don't have any friends any more because I am just too tired to chat and I never have the time to go out and socialize. I have to cut out anything that's unnecessary, and that means most things apart from eating.' Kylie's parting words to Jane were particularly poignant in a seventeen-year-old girl: 'One day I'd like to lead a normal life and not be nagged by people about losing weight.'

Skip nearly fourteen years, and Kylie is back at the top of the tree and enjoying a greater popularity than ever. *The Face* magazine observed, 'She can't sleep, can't remember what day it is, gets up and cries in the night.' The writer Chris Heath reported that Kylie was running on empty, over-busy and a little ill. She had, in fact, spent much of 2001, arguably her most successful year since 1988, battling many of the same problems of physical exhaustion as she did back then. The incredible thing is that nothing much seems to have changed. She punishes herself, so that she can continue to drink the elixir of fame. Her 2002 World Tour also left its mark on her brittle constitution. When it finished in August the gruelling schedule combined with the emotional fall-out from her breakup with boyfriend James Gooding found Kylie again seeking comfort and rest in the bosom of her family. This time she and her mother Carol headed off to a retreat in the Western Australian outback. Once more Kylie had reached breaking point.

One thing, however, has changed for the better. Kylie may have been a phenomenon under the guidance of Stock, Aitken and Waterman, but her treatment in the early days, by both press and public, was quite shameful. The legendary Fleet Street columnist Jean Rook of the *Daily Express* was perhaps the chief culprit. Rook was the very worst kind of bullying old dinosaur, coasting by on a reputation that sometimes bordered on parody. Not for nothing was she the inspiration for the satirical Glenda Slag in *Private Eye* magazine. She targeted poor Kylie, who was completely unprepared for the poison pen of this wrinkly Rita Skeeter. It was just a month after Jane Oddy had seen her in Melbourne, and Kylie was still exhausted. She flew in to Heathrow to finish the vocals for her first album and to do some publicity because, after all, she was number one in the UK. Kylie was shocked by the microscopic scrutiny afforded every celebrity by the British press, and this was the start of a lifelong hate affair with the tabloids. To a certain extent, she was the target of innate racism by good old Brits against all things Antipodean. It's not something Australian visitors to the UK expect, but it is by no means reserved for the non-white population – because it is white on white, it is ignored and laughed off.

It was naïve, however, of Kylie and her management to think the latest pop sensation and soap star would in any way escape media attention. Kylie asked her manager what she could expect at the airport. Blamey told her to relax and get some sleep, because nobody knew she was arriving on that flight. He had taken the precaution of booking the seats only a couple of hours before take-off. Unfortunately, it would have made no difference if he had booked them two minutes before departure – the telephone lines between Melbourne and London were buzzing, and Fleet Street's finest had plenty of time to trickle out along the M4 to wait for their prey. Kylie stepped off the plane in dark glasses, an old pair of scruffy sandals and a wraparound skirt.

It had not helped that Kylie was escorted by burly minders the size of Ayers Rock, who were not exactly the type you would want to invite home for tea with mother. Minders behaving badly has always been a sure-fire way to achieve newspaper coverage, as a list of other over-protected female stars from Madonna to Britney Spears illustrates. On this occasion, it just irritated everyone.

Jean Rook commented, 'Maybe getting off a plane looking as if you've just crawled out of a kangaroo's pouch is Australian style but Kylie Minogue's disappointing arrival at

Heathrow was worse than just the sloppily-dressed girl-next-door. She looked like a slept-in Qantas blanket.' That was the kindest bit. She went on to describe Kylie as a 'filthy-mooded funnel-web spider' and suggested that Kylie could take lessons from a real high-flying star, like Joan Collins. Poor Kylie probably did not have a clue who Joan Collins was. Rook's assassination coincided with the publication of topless pictures of Kylie in the *Sun*. They were the ones that had been taken when she was holidaying in Bali with Jason Donovan, some eighteen months earlier.

It was time for the shutters to come down. Terry Blamey decided, at least temporarily, that Kylie was receiving too much publicity, and that her audience was in danger of getting sick of her. Officially, she refused all interviews for a while, because she needed rest to recharge her batteries. The publicity bandwagon had been temporarily derailed, and even requests from Australian media were turned down. One of the few newspapers to achieve access was the *Melbourne Sun*, which had carried 150 stories about Kylie in one year. The editor Colin Duck explained that featuring Kylie meant they sold more papers. It was as simple as that, and very much the same formula that accounted for the enormous coverage the late Princess Diana always received.

And it was not just the Press giving Kylie a tough time. She went with Pete Waterman to Peter Stringfellow's Hippodrome nightclub off Leicester Square, and was allegedly spat on, full in the face, by a drunken mob of jealous girls. The story may have become exaggerated in the retelling, but one eyewitness said that the girls called her names and were jostling her: 'She didn't say a word – just struggled out of her seat and was ushered out.' Kylie learnt a valuable lesson that night – nobody cool ever went to the Hippodrome. It is also interesting that, after the early mauling she received in London, Kylie chose within a few years to make her permanent home in the city.

Success and survival have come at a price, as her continuing health battles and the general brevity of her relationships illustrate. She literally began her musical career at the top of Mount Everest, having reached the summit in a comfortable cable car. The only way was down. Kylie is not renowned for revealing too much in interviews, preferring to give, broadly speaking, the same answers in rotation. But her view of success is one that anybody who has tasted fame will know all about: 'I climbed the ladder of success. Now I'm right at the top, but when I look down from the dizzy heights there is no one there except me.'

Loneliness is a common theme running through Kylie's life. At the height of her fairytale return to the top of the charts in 2001, she confessed how isolated she felt as a star, especially when she faced night after night of hotel rooms in an energy-sapping tour: 'For two hours you are the greatest woman there is. You get such a kick and then it is all over.' Kylie finds herself alone in her room, wondering who she is and where her friends are. And then, more often than not, she will have a weep.

Tears have always come easily to Kylie. She cries a lot. She cried when she was discovered having sex with Paul Marcolin. She cried when she split from Michael Hutchence. She cried when she split from Jason Donovan. She cried when a journalist suggested that her biological clock was ticking and that, perhaps, she should think about settling down. She burst into tears three times at her farewell party from *Neighbours*. She left a restaurant in tears after a row with James Gooding. She cries when she cannot sleep in the middle of the night. She gives the impression of living her life right on the edge of her physical and emotional capabilities. As her great friend, confidant and style director William Baker observed, 'Everyone thinks she's smiley, happy people all the time.'

There is a certain neat irony about one scene from *The*

Henderson Kids, which Kylie has acknowledged was a turning point in her career. It was her first screen weep. She had made a mess of dyeing another character's hair and, distraught, ran off into the bushes where she was later discovered in tears. Kylie recalled, 'I was really nervous but found I could do it. The scene worked really well. Now I can get to those emotional moments and I can express them.'

The problem with being a celebrity is that you are always on show, even if you are tired, exhausted or upset. Once, she was openly crying in the street in Melbourne after some boyfriend trouble when a man came up to her, bold as brass, tapped her on the shoulder, shoved a piece of scruffy paper under her nose, and demanded an autograph. Kylie was so shocked she just signed it, so he would go away and leave her alone.

✳

Kylie's physical condition has always given the people around her plenty of cause for concern. When she was in *Neighbours*, her doctors were so worried about the physical stress her small frame was suffering, and her inability to keep her weight up, that they devised a special high-energy diet. This 'brown rice' regime was not something she enjoyed, especially as it was during this period that rumours surfaced about her suffering from anorexia nervosa. This is one of the few untruths about her that have really got under her skin. The fascination with her weight has continued year after year. She fluctuates between six and a half stone and seven stone (forty-four kilos). Food has been a constant worry over the years. Kylie was vegetarian for seven years in the nineties, until nutritionists insisted she needed to eat meat, because the stress involved in performing, combined with her light frame, meant that the weight would be burned off in a couple of days and she had to replace it.

The year 2001 may have been one of Kylie's most successful ever in terms of career – and in terms of a settled love life – but it was not good on the health front. She had no energy and her voice was giving way under the strain. It was a voice coach, rather than a doctor, who suggested there might be a problem with her protein intake, and advised that she should eat chicken regularly during the day to bolster her protein level. As a result, she started to feel much better towards the end of the year.

One of the amusing side-effects of this constant examination of her physique is that Kylie either eats or talks about food in the majority of her interviews. If she really put away this much grub, her famous rear end would be dragging along the ground by now:

February 1988: Jane Oddy notes that Kylie was 'tucking into calorific profiteroles'. The same month, the *Melbourne Sun* breaks off from congratulating her on reaching number one in the UK, to note that she was 'nibbling on a sandwich after having complained of hunger while having her photograph taken'. She dismissed concern that she now weighed six stone (thirty-eight kilos): 'I'm skinny, that's all.'

February 1989: A year on and she is telling *Smash Hits* that she tries to eat healthily: 'I'm not a vegetarian,' she insists, 'but I try not to eat things with too much fat or sugar.' She then proceeds to pass on the recipe for 'yummy' banana cream pie, of which sugar is a principal ingredient. At the time, she is sipping a strawberry-flavoured soya milk shake.

May 1989: Kylie is filming *The Delinquents* in Thailand, and tells a magazine journalist on the phone, 'Oh my God, a tray of strawberry cakes has just arrived.'

October 1996: The *Daily Mail* is shocked at 'how painfully thin, even ill, Kylie looked as she toyed with a rocket salad.'

August 1997: Kylie meets David Thomas of the *Daily Telegraph* at the trendy Soho House in London. She demolishes 'an oversized ravioli, prior to polishing off a plate of penne and a crème brulée.'

September 1997: In a private dining room at an exclusive Soho club Kylie is spotted by *MixMag* 'demolishing a plate of nouvelle cuisine noodles and sniggering over newspaper reports that she is anorexic.'

October 1997: She talks to *Esquire* magazine at Soho House. This time, 'She has a small portion of tagliatelle, eats half a dozen mouthfuls and pushes the plate aside.'

November 1997: Kylie, says *Cleo* magazine in Australia, is in the kitchen 'having a discreet nibble of pasta.'

June 1998: Kylie tells Swedish magazine *Solo* that she enjoys dinner at the fashionable London restaurant Nobu, where she always has yellowtail sashimi with jalapeno.

June 1999: An interview with both Kylie and Dannii for *Esquire* magazine. Kylie leaps from soup to chocolate cake. Dannii has cheese.

October 1999: Kylie tells *UK Style*, 'I'm cooking a family dinner tonight, so I've got to pick up some tuna steaks and wine.'

June 2000: *The Big Issue* magazine observes, 'She crams fruit salad into her mouth and pretends to talk through it.'

June 2000: The Australian magazine *Who Weekly* reports, 'Kylie is toying with her tomato and herb penne at Lunasa, a stylish bar in London's Fulham.'

July 2000: She tells Tony Romando of *Minx* that after seven years of being a vegetarian she has changed back to meat. 'I'm far healthier,' she confides.

September 2001: The *Daily Mirror* reveals, 'Despite her childlike physique, though, she has a mammoth appetite and has just finished a huge steak and chips.'

October 2001: Kylie recalls in *Time Out* that she had been camping eighteen months earlier and had spent the time cooking 'eggs and bacon on the fire'.

October 2001: She informs *Rolling Stone* that she enjoys working in Peter Gabriel's Bath studio because of the kitchen. She enthuses, 'There's really good food in there.'

December 2001: A comprehensive feature appears in *The Face*, chatting to Kylie over a couple days. Kylie starts off by munching an apple, she eats toast as her hair is done, she has chicken for lunch, she eats a bacon sandwich as her plane takes off for Germany, orders a rump steak in a Berlin restaurant, nibbles chicken pieces during a costume fitting to keep her energy levels up and, for good measure, confides that she loves bangers and mash.

Winter 2001: *Now* reveals that Kylie does not diet especially. 'I do eat junk food like chips and ice cream,' she confides.

December 2001: *TV Hits* magazine asks Kylie what she eats. 'I tend to eat little amounts all through the day but I've had occasions when I order a huge meal and people look at me at the end, absolutely shocked.'

February 2002: Kylie tells *heat* magazine that she is now following a diet called Eat Yourself Slim, in which you can eat as much as you want, as long as you don't eat certain foods.

February 2002: Kylie tells *heat* magazine, in another interview, that the previous night she ate a dark chocolate truffle cake: 'My main course wasn't very nice, so I moved straight on to dessert.'

How on earth does Kylie fit in singing and performing, when so much time is taken up with eating?

There is a serious side to this obsessive reportage of Kylie's eating habits. She does need to eat regularly, to stave off the old enemies of tiredness and exhaustion. And the more articles that mention her Billy Bunter appetite, the less likely it is that the dreaded spectre of anorexia will ever be mentioned again.

Confidentially: 'I love my food, actually.'

kylie
unexpected

KYLIE WAS INCONSOLABLE. Her friends were offering as much support as they could, but she was heartbroken. Even those who were little more than work colleagues found themselves providing a shoulder to cry on. One who had never had a real conversation with the singer recalled, 'Kylie actually sobbed on my shoulder. It was very unusual for her because she wasn't that kind of person, but for me it was sort of a special moment that she was talking to me 'cause she didn't, she wasn't a natural, she would have her select people she'd talk to and I wasn't one of them, so she was obviously very down indeed for her to talk to me. It just started with "I'm feeling down" and went from there.'

The reason for Kylie's despair was the disintegration of her relationship with the man who was the love of her life, rock singer and sex god Michael Hutchence. The front man of Australian rock band INXS oozed sex and charisma in bucketloads. He could fill a stadium with his presence, fill a room with his wit and charm and, famously, fill his shorts. He was dangerous and exciting to know and, less than two years previously, he had chosen a suburban girl from Melbourne as his next conquest, a decision that would turn her whole life on its head. No wonder Kylie was so unhappy when she discovered he could not keep his fly zipped.

To understand the cataclysmic effect the tousle-haired Hutchence had on Kylie, it is essential to take a step back and examine where both stars were in their respective careers, and how they had achieved fame. The simplistic approach favoured by tabloid newspapers is that Kylie was a virginal girl-next-door, giving herself up to be sacrificed on the altar of perversion by the demonic Hutchence. Lurid tales always accompany the Hutchence name. Suggestions abound that he liked three-in-a-bed sex, was more than intrigued by sado-masochism and had a taste for heroin. He certainly confessed to his family that he tried heroin. As for sexual shenanigans, he himself would tell the story of how, once when he was on tour, he was presented with a seventeen-year-old nymphet wearing nothing more than a dog collar and lead. For the most part it is all hearsay and innuendo, mainly third and fourth hand – the traditional stuff of rock myths. Hardly any concrete evidence exists of his debauchery. Newspaper articles and books about the dead star are not littered with kiss-and-tell tales supporting the popular view of his lifestyle.

Kylie was not a virgin – in fact, she was already quite an expert. She had enjoyed a full relationship with Jason Donovan, and flings with other teenage boys. She was, perhaps, developing a taste for the dangerous side of sex, the thrill of getting caught. She was like a naughty school-girl, with a lollipop in her mouth and the Kama Sutra in her satchel. This is not to suggest a fascination with the Marquis de Sade, more a desire to seize the moment when passion presented an opportunity. Kylie's most revealing observation about her relationship with Hutchence remains, 'Michael was not as bad as everyone thought, and I was not as good. We met somewhere in the middle.'

Michael Hutchence was a classic leader of a rock band. He enjoyed taking his pick of girls and narcotics. He had the arrogance and exhibitionism of a born performer, but cloaked them in an almost childlike enthusiasm that made him fun to be with. When he first met Kylie at a club in Sydney's King's Cross area, where the city's most fashionable and exciting nightlife is to be found, he stunned her by making an outrageous sexual suggestion. It was the sort of blatant swagger of a remark, which many a teenage boy has tried once, only to get a fat lip for his cheek. But Hutchence was no teenager. He was twenty-seven and the most famous rock star in Australia. Exactly what he said is one of those urban myths that changes in every telling and retelling. The clean version is that she was standing self-consciously against a wall surrounded by minders when Hutchence, in typically worse-for-wear mode, lurched over and declared, 'I don't know what we should do first – have lunch or have sex.' Kylie was completely tongue-tied. She was not remotely equipped to deal with this approach from such a famous person: 'I couldn't believe he would talk to me, and I couldn't believe what he'd just said. I was speechless.'

Kylie was a very suburban young woman from a city which, at that time, was hardly cutting-edge. Her acting career had led to abnormal teenage years. Being a young actress, almost a child star, is like being a boy wonder at football – you don't live in the real world, but in a strange,

timeless environment, where you are cosseted and protected. Kylie had the qualities of an ingénue. She had
intrigued Hutchence. Before he crossed paths with her
again, he mentioned her name in an interview in *Smash
Hits* magazine: 'Kylie Minogue . . . hmmmm . . . she's got a
horrible voice . . . actually I met her once and she was very
sweet.'

While Kylie was growing up, protected in the Melbourne
suburb of Camberwell, Michael Hutchence was already
travelling the world, and had enjoyed a cosmopolitan and
enlightened upbringing. He was born Michael Kelland
John Hutchence, in Sydney on 22 January 1960. The name
Kelland was after his father Kell, an international business-
man who bears a passing resemblance to David Niven. His
glamorous mother Patricia was a model, and also ran a
modelling school in the city. When Michael was four, his
father accepted a job as managing director of a firm import-
ing whisky and champagne for restaurants in Hong Kong. It
would mean a major upheaval for the family.

It was a very urbane ex-pat world in which Michael, his
younger brother Rhett and teenage stepsister Tina found
themselves. After a nine-hour flight from the January sun
of Sydney to the bustling, humid, Far East metropolis, the
family checked in to the Hong Kong Hilton. Michael
Hutchence seemed to spend a good deal of his life in the
impersonal environment of an expensive hotel room. The
family settled in to a life of cocktail parties and afternoon
tea. And soul music. Michael recalled, 'There were loads of
parties and good music like James Brown and Aretha
Franklin. Mine were hip parents.' His mother found work
as a make-up artist on movies being shot in Hong Kong.
The actress Nastassja Kinski was the same age as Michael
and was a guest at his sixth birthday party, when her father
Klaus was starring in a film called *Sumuru*. When the family

moved in to their own apartment, they employed two servants, who would address young Michael as 'Master'.

He may not yet have been a 'man of the world', but Michael was certainly a 'boy of the world' by the time the family returned to Sydney in late 1972 when he was twelve. He was more an international citizen than an Australian. He explained in *Spin* magazine, 'I had a problem with Australia. In the first place, I hated it. I had all the same prejudices in my head that the English have about it – hats with corks dangling to keep the flies away and kangaroos. Once I got there I realized it was different, but I couldn't believe the people where I went to school. I just hated the place.' One saving grace was that his best buddy at the school was Andrew Farriss, equally shy and even more serious, who would join Michael in finding fame with INXS. The pair would chat for hours, discussing poetry and music.

Michael, already a shy boy with a subtle lisp, retreated further into the world of books and, in particular, poetry, which remained a constant love in his life. He was soon to suffer another upheaval when his parents' marriage, which had been rocky in Hong Kong, collapsed completely with Patricia leaving for Los Angeles with Michael, now an impressionable fifteen, in tow. Michael took to life in LA like a duck to water, and began a lifelong enjoyment of girls and marijuana. But, at seventeen, Michael was back in Sydney and had decided a career in music was for him, especially when he discovered how easy it was to get girls, as the singer in the band. He played his first gig on 16 August 1977, the date Elvis Presley died. They called themselves The Farriss Brothers, an uninspiring name, which would eventually be ditched in favour of INXS. As soon as he finished school later that year, Michael was off again, this time to Perth in Western Australia, with Andrew and the rest of the 'brothers'. Another year, another home.

By the time he reached the age of twenty, INXS had taken off, and were playing nightly gigs all across Australia. Michael was living with a girl called Vicky in Sydney. However, he had met another girl with whom he was to spend seven years. His relationship with Michele Bennett – tall, leggy and brunette – was arguably the most important of his life. They lived together in a two-bedroomed terraced house Michael had bought in the Paddington area of Sydney. The relationship was very stable and loving, even though Michael was prone to infidelity. For all his reputation as a great womanizer and hellraiser, Michael had a surprising number of stable, important relationships throughout his short life. Michael's friends and family assumed that, one day, he and Michele would marry. Revealingly, his legendary status as a serial cheater on the road with INXS owed much to his fear of being alone. Even after their split, he would remain in constant touch with Michele – including the night he died – ringing her from all over the world, to seek reassurance and to help him get to sleep. His mother Patricia recalled that just hearing her voice would calm him down. She also described poignantly in her memoir to her son, *Just A Man*, how Michael had told her of their split: 'I watched him walking away, looking so lonely and, somehow, had a feeling that he and Michele would never, ever break off their relationship. I was right, they never did. Until the day he died, Michael loved her.'

Intriguingly, in the light of his future break-up with Kylie, infidelity was only part of the problem with Michele. She wanted to pursue her career as a video and film producer, and he wanted someone to be with him, pandering to his every need, twenty-four hours a day. That person was not Michele Bennett and it certainly was not the ambitious Kylie Minogue. It may well have been his last love Paula Yates, but fate would cruelly intervene.

Hutchence was carrying a great deal of emotional baggage by the time he stumbled up to Kylie in that King's Cross club. This was no shallow Casanova. He was very well read, a pop philosopher, as well as a collector of fine art and beautiful things. Kylie Minogue was very collectable. The club where they met was hosting the party after the annual Countdown Music Awards ceremony, the Australian equivalent of the Grammys or the Brits. INXS had already collected a sackful of awards, but Kylie was a musical novice. She had won the TV Logie for Most Popular Actress in Australia for *Neighbours*, but had been invited to this event because 'The Loco-Motion', her first single in Australia, was the current number one. By contrast, INXS had produced one of the biggest albums worldwide in 1987, in their enduring rock masterpiece *Kick*, which sold eight million copies. Hutchence, never prone to public self-doubt, once boasted to a journalist, 'I am a f***ing great rock star.' And he was. No wonder Kylie was starstruck. But, amazingly, it was Kylie who made Michael Hutchence a 'celebrity'.

After that first unforgettable encounter, it would be another year before Kylie and Michael met again, this time in Melbourne. It was towards the end of 1988 and the mammoth INXS Kick tour was coming to an end. Kylie and Jason had gone to the concert together and been invited to the end-of-tour party afterwards. Kylie's career had gone into overdrive during the past year, with her Stock, Aitken Waterman alliance in the UK triggering an enormous press interest. Her British debut single 'I Should Be So Lucky' was the biggest-selling record of the year in the British charts. Hutchence had not stood still either. The aptly named single, 'Need You Tonight', was a number one in the States and reached number two in the UK (only to be outsold a couple of weeks later by 'Especially For You' by Kylie and Jason). Kylie had even admitted in a pop profile that INXS was her favourite band. Kylie still was not at ease at celebrity functions, as if, in some way, she did not have a right to be mingling with so many famous people. The irony of her reticence was that she and Jason, the old married couple from *Neighbours*, would be the only guests recognized in every supermarket in the land – and probably most of the world.

During this second chance meeting, the conversation was more civilized. Hutchence apologized for his derogatory remarks about Kylie's music and proceeded to turn on the charm like a 200-watt bulb. He was not particularly handsome, with the thin frame of a rock star heavily involved in drugs. His intake had markedly increased during the tour, and he was seen literally knocking back a handful of ecstasy tablets before he went on stage. His face bore the residue pock marks of bad teenage acne and had led to him unkindly being called 'crater face'. He could not compete with the blond surfer-boy looks of Jason Donovan. But few women could resist his doleful eyes, or the feeling he gave them when he was talking to them that they were the centre of the universe.

Kylie has never been a heavy drinker and, while everyone else was over-indulging in the substances on offer, she allowed Hutchence to fetch her a Bailey's to sip. Kylie was not head-over-heels at this point. This was a rock party and she was not totally relaxed. Michael's mother Patricia recalled, 'Wholesome Jason and Kylie looked so out of place amidst the heavy rock and rollers.' Amusingly, she broke the habit of a lifetime to ask Jason and Kylie for an autograph and was deeply embarrassed to discover they were in the middle of an argument. Especially for you?

The romance so far had been such a slow starter that it resembled the desultory meetings of the film *When Harry Met Sally*. Kylie was actually asked by a teen magazine to comment on the INXS singer's new shorter haircut the following May: 'I think people really liked his long hair. I'm not really interested in Michael Hutchence, but I'm sure people will get used to it.'

When Michael next met Kylie, things began to move. It was late September 1989 and this time the city was Hong Kong. Intriguingly, Kylie had given an interview earlier in the month, in which she confided that she wanted to meet more pop stars because it would be interesting to talk to other people in the same business. But, she said, not about work: 'Talking about work is so boring!' She was about to get her chance. Michael's latest relationship with the svelte American model Jonnie had finished when he walked out, leaving her devastated in New York. He had a home in Hong Kong, a welcome haven where he could escape the glare of western fame, and indulge a passion for opium.

Out of the blue, he heard through a mutual friend that Kylie was coming to Hong Kong on her way to perform four concerts in Japan. He cleared his diary to make sure he was around when she visited. A dinner date was arranged and Kylie waited patiently in her hotel suite for the singer to pick her up. She waited and she waited. Hutchence had never been on time for anything and he was not about to start now. This did not go down well with 'Kylie Minogue Limited', who had formed their usual protective shield around her. When Hutchence eventually showed up, he was greeted by a gallery of angry faces – Kylie's mum Carol, manager Terry Blamey, a personal assistant and four dancers. The atmosphere failed to faze the rock star, who whisked Kylie off to a local restaurant and completely charmed her, despite the meal making her feel queasy. 'From that terrible start, we had a fantastic time,' she said. 'We talked and talked into the night until we literally had to be separated.'

Kylie was just twenty-one, famous but unworldly, and thus fascinated and overpowered by her companion's articulation and knowledge. Hutchence had a view or a witty comment on every subject, and Kylie was a blank canvas on which he could work. This time Kylie was completely hooked. But what was more surprising, so was Michael. He found her fun, fresh and genuine in a world full of fakes: 'She's a very underestimated person, she looks absolutely fabulous, she's very honest, she has no pretensions, she's unjaded. The amount of people in her position I've met and I wouldn't want to spend thirty seconds with. There is nothing worse than successful people who are miserable.'

After some sightseeing in Hong Kong, with Michael as the perfect gentleman guide, the Kylie circus moved on to Japan for a gig at the Tokyo Dome in front of 38,000 fans. She was, and remains, an enormous star in Japan. After the show she was back in her hotel room, relaxing with her entourage, when Hutchence walked in. He had followed Kylie from Hong Kong, a clear indication of his intentions. Everyone decided to go out clubbing. Michael romantically kept trying to hold Kylie's hand like a lovestruck kid and Kylie kept slapping it playfully away. By the end of the evening, however, her resistance had melted. This night marked the start of a relationship which would blossom and flourish, making the year 1990 one of the happiest of Kylie's life. She fell deeply in love with her rock star. For his part, as his mother Patricia once wisely observed, 'Michael loved being "in love".'

Rumours that Michael and Kylie were an item quickly spread throughout the music world. Nobody could believe it. The public perception was that Michael was so cool and Kylie was so uncool. 'It was shocking for everyone,' she admitted, 'including me.' Even their respective families at first dismissed the rumours as pure gossip. By Christmas of that year, however, everyone knew. Already the famous couple had been playing a game of cat and mouse with the world's paparazzi, with photographs of them together being bought and sold for vast sums. Kylie was already accustomed to this daily intrusion, but it was new to Michael. He would find himself even more the focal point of long lenses during his notorious relationship with Bob Geldof's wife, Paula Yates.

While Kylie's romance with Michael was blossoming, Jason Donovan was being portrayed as some sort of cuck-olded fool. This is very unfair on Kylie, as her relationship with Jason had been drifting ever since their pop careers had exploded into life. Jason has admitted, 'I found it really hard to deal with her fame at the time. We broke up and she went out with Michael and it was splashed every-where, I was the one that copped that. It was a hard time for me, having spent personal time with her and then her moving on to the guy that I wanted to be. That was pretty hard.' Kylie's friends are adamant that her relationship with Jason was over before her affair with Hutchence ignited. One explained, 'Kylie is quite moral.' Kylie did see Jason soon after she had fallen in love with Michael Hutchence. It was at the recording of Band Aid II's version of 'Do They Know It's Christmas?', destined to be the 1989 Christmas number one. An eyewitness observed that both Jason and Kylie were in tears: 'It was very awkward because they hadn't seen each other for some time. It was quite emotional.' Kylie and Jason had begun the year on top of the world with 'Especially For You', but ended it apart. Kylie was with Michael and a changed woman. It is a cruel irony that Jason enjoyed his first solo number one during the year – 'Too Many Broken Hearts'. Kylie, too, had a chart-topper with 'Hand on Your Heart', a plea to a lover to confess that their relationship is really over. Pop music, so often accused of being shallow, can often provide a commentary on life and lives, as Kylie was soon to prove again with 'Better The Devil You Know', a song which appeared to encapsulate the image of Michael Hutchence.

Kylie was behaving like a teenager in love, even though she would soon be twenty-two. She had to fulfil commitments in the UK, including a short concert tour, but she was constantly on the phone to Michael, displaying a mixture of excitement and insecurity. In fairness, Michael did his share of calling her, and her entourage were getting used to his familiar greeting, 'Hi Babe', if one of them picked up the telephone when she was busy. When Kylie grabbed the phone, she would always leave the room so that she could talk privately. No one could fail to notice the immediate change that had come over Kylie. She described it as having had her blinkers taken off. During the next six months she would, under Michael's influence, start reshaping her life and taking control of her own destiny. It was this period, which so many perceived at the time as Kylie firmly going off the rails, which actually sowed the seeds of survival. Back at PWL in London, they were noticing a complete personality change: 'After she met Michael, you could tell that she was stronger. Before, she might have said if she didn't think something was a good idea, but afterwards she just wouldn't do it.' The Hutchence philosophy was that she was a star, *the* star, and everyone around her was serving her, not the other way round. He described it as wearing an 'ego jacket' – whenever she messed up it was not her fault, it was the person in the jacket.

After her London commitments, Kylie was able to spend some quiet time with Michael in Hong Kong before they both flew on to his home in Sydney to prepare for Christmas. The romance was already public property, something denied her fans during her relationship with Jason

Donovan. Kylie was used to the persistent press scrutiny and had managed it successfully during her time with *Neighbours*. Hutchence hated it. He was mortified when they were secretly photographed enjoying each other's company in Sydney's Centennial Park. The Australian magazine *Woman's Day* devoted three pages to a set of pictures showing the couple happy and embracing, with Kylie soaking up the sun in a bra top. They also appeared in the *News of the World*.

The cameras followed them everywhere – taking rides around the city on Michael's Harley-Davidson, going to the movies, or just hanging out in cafés, bars and clubs. Michael would recommend books for Kylie to read, or he would rent classic films like *Casablanca* and *Citizen Kane* for them to watch together in his minimally furnished apartment. Kylie revelled in Sydney's more cosmopolitan culture and, away from the camera shutters, she was having the time of her life. Such was her lover's influence that she broke her personal ban on taking drugs. It was not the sort of intake to persuade rehabilitation centres to put out a welcome mat. It amounted to no more than a little dope and the occasional ecstasy tablet, but it didn't stop the now notoriously false rumour spreading that Kylie was rushed to hospital to have her stomach pumped after her experimentation went wrong. She was most displeased, and just last year stated categorically, 'I was not even in the country at the time!'

Drugs have never played a major part in Kylie's life. She was not happy about Jason's consumption and, even under the influence of Hutchence, she never went through an opium-den phase. She did, however, appreciate her lover's point of view concerning freedom of choice. Drugs and, in particular, ecstasy were an essential ingredient of the rock-star lifestyle in the nineties and, in Sydney, Hutchence and his friends would indulge before hitting the clubs and staying out most of the night. It was exhausting and repetitive but, as Kylie explained to *Q* magazine, 'I've experimented, yes; some things you can only talk about if you've had experience of them – so I'm thankful for that experience. But I would condemn drugs now. I guess there's a drug for each decade and ecstasy is this decade's drug.'

Those who try to pin down Michael's influence on Kylie to one thing are missing the point. It was not just about popping a few pills or a more adventurous sex life. That was part of it – not least when Kylie's luggage revealed a pair of handcuffs in an airport security check. It was a life change. Kylie liked her new friends. Through Hutchence, for instance, she met Nick Cave, poet and Gothic Prince of Darkness, who was to have a huge creative influence on Kylie during the mid-nineties. This new 'circle' embraced Kylie. They did not treat her like a miniature Barbie doll or a trophy girlfriend for Michael. They found her bright, fun and a tonic for their jaded palates. As Tim Farriss, INXS guitarist and brother of Andrew, told music journalist Adrian Deevoy, 'Kylie's a lovely girl and Michael really loves her. So if you were thinking of writing anything smart arse about them, prepare to have your legs broken slowly and painfully.'

The rest of the world became aware of the change in Kylie at the Australian première of her first starring role in the feature film *The Delinquents*. Hutchence was there, looking every inch the dissolute rock star, complete with garishly patterned trousers, a waistcoat for a shirt and a pair of ill-fitting army boots. Next to him was a girl no one recognized, his latest conquest no doubt. She was petite, fit-looking with a tight 'suicide blonde' wig and a micro-dress with a pattern of noughts and crosses. The photographers took her picture in the weary way they reserved for nameless rock chicks, until the whisper went round. It was Kylie! Gone were the bubble haircut, the comfy denim teenage outfits and the self-effacing cheery smile. This was a sex bomb at a première, years before Liz Hurley and her ilk used such occasions to get noticed. It was a bold, rebellious statement, not just challenging the public perception of Kylie and that of her fans, but also making the powers that be at PWL sit up and splutter into their morning tea. It was a watershed moment in Kylie's career, and Hutchence gave her the courage to go through with it.

This was one of the few moments in Kylie's career when her private and public life dovetailed neatly together. She wanted everyone to see her and to realize that she was now with Michael Hutchence: a new independent, grown-up Kylie. Soon, their respective careers would mean they would be apart more than they were together. Kylie was preparing for her first real tour, when she would be singing live with a full band instead of using backing tracks. She spent Christmas, as she always preferred to, with her family back in Melbourne and then plunged into rehearsals for her tour's first night at the Brisbane Entertainment Centre. She did, however, drop everything to fly into Sydney for Michael's thirtieth birthday party, which she helped organize in a large warehouse, a favoured venue for rock events. Her sister Dannii had helped her bake a special chocolate cake which, candles ablaze, Kylie brought into the room, followed by a boisterous conga line of most of the 200 guests.

Kylie told Pete Waterman that she wanted some time off from recording in the early part of 1990. She stayed in Sydney, while Michael and INXS worked on a new album, which would eventually be entitled X. Kylie would spend most of the days hanging around the studio, grasping the opportunity to watch and learn, in a way she had never been allowed to in the studios of Stock, Aitken and Waterman. They took time off to travel back to Hong Kong and also took a holiday on Great Keppel Island on the idyllic north-eastern coast of Australia. Kylie travelled with Terry

Blamey, but without Michael, to Los Angeles, to work with some American producers on tracks for a new album. She dedicated one of the songs called 'Count The Days' to the lover she was missing.

Kylie soon had to fly back to the UK for spring tour dates and the full extent of her 'change' was becoming apparent. In May, her new single 'Better The Devil You Know' was due for release and, for the first time, Kylie exercised control over her image. She presented Stock, Aitken and Waterman with the video for the song, which she had filmed in Melbourne, and they had little choice but to accept it. It was noticeable for the new, raunchy Kylie, dancing seductively in the arms of a muscular black dancer, and also for the large ring on her finger, a gift from Michael, which she seemed to be flashing for the camera at every opportunity. It was emblazoned with the letter M.

Michael joined her in London at the end of her tour. The relationship looked set to last, as the couple began a continental holiday by travelling on the romantic Orient Express. Kylie helped Michael choose a $500,000 villa to buy in the French village of Roquefort les Pins, on the Riviera between Nice and Cannes. It was a magnificent 400-year-old farmhouse, with five bedrooms. Kylie and Michael would speed up and down the coast on a motorbike. Back in London, they were in danger of becoming a familiar showbiz couple; Michael took Kylie to see John Malkovich in *Burn This*, a theatrical *tour de force* and one of the West End hits of the year. Eyewitnesses in the audience reported that he spent most of the performance twanging Kylie's bra strap. There was still time for another legendary story to emerge: this time it was that Michael and Kylie had joined the 'mile-high club' on a jumbo jet when the Australian Prime Minister Bob Hawke was seated a row in front. According to one of Michael's entourage, they had just a blanket to cover their modesty. Kylie is petite, but this is not something that should be attempted in economy seats. The whole incident was given a 'Carry On' flavour, with the suggestion that Mr Hawke had turned round and winked at them.

Kylie's life could not have been more perfect, or so it seemed. She now had control of her career for the first time. She was a multi-millionairess. And she was in love. The only cloud on the horizon was the fact that Michael was back on tour, promoting the new INXS album. It began in Europe but, over the coming months, would take him all over the world and keep them apart. Kylie could be forgiven for feeling insecure, considering his past reputation. The couple spent Christmas together at the farmhouse and Michael gave her a Gucci watch as a present. They were joined by fellow musician Chris Bailey and his wife Pearl, old friends from the time Michael was with Michele Bennett. Kylie cooked for everyone, and did her best to make it a happy, festive time, even though it was the first time she had spent the holiday season away from Melbourne and missed having her family around her.

What Kylie did not know was that the famous celebrity photographer Herb Ritts had introduced Michael to the breathtakingly beautiful Danish supermodel Helena Christensen, who was just nineteen. By the time he had crossed the Atlantic for January dates in Mexico and the States, he was spending almost as much time on the phone to Helena as he was to Kylie. Rumours of his womanizing – including with singer Belinda Carlisle – and pictures of him with glamorous companions were not helpful, but it is always one particular fixation which is the most dangerous for a relationship. Michael Hutchence loved being 'in love'. Kylie, promoting her new album *Rhythm of Love*, was more independent now than when she first met Hutchence. Did she still need him as much as she had done a year ago? Was Helena about to become his next 'work in progress'?

In New York, in February, events took a complicated turn with both Helena and Kylie in town at the same time. Michael's mother Patricia recalled meeting Helena at the INXS concert at Meadowlands, the first time the model had seen the band. The next day, Patricia was expecting Michael to arrive for lunch with Miss Christensen and was stunned when he appeared with Kylie, for a distinctly frosty meal. She did not see Kylie again. Michael and Helena stayed together for four years, until Paula Yates arrived on the scene. Although Kylie was distraught by what had happened, and did not speak to Michael for many months, she emerged from their relationship a stronger person.

*

On a late November day in 1997, Kylie was awoken at 4 am by a telephone ringing persistently. Calls at that time in the morning are never good news. Michael Hutchence was dead, at the age of thirty-seven. He was the first person to die whom she had loved and, understandably, she was completely devastated. Michael had been found naked, kneeling on the floor behind the door of his room at the fashionable Ritz Carlton Hotel in Double Bay, Sydney. His belt was around his neck, the buckle apparently having broken under his weight as he dangled from the hook on the back of the door. There was at the time, and remains to this day, intense speculation as to the reason for his death. The most controversial is that it was an act of auto-eroticism that went wrong.

The New South Wales Coroner Derek Hand decided a full inquest was not necessary. In his report, he stated, 'I am satisfied that the standard required to conclude that this death was a suicide has been reached.' Hutchence's blood contained a cocktail of cocaine, alcohol, Prozac and other prescription drugs. He was involved in a difficult custody wrangle with Bob Geldof over Paula Yates' children. One of the saddest aspects of the tragedy was that he had twice called his first serious love, Michele Bennett, but both times only connected to her answering phone. On hearing the messages and how upset he sounded, Michele rushed round to the hotel but could not raise him when she banged on his hotel door. Reluctantly, she left a message at reception and went home.

The untimely deaths of rock heroes seem to make time stand still: John Lennon, Kurt Cobain, Jim Morrison and Jimi Hendrix are just part of a list that will now for ever include Michael Hutchence. If his death was suicide, it is even more distressing, because he had deserted his eighteen-month-old baby with Paula Yates, Tiger Lily. Just a short time before that fateful night, he had told journalist Sharon Klum that he 'would jump in front of train for his daughter'. Kylie was once asked what she thought of the idea that Hutchence was just in search of an orgasm – something which Prozac could sometimes inhibit. She thought it made it more bearable to think that he died for that reason, rather than killing himself because he was in so much pain.

When you are a celebrity, you are never allowed to forget a relationship. Not one. Kylie would never want to forget Michael Hutchence, but she has scarcely given an interview in the past ten years, both before and after his death, where his name has not been mentioned. The only time they had reportedly got close since their break-up was after an INXS concert in 1994 when, at the subsequent party, they were spotted disappearing into a toilet cubicle for nearly an hour. It may have been a sexual encounter, or Michael may have just wanted to chat to Kylie while he got 'off his face' on one drug or another. She was now firmly filed in his mind under 'f' for 'friend'. In fact, they saw each other fairly regularly and remained on good terms until his death. Kylie has always politely explained that Michael was a great influence on her life, and helped her to make the change from girl to woman. Many tears have been shed, some in public and many in private. But they are not bitter tears.

The most poignant memory came on New Year's Eve 1998, when she was celebrating in the town of Whistler in Canada with her then boyfriend Stephane Sednaoui. Out of the blue, an INXS record came on the radio and she heard Michael's voice once more. Out loud, she exclaimed, 'Of course, you turn up now!' She has sensed him with her on several occasions since his death. Hutchence remains a strong presence in her life, a little like a guardian angel, but more an intangible reassurance that life will continue to move forward, if she takes control of her destiny. She told Kevin O'Sullivan of the *Daily Mirror*, 'I don't mind talking about Michael, but please don't say I cried. I am a big girl now.'

At Michael's funeral Kylie was quiet, dignified and did her best to support his grieving family. With masterful timing, which would have tickled Hutchence, the heavens opened and a loud crack of thunder greeted the arrival of his coffin. Kylie even managed a smile at the celestial intervention. Michael Hutchence was most definitely not saintly, but nor was he the devil. His throwaway line that his hobby was 'corrupting Kylie' was nothing more than a soundbite. Kylie is demonstrably a stronger, more focused individual than he ever was. Ironically, her romance with Hutchence turned out to be a brilliant career move, something which hardly seemed the case at the time.

Confidentially: 'I would not have missed our relationship for anything and I miss him'.

kylie

stylish

IT WAS AN UNDERCOVER OPERATION. Kylie was smuggled into Raymond's Revue Bar, home of the famous Soho sex show, for a photo shoot. She was not exactly hiding underneath a blanket, but it would have ruined the surprise if the newspapers had been tipped off that she was seen going in. Kylie has never been short of a few surprises, but this was one of the last places the Stock, Aitken and Waterman star would have been expected to frequent. Kylie was very excited about the whole thing. This was to be her first fashion shoot for *Vogue* and she was desperate for it to be a success. The front cover of *Vogue* would be a credible fashion statement, at last. And it would add weight to her ongoing bid to break into America, and help set up her imminent move away from PWL.

The idea of photographing Kylie in a slightly seedy setting was an enterprising one, and she threw herself into a series of poses, wearing an alarming array of feathers. Everybody was waiting excitedly to see the finished result when the magazine hit the news-stands, especially the choice of picture they had decided to use on the cover. Disappointingly, the magazine arrived and the cover picture was of a standard, glossy model. Poor Kylie had been dumped inside, admittedly over eight pages. One of her entourage recalled, 'She could not understand why. But the magazine seemed to have the attitude that "we take the pictures and if there isn't an appropriate one for the cover, then we will use something else." Kylie was disappointed. We all believed when she did the shoot that it was for the front cover.'

Kylie had been on more than twenty front covers in Australia alone during her first year in *Neighbours*, so she was not used to being featured on the inside. It seems an incredible decision now, nearly ten years later, when Kylie's image is one of the very few that can add sales to a publication. The queen of magazine and newspaper covers at that time was Diana, Princess of Wales. But, since her death in 1997, only Kylie has come through to stake a claim to the crown. Pretenders to the throne, like Victoria Beckham and Geri Halliwell, have become tiresome to the public. Kylie's great strength is that she appeals to male and female in equal measure.

Leading fashion writer Alison-Jane Reid explained, 'Kylie is ideal cover material because she is an established star who has re-invented herself with the help of the world's best designers and stylists. She is sexy and womanly and totally comfortable in her own skin. Lately she has been like a cheeky pin-up girl from the 1940s and it's an image that really suits her.'

The camera has always loved Kylie. It was something Jan Russ, the casting director for *Neighbours,* had specifically noticed at her first audition. The plain, mousy girl was totally transformed by the time her image appeared on a television monitor. Kylie has always had the gift of being able to flirt with the camera. It was the same when she came to London. One stylist recalled, 'Put Kylie in front of a camera and she becomes alive. She makes love to the camera. She is fantastic at posing, as if it is the most natural thing in the world. Not having any inhibitions about your body helps.' Not surprisingly, Kylie has formed close bonds with photographers, not only ex-boyfriend Stephane Sednaoui – she learned a lot of her poses from him – but also with Katerina Jebb, whom she met in Paris in the early nineties and with whom she has a fantastic rapport. Kat, as she is known to friends, has taken some of the most moving and erotic pictures of Kylie.

The camera does not care whether Kylie is short or tall, voluptuous or slim. She is styled to appear stylish. Kylie's physique is, on first appearance, an unpromising one for a style icon. Traditionally, catwalk models are elegant, long-legged and svelte, as, of course, was Princess Diana. Kylie's legs are so little that sport was something to be avoided at all costs at school. 'It was the worst thing ever,' she said. She was always the puny one who was last to be picked for any team game.

Kylie has probably suffered more barbs – and allegedly funny allusions – to her size than any other star. She has had to bear every conceivable description of her lack of stature: 'pint-sized chartbuster', 'diminutive diva', 'pop pixie', 'perfectly tiny', 'pop trinket', 'wee Kylie', 'miniature Madonna', and, unsurprisingly, the well-worn remark that she is always the last to know it's raining. Sometimes Kylie can be quite coy about her actual height, stating enigmatically that 'it varies'. She is actually 152 centimetres high, just a hair above five feet, a height she shares with her mother Carol. Sister Dannii is also petite. Kylie used to hate being small, especially as she was easy to spot in school photos: 'I was usually the one holding that darn board in front.' Kylie is by no means the only pop star who is on the small side, but she is the one who has had her height alluded to in almost every newspaper article from the time of 'I Should Be So Lucky' to the present day. But no one can tell how tall you are if you are the only person in front of the camera and, eventually, Kylie realized that being small actually made her stand out in the crowd.

When Kylie first arrived in London, her look was the responsibility of the PWL team, just as it might have been at a Hollywood Studio. Kylie has changed her image so many times, it is impossible to keep up. She might decide to change her look twenty minutes before going on stage.

The man responsible for Kylie's image is William Baker, her style guru and the man who converts her whims into reality. Baker, very camp and very gay, has seen Kylie's boyfriends come and go, but he is always there with a safety pin, some toupee tape or a sequin. His friends call him Joan, a tribute to his own personal icon Joan Collins. On the payroll he is Kylie's 'creative director', and she admits that they have such a close relationship that 'they are practically joined at the hip.' He is the kid sister Dannii was always too busy to be.

Baker met Kylie in 1993, when he was nineteen and working in the Vivienne Westwood store in Chelsea. Technically he was still at university in London studying theology, but he worked part-time as the 'Saturday boy' and dreamed of getting a break in the world of design. Kylie was already revered in the gay community. Baker had loved the video for the perennial gay favourite 'What Do I Have

To Do?' in which Kylie does some ironing. He loved the image of a superstar doing domestic chores. On a whim, he rang Kylie's record label deConstruction, and asked if she needed a stylist, only to learn that she was abroad. He left his name, number and the name of the shop and never expected to hear anything more. Three weeks later Kylie calmly walked into the store. William could not believe it, but boldly seized his opportunity: 'I leapt from behind the counter and bombarded her with ideas, and somehow persuaded her to go for a coffee.' The pair adjourned to a café across the road and Kylie listened intently to William's ideas. 'She probably thought I was mad,' he told Kylie's website, *Limbo*. Fortunately, she thought no such thing. Kylie, though initially reserved, is very astute at sizing people up and knowing who might be useful to her, and the obviously bright, witty and enthusiastic Baker looked a promising addition to 'Team Kylie' post Stock, Aitken and Waterman.

Kylie suggested Baker might want to meet her friend Katerina Jebb, who was photographing Kylie at the time. From that meeting came the idea of a shoot based around a Debbie Harry theme – the glamorous singer from Blondie whom Kylie had long admired and regularly watched on old videos. Baker dashed home and raided his boyfriend's old punk-era wardrobe for costumes for Kylie. He settled on a pair of ripped tights and a sleeveless Marilyn Monroe T-shirt which had once belonged to a girl who had worked at Andy Warhol's New York factory in the early seventies. Kylie loved the pictures, which were arty enough to fit into the overall strategy of her mid-nineties creativity, and they appeared in a small limited edition book that accompanied the release of the *Kylie Minogue* album.

Baker and Kylie became great friends and confidants. She calls him Willie. He is able to tune into her creative wavelength, as well as sharing her sense of campness. Kylie is *very* camp and always has been. She loves feathers and diamanté and dressing up. Her mother Carol, who helps with the costumes when Kylie goes on tour, also adores William. On the Intimate And Live box-office-busting tour of Australia in 1998, Kylie was on stage performing, while her mother and William were enjoying a drink backstage. 'After all,' he recalled, 'it was sponsored by Absolut vodka.' They decided it would be a hoot to dress up in wigs and costumes – Carol was Baby Spice and William was Boy George, whom he used to follow about when he was younger. Kylie bounced off stage to be greeted by these two 'stars', acting up like a pair of old drag queens. She was laughing so much that she had to be pushed back on stage for the encore.

Kylie does not take herself as seriously as some observers believe. She takes her career much more seriously than she takes herself. The images that she and Baker have come up with over the years are often no more than hammy pastiches of a look they picked up on from watching an old episode of *Dynasty*, or even *Doctor Who*, on the television. They are style magpies with attitude – if it's funny or different, then why not try it? Baker has likened their approach to the tongue-in-cheek style of a Hollywood B–movie actress. For the concert celebrating twenty-five years of Mushroom Records in Melbourne, Kylie was a geisha, emerging slowly from a pink glitter birthday cake, singing 'You will like my sense of style . . . . You will like my sense of style.' It was camp of the highest order.

In addition to the sense of fun that Baker brings to the party, he is also fiercely protective of his friend and style collaborator. He was incandescent with rage at the creation of the sobriquet 'IndieKylie' as a label hung on Kylie during the *Impossible Princess* project. He echoed the views of

Steve Anderson from Brothers In Rhythm, who believed the record company put too much emphasis on her Manic Street Preachers tracks, which were unrepresentative of the whole work. Kylie, diplomatically, has left it to these two friends and advisers to put across that particular point of view. Baker declared, 'Kylie has never been, and never will be, indie.'

One of the more popular and patronising ways of explaining 'Kylie chameleon' is that she is constantly being defined by her boyfriends. This is really only true of Michael Hutchence and Stephane Sednaoui, two of only three men for whom she has publicly declared her love (the other is James Gooding). They were able to influence her because she looked up to them. But Kylie has always been her own woman, absorbing ideas from others and putting her own spin on them. The sexy, rebellious look of the Hutchence era had already been brewing before they became a couple. The more curvaceous shape of her *Street Fighter* era was down to martial arts training. She went up three bra sizes, prompting the usual speculation that she had been cosmetically enhanced. Perhaps her least successful look was as a street waif when she was with Stephane. To a certain extent it was 'heroin chic' but everyone thought she was ill. At least it was different, and she did not look like Madonna.

By the time of the 1998 tour, Kylie's image needed a kick up her very famous backside. The Kylie that she and William Baker proceeded to present to the world was a camp classic, her stage show was like a Las Vegas cabaret extravaganza, nothing like an average pop concert. The disappointingly received *Impossible Princess* album may have been the most interesting she had ever done, but it did not lend itself to visually exciting presentation. It was brooding and introspective, and not in the least Liza Minnelli. Kylie began the set by showcasing some of the album, opening with a moody rendition of 'Too Far', Kylie clad in black descending a silver staircase in impossibly high heels. But the style momentum clicked into gear when she appeared underneath a glittery pink 'K' and sang 'I Should Be So Lucky', wearing a tiny, spangly showgirl's dress that revealed her perfectly proportioned legs. But she did not just belt out 'Lucky' as she had a thousand times before. This was a new jazzy arrangement, a putting-on-a-show Broadway Ballad, and it was thrilling. It absolutely brought the house down at every concert on the tour, from the Palais Theatre, Melbourne, to the Shepherd's Bush Empire in West London. Not only was it fun and kitsch, but it was also brilliantly done and caught the attention of all the jaded reviewers. The *Independent on Sunday* purred, 'It was fantastic. An inspired arrangement and Kylie even sang it well. The helium she overdosed on in the late 1980s has worn off.' Kylie was reclaiming her audience, the fans that she has said 'grew up with her'. Her image and music had finally fused into one, and this is the crucial element in her rapid rise to style icon in the last four years.

After 'Lucky', the show hurtled into Abba's 'Dancing Queen', an honorary Australian anthem since it featured in the film *Muriel's Wedding*. Kylie was flanked by two male dancers, wearing little but a few peacock feathers and some lurid pink shorts that left nothing to the imagination. They were pure Baker who happened, at the time, to be the boyfriend of one of the well-toned, well-muscled boys – the Fabulous Baker Boys. Tongue-in-cheek renditions of 'Shocked' and 'Better The Devil You Know' pleased her devoted fan base before 'Confide In Me', arguably her strongest song to date, provided a sultry encore. The show was a triumph and proved that Kylie was back. It was a daring return to form and demonstrated that the thirty-year-old Kylie had the maturity to carry off any design William Baker cared to throw at her.

The size of the venues in Australia gave Kylie enough space to exploit her own and Baker's ideas to the full. They had wanted to depict all the different images, or incarnations, that Kylie had brought to life over the years – rock slut, show pony, stripper and even cowgirl for the track 'Cowboy Style', well before Madonna adopted this look in 2000. Baker himself had painstakingly covered all the hats in sequins and silver glitter. He remembered giving some away to Kylie fans in Australia, who went to every single show, stood at the front and cheered their heroine. Even Cliff Richard fans are not this devoted. Not everything went smoothly. On one memorable night, Baker had omitted to properly fasten the zip holding up Kylie's cowgirl costume. The zip ever so slowly came undone, gently lowering the costume towards the floor. Underneath, Kylie was 'stark bollock naked', so Baker and Carol Minogue were in a state of high panic. Fortunately, Kylie's PA Natalie seized the initiative and ran on to the stage to save her employer's modesty, much to the disappointment of the vast majority of the audience.

The Intimate And Live tour was of enormous importance to Kylie's career and the public's perception of her, because it allowed her to reposition herself in the market place. It was her first major tour for seven years, and she was able to deliver the present without deserting the past. Formerly, she had been embarrassed by her previous incarnations, but now she gloried in them. She had the confidence not to reject 'I Should Be So Lucky', although she drew the line, on this occasion, at 'The Loco-Motion'. Steve Anderson, who produced the show, was determined that there would be no song involving moving your arms like a train, and threatened to stay behind in the UK if it found a slot.

*

When the triumphant tour was over, Kylie faced the problem of cashing in on that success. She had re-found her gay fan base, who loved the even camper versions of the songs they already considered classics. She had acquired many new fans who were oblivious to the vitriol previously heaped on the Stock, Aitken and Waterman song book. But there was no hit album to back up her rediscovered popularity. That would have to wait until the next tour. Instead, Baker persuaded Kylie that she should do a book. Everybody was always saying what a chameleon Kylie was, so why not present those changing images in one coffee-table book of photographs? It would be a voyage of discovery and consolidate the good work of the tour – namely, that Kylie was now a much-loved institution, entirely at ease with all her previous images.

The book, *Kylie* – titles have never been her strong point – was a study in reinvention, with images from throughout her life and career, and featured close-ups of most parts of her body, many life-size, including arm, foot, ears and bottom. The final product revealed that Kylie was reconciled with her past. In many of the previously unseen photographs, many taken by Baker, Sednaoui and Jebb, Kylie looks absolutely fabulous. She observed that she had to 'learn' how to have a photograph taken in the early days of her career. She also knows her best angle, such an important consideration for celebrities: 'Years of experience have taught me that angles do exist – everyone has one. Sometimes I'll get photographers trying to do things and I'll be like "I don't want to be rude but take my picture from the front and a little to the side and that's it." People say I do this arched eyebrow thing but they just take over.' Kylie's own favourites among her pictures are the ones in which she is laughing.

The project was rather egotistical, and strictly for devoted fans, but had some worth as a social document. Just as interesting as the pictures was the text – eulogistic vignettes from friends and admirers, like Baz Luhrmann, Nick Cave, Julie Burchill and Katerina Jebb. The violinist Nigel Kennedy revealed that he called his violin 'Kylie' because it was 'small, beautiful and portable'. Baker was fulsome in his praise of Kylie, asserting that her image changes were not cleverly orchestrated publicity stunts. More pertinently, he recognized that fashion had moved on, and that what was considered banal in the nineties was now thought to be fabulous, which is exactly what happened to Kylie herself in the latter part of the decade. *Kylie* was all about image and a life lived in the public eye, but seemed too posed. There was little private information.

Kylie even took to the catwalk in July 1999, at an Aids charity fashion show in Vienna. But for most of the year she was working on a new album, hoping to bury the memory of *Impossible Princess*, a title which, even before the untimely death of Princess Diana, suggested that Kylie was some kind of petulant prima donna. Part of the secret of being a style icon is to anticipate a fashion or a trend, so that you appear to be the leader and everyone who follows is copying you. Madonna has always been expert at this, whether as the 'Like A Virgin' slut or wearing a conical bra. Kylie's next reincarnation was as a disco diva for her frothy, retro album *Light Years*. The first single 'Spinning Around' went straight to number one in the UK and, from this position of strength, the new-look Kylie was every magazine editor's dream cover girl. Baker had worked out that Kylie's bottom was her best feature, and would give her an edge whenever she wore an outfit that showed it off.

Disco was cool once more, providing it was approached in a knowing fashion, with a wink to the audience. Kylie tapped into the trend by appearing in Ibiza at Privilege, which billed itself as the largest nightclub in the world. The fact that Kylie was chosen as the inaugural live act at the venue was testimony to the fact that it was now officially OK to be a fan. The 'K' from Intimate And Live had been replaced by 'Kylie' in neon bulbs, very seventies disco. Her dancers, clad in black, made robotic moves close to the swimming pool at the front of the stage. And there was Kylie at the top of the stairs – Tinkerbell herself – dressed in a pink vinyl jacket, pink micro-skirt with a slit up the back and little pink boots, giving the crowd a big, cheesy 'Lucky' grin. How times had changed. Or had they? In 1990, almost exactly ten years earlier, Kylie was asked what her latest fashion buy had been – it was a pair of pink ostrich feather hot pants. Perhaps Kylie was just not cool enough for them in those days.

The last time there had been live music on the Mediterranean DJ Mecca of Ibiza was in 1988, and you can bet nobody would have been seen dead turning up to watch Kylie Minogue and her gruesome Stock, Aitken and Waterman fodder. This island prides itself on a reputation for hedonism and Kylie was at that time too naff for that – not any more. The high spot was the track 'Your Disco Needs You', which outcamped the Village People for slightly sleazy fun. The dancers removed their tops to reveal oiled pecs (men) and powdered breasts decorated with black tassels (women). Kylie, meanwhile, had changed into a gold bikini top and frilly hot pants. There was the decadent air of *Cabaret*, with none of the threatening overtones. One reviewer noted, 'No one really dances during Kylie's set – they're too busy leering.'

After *Light Years*, her first album for major record label Parlophone, it was just a year before Kylie was back with *Fever*, and the single which has transformed Kylie's career yet again. In the wake of the incredible success of 'Can't Get You Out Of My Head', Kylie has become the number one style icon in the land. The stage costumes are getting even more outlandish – the famous revealing white ensemble for the video looked like a pastiche of something a scene of crime officer might wear. For *An Audience With Kylie Minogue* on television, she began by singing 'Spinning Around', wearing an exotic head-dress that looked like something out of a Busby Berkeley movie of the 1930s. More importantly, Kylie was beginning to make the fashion pages because of what she was wearing away from her stage persona. Her choice of dress for any occasion was being afforded the attention that in the past had been reserved for the Princess of Wales.

Kylie's people

Kylie's first stylist in London was Kelly Cooper Barr who looked after the Stock, Aitken and Waterman stable – never the most stylish bunch. Cooper Barr was presented with a well-scrubbed girl with unruly hair, who looked about twelve. She was instructed to 'turn her into the next Olivia Newton-John.' Kylie would have been delighted to emulate the star of *Grease*, a childhood heroine, but the willowy Newton-John and the diminutive Kylie were poles apart. 'I remember looking at Kylie,' said Cooper Barr, 'and thinking it was never going to happen. She was a soap star and I could never imagine her being as big as Newton-John.' But she had her instructions, and Cooper Barr was determined to do her best, although it never occurred to her to try and make anything sexy of Kylie: 'I despaired of turning this childlike figure into anything approaching a star.' Kylie was so small – sometimes a size six would fall off her – that they struggled to find outfits for her, most of the time resorting to figure-hugging Lycra, topped off with huge platform shoes and knee socks. Kylie can laugh about it now, but at the time she looked a sight.

Kelly and Kylie used to go to clubs together in the late eighties and it was always the make-up artist who would get chatted up, because the wolves on the dance floor would invariably assume that she was the famous pop star. Nobody recognized Kylie. Nearly fifteen years later, Cooper Barr believes the secret to Kylie's current irresistibility is her age. She explained, 'Most women don't smoulder until they get to their early thirties and reach sexual maturity.' In other words, sex appeal has given Kylie style. And style has given Kylie sex appeal.

She was named Style Icon of 2001 in the *Elle* Style Awards, while *heat* magazine made Kylie their most stylish woman of the year for the outfit she wore to an It's Fashion charity party, where she chatted easily with Prince Charles. Her Ungaro-designed dress, embroidered with beads and embellished with flowers, simply floated above the ground, although one wondered how Kylie managed to walk in such high heels. She made everyday fashion look both wonderful and accessible at the same time – everyday, that is, if you can afford Ungaro, Dolce & Gabbana and Colette Dinnigan.

Alison-Jane Reid observed, 'When a star looks good and her career is on track the whole world wants to dress her. That's what's happened to Kylie.' Her status within the notoriously fickle fashion world shows no sign of diminishing. At the 2002 Elle Style Awards Kylie won again – this time she was named Woman of the Year.

Kylie has a perfectly proportioned body, seventy-five per cent of normal size, but perfect nonetheless. She is only a size six to eight but now, with designers working especially for her, clothes always hang perfectly on her. She can be outrageous or demure, camp but never vulgar. Even the transparent toga dress she wore to the MTV Awards was acceptable because it was 'our Kylie' wearing it. Eleonore Crompton of *heat* magazine observed, 'She's the kind of girl you're sure wears a matching bra and knickers every day.'

Kylie's favourite designers include her friend Julien Macdonald, Chloë, Mark Jacobs and the master couturier Ungaro, whose romantic and sensual clothes are perfect for modern goddesses. She paid £6,000 for a Macdonald-designed lurex dress woven with twenty-four carat gold thread and precious stones. She is a big fan of Colette Dinnigan, the hip Australian designer favoured by Nicole Kidman and Cate Blanchett. Colette created the devastatingly pretty black and beige sequinned dress that Kylie wore to the London première of *Moulin Rouge*. But her principal supplier is Dolce & Gabbana, where Fiona Doran works hard to make something of William Baker's outlandish ideas. The Milan-based designers Domenico Dolce and Stefano Gabbana became the most fashionable designers for women after Madonna endorsed one of their shirts – a present from Warren Beatty – in her movie *Truth Or Dare/In Bed With Madonna*. She thought they made clothes 'for a womanly body'.

Doran devised the hooded white gown that was falling off Kylie in the video for 'Can't Get You Out Of My Head'. The dress she wore on stage at the Brits 2002 was also a £1,000 D&G number which consisted more of air than material, and showcased the Minogue thigh and bottom.

Just by chance, she was asked by *Vogue* in June 2001, eight months before the Brits, which was her favourite outfit of all time. She replied, 'A vinyl bib-front mini dress with matching white knee-high boots with "smiley" on the toes, that I had at the age of four.' The boots Kylie wore at the Brits were adapted from a pair of £900 zip-up boots from Jimmy Choo. William Baker sprayed them with silver paint, so that she would have matching new boots and panties. Kylie takes a tiny size three, so many shoes have to be adapted. She may not be a collector in the Imelda Marcos bracket, but Kylie is a devourer and hoarder of shoes, her major fashion weakness. Her favourite designer is Manolo Blahnik, so in vogue because his is the worshipped footwear of the girls in *Sex And The City*, a programme, incidentally, that Kylie likes to watch. Kylie believes her pretty feet, and not her famous *derrière*, to be her best body feature.

Kylie has forsaken the enormous false eye lashes, Dusty Springfield-look she favoured in the bad old days of her rock chick phase. Her eyes tend to be outlined in black to accentuate their almond shape. But her make-up focuses primarily on her lips and impossibly high cheek bones. Suggestions that she has had cosmetic surgery are unlikely ever to be proven. She has always had great lips and her choice of bold lipsticks allows for a glossy, thoroughly modern, accentuated look. Her favourite make-up item is Bloom clear lip gloss. Kylie's line-free skin continues to give rise to rumours that she is the Queen of Botox, a series of injections which freeze the skin, rendering it impossible to furrow and wrinkle. Unlike English women, for whom sun is a rarity, and who like to fry like kippers the moment they hit a holiday beach, Kylie is an Australian brought up in a sunny climate where shorts could be worn most days of the year. Consequently, she is a sunblock aficionado, never applying anything less powerful than factor thirty and gave ex-boyfriend James Gooding a tough time should he ever try to catch a tan. Kylie is a great lotions and potions buyer. Her biggest extravagance is the fermented seaweed-based Crème De La Mer moisturiser, which costs £135 for a 60 ml pot. Kylie prefers her skin to have a dewy glow to it and eschews heavy foundation bases.

*

We live in a cynical age, and Kylie is thirty-four in 2002, so the more incredible she looks, the more innuendo she will have to dodge. She does not appear to have any cellulite. Hairstylist Caroline Barnes, who has worked with Kylie, observed, 'It's totally sickening, but she doesn't have a scrap of orange peel skin in sight.' On one occasion, Kylie thought she might try some anti-cellulite cream, but Caroline told her, 'You can if you like, but there's really no need.'

Confidentially: 'I changed my image so much because that's all I had control over.'

kylie
selective

THE SCENE WAS VERY HOLLYWOOD. Kylie Minogue, famous but not a household name across the Atlantic, was eating lunch in a fashionable restaurant in Beverly Hills, when she was asked if she would like to join another table, where she could meet and chat to film star Jim Carrey, the plasticine-faced star of *Dumb and Dumber*. This is an example of a social nicety played out constantly in the upper echelons of the movie capital – a case of it being good celebrity manners to acknowledge another well-known face in public. His people check with your people and then, when the meeting happens, it all looks very spontaneous, as the air is kissed to death. It is just a game. Carrey instantly became the media's new man in Kylie's life, even though this very public lunch where they were not *à deux* is the one and only time that he and Kylie have met.

A public fascination with her love life is something Kylie has always had to put up with. She is thirty-four now, and still single. If, as we now know, she was sexually experienced at sixteen, then that makes something like eighteen years of being young, free and available. It would be very sad indeed if she had been a nun for all that time. Fortunately, that is not the case, and Kylie has, as she likes to put it, 'a healthy appetite for most things'. She finds sex very enjoyable and once gave herself a performance mark of seven out of ten – eight on good occasions – so that there was always room for improvement. So far, two years seems to be the cut-off point for any relationship, although her fifteen-month affair with Michael Hutchence has a disproportionate importance in her life. Jason Donovan was around for longer but, these days, Kylie appears faintly embarrassed by that, as if their romance was something she was involved in when she was just a kid, and before she became a woman. Perhaps it was Jason's own fault for blabbing a couple of years ago that he and Kylie had sex 'many times, four years' worth, actually.'

Even worse, Jason brought Michael Hutchence into the mix by declaring, 'He was my hero, the man I wanted to be. All I can say, and this is terrible, is that I was in there first. I can discover talent better than most.' Jason may have been 'in there' before Hutchence, but he was not the first. His remarks appear rather juvenile and boastful, and not exactly in keeping with his reputation as a good guy. When he had been asked previously about Michael and Kylie, he had answered more diplomatically, 'I wish them luck, any jealous thoughts don't even go through my mind,' a sentiment which he later contradicted. Rick Sky, who has interviewed Kylie and Jason on many occasions, always found him much the easier of the two to get along with: 'Jason's a lovely bloke, much softer than Kylie, and much more giving.' Perhaps Jason was, ultimately, too soft for

Kylie. He has said that he prefers women to be difficult, dominant even: 'I'm a bit of a sucker for someone who gives me a hard time, maybe I'm a masochist. If someone's pulling you along by a a string, you want it more, don't you?'

Kylie's own attitude to Jason these days is that of an aunt who might see a nephew once in a while. They stay in touch, but their paths cross very rarely. She did not even know he was going to be a Dad until she bumped into him by accident in the street.

Kylie's list of men who may have been 'in there', to use Jason's elegant phrase, includes model Zane O'Donnell (on-off, 1991–1993), singer Evan Dando (one-off, 1993), singer Lenny Kravitz (1993), actor/model Mark Gerber (1994), playboy Tim Jeffries (occasional, 1993/4, again in 1998), idiot comedian Pauly Shore (1995), photographer and video director Stephane Sednaoui (1995–7), music director Cassius Coleman (1998-9), actor Rupert Penry-Jones (1999) and model James Gooding (2000–2002). Numerically, it's more than the Virgin Mary and fewer than Marilyn Monroe.

There are some possibles, like Scott Bradley, Daniel Lapine and Brent Wahling, but much more entertaining is the list of men she has been linked to, but who are, in fact, a definite NO!: Jim Carrey, Chris Evans, Julian Lennon, Jay Kay, Roger Lloyd Pack and Prince. Disappointingly, it is also a negative for Kylie and Robbie Williams, a liaison which would have made them pop royalty and might have taken David and Victoria Beckham off the front pages.

And then there are the men we know nothing about, the secret admirers. Soon after she had split from Hutchence, she was seen leaving her Chelsea apartment with one of her dancers. The couple, scruffy and casual, had only managed a couple of steps down the street when a paparazzo was in their face taking pictures and a statuesque blonde reporter was firing questions. Kylie hared off in one direction, while the dancer bolted the other way. Running has never been one of Kylie's strengths and the journalist, despite wearing high heels, soon overtook her and pinned her up against a wall: 'Look,' said the reporter, 'I'm just going to ask you a couple of simple questions, so there's no point in either of us getting out of breath, right!' Poor Kylie had no choice other than to comply, and an article appeared in the *Daily Star*. It was a rare glimpse of the secret Kylie, someone who suffered from spots, and could not be bothered to do her hair when she was going out to grab the first coffee of the day. And why on earth should she be on show twenty-four hours a day? It was a similar situation to the one that she had found herself in at Heathrow Airport, when she had been mugged by Jean Rook and others. The secret Kylie, when discovered, is like a rabbit trapped in a car's headlamps. She does not mind divulging a little of her private life – but it is always on her own terms.

The men in her life seem to fall into two categories. Either they are drop-dead gorgeous, or they are larger than life. Kylie says the most important qualities she looks for in a man are charisma and humour, a rare combination: 'I'd like him to be artistic, too. I like to be swept off my feet.' There is one other credential shared by at least three of her lovers – they were more renowned for what was between their legs than between their ears.

O'Donnell met Kylie on the video shoot for the single 'What Do I Have To Do?', a great gay favourite. O'Donnell was a strikingly handsome and well-built model from South Africa, who was blind in one eye, and who was best known for showing off his physique in a Levi Jeans ad. It is an amusing coincidence that several of Kylie's boyfriends grabbed her attention after they had removed most (or all) of their clothing in front of a camera. Even Kylie let the cat out of the bag about his attraction, when she admitted that they had 'discovered sex'. O'Donnell had a considerable reputation as a ladies' man. He had left his wife Lauren and their young son as his career began to take off. Lauren got something of her own back by declaring, 'The only way to stop him going off with other women is to castrate him.'

His relationship with Kylie was a stormy one, and they would split up and then get back together again, declaring undying love. They once separated on Valentine's Day in Paris, where Kylie was filming the video for 'Finer Feelings', her eighteenth UK single in just four years. A confidante observed, 'They spent a long time locked in deep conversations. I believe it was a mutual agreement, but Kylie was very down and almost tearful at times.'

Kylie, who too often for her own good can wear her heart on her sleeve when she is involved with someone, was also in floods of tears after they had a blazing row at a party given by fellow Australian, former Wimbledon champion Pat Cash and his then wife Emily, in Kingston upon Thames, near London. A friend of Kylie's confided how distraught she was, because she really wanted to make things work: 'She is still very fond of him, but the relationship is just not happening.'

That particular row was just before Kylie flew off for her annual Christmas break in Melbourne, at the end of 1992. It really was the death knell for their relationship. O'Donnell's career never amounted to much subsequently, and he only became newsworthy once more for discovering God and abandoning advertising jeans, in favour of a campaign to try to attract young people to church.

For someone so careful about her private life, sometimes Kylie can be astonishingly indiscreet. It is as if, every so often, she gets the devil in her, and hang the consequences. There was the sexual activity with Paul Marcolin in a passage next to a house where a party was in full swing; there was the full-blown sex with Michael Hutchence on a plane, in a seat within winking distance of the Australian premier and then there was Lemonheads singer Evan Dando, with whom she disappeared into a toilet at a party. This was an incident that soon achieved legendary status.

In 1993 Evan Dando had looked like he might follow the Michael Hutchence path to rock god. He was flavour-of-the-month after the release of the album *Come On Feel The Lemonheads* – and the classic rock ballad 'Into Your Arms' – and could be seen out and about with Johnny Depp and Courtney Love. Besides Kylie, he shared one other thing with Hutchence – a love of hard drugs. He once admitted that, during one binge, he had smoked so much crack that his voice was ruined for weeks. Dando was from Boston, but spent a good deal of the nineties in Australia. He is now back living in New York, planning another comeback and receiving some press coverage for living five blocks away from the destroyed Twin Towers, but not much else.

Kylie has admitted that there is some truth in the Evan Dando story, although they were never boyfriend and girl-friend. They were not really a one-night stand either – more a one-hour stand. The last time she was asked about it, she blushed and giggled: 'What can I say about it? There was some frivolity.'

*

Prince had been a childhood hero of Kylie Minogue. In all her early fanzine interviews, she answers the frequently asked question: 'Who are your pop idols?' with an acknowledge-ment of the influence of the petit purple one. He may have been a hero with charisma to burn, but there is no evidence that Kylie actually fancied him, although she once famously described him as being 'sex on a stick'. In fairness, Kylie never actually said that she thought he was a sexual lollipop. What she actually said was: 'He's an interesting person and the only person I really admire as a fan. He's so outrageous and different. It's funny. He revolts some people but others think he's sex on a stick.' As a small girl herself, Kylie tends to prefer taller, well-built men – so Tom Cruise need not apply.

She met Prince backstage at one of his London concerts, after an introduction from a limousine driver they shared in London. Kylie remained virtually unknown in the US – The 'Loco-Motion Girl' – so Prince did not wholly realize what a big star she was. 'I don't think he knew much about me,' she confessed. At the time, Kylie was looking for more artistic credibility, following her split from Stock, Aitken and Waterman and her new alliance with deConstruction Records, so it would not do any harm at all to be placed next to Prince by the media. She visited him at his London studios, where he playfully suggested she write some lyrics for him. Kylie may have been seeking some working endorsement from Prince but, at the end of the day, this was the same man who had taken Sheena Easton under his wing.

Although Kylie has always protested there was never anything between her and Prince, that did not stop her fuelling the rumours herself with some typical celebrity behaviour. They spent half an hour chatting at Tramp nightclub in London's West End before leaving separately. Prince set off for his hotel, the Conrad in Chelsea Harbour, in the back of a huge chauffeur-driven limousine. A hundred yards or so down the road, the car pulled up and Kylie darted from out of the shadows and jumped in. They got out together at his hotel, although, to be fair to Kylie, it was only ten minutes from her home, should she have tired of massaging the man's ego.

She did visit his famous home, Paisley Park in Minneapolis, although she is adamant she was not another conquest. She assuredly did not want to be on that list. They did, however, enjoy a game of table tennis together,

'He's very good. I consider myself quite good at pool and table tennis, but he slaughtered me. I let myself down there. I remember doing one glorious flying leap and landing in the shagpile.'

Kylie did find the right moment to present Prince with the lyrics she had written to a song 'Baby Doll', which was pleasant enough without being Lennon and McCartney. Prince took it away and bashed out a melody to go with it, although it has yet to see the light of day on an album.

By coincidence, Kylie did have a minor fling with Lenny Kravitz, another talented and charismatic black artist but, once again, it did not produce any artistic sparks. He was enlisted to write a song for Kylie's first deConstruction album. The song never materialized but Kylie admitted, 'there was a little bit of truth' in the rumours that they had connected on a physical level. Coincidentally, Kravitz was a good friend of Michael Hutchence and a regular visitor to his French villa. Like all rock stars, Kravitz has a certain wild image to maintain, but he is one of the very few known to have taken his grandfather on tour with him.

Both Prince and Lenny Kravitz have enjoyed a great reputation as rock Don Juans over the years, but even they must step aside for Tim Jeffries or 'Tim Who?', as he might be better described. 'Nice But Tim' ostensibly has nothing on his CV until it comes to the page detailing lovers and then he can fill in, among others, the names of Koo Stark, Elle Macpherson, Claudia Schiffer and Kylie. The reality is that Jeffries is amusing and congenial company, and works hard as a director of the London photographic gallery Hamiltons. He is a great friend of the couturier Valentino and moves easily in the world of fashion and photography, two of Kylie's great interests. He abhors the label 'playboy', but is stuck with it: 'A playboy is a relic of the 1950s, someone who was unbelievably rich, didn't work and who travelled the world in a private plane and that's not me. I am not a playboy – I am a hard-working art dealer.'

Jeffries has the priceless attribute, as far as his conquests are concerned, of being absolutely discreet, and has never blabbed about the beautiful women with whom he has been involved. In the mid-nineties, Kylie began to move away from the rock world to a more creative and fashion-based circle of friends – people who could satisfy her endless fascination with image. Jeffries was one of the friends who could open up that world for Kylie.

Kylie's next conquest was a former model-turned-actor called Mark Gerber, who bore a passing resemblance to Zane O'Donnell, and who had also revealed a prodigious endowment in the acclaimed Australian film *Sirens* in which he stripped off in his role as a stablehand. Coincidentally, the film also featured Tim Jeffries' ex, Elle Macpherson. Kylie rang Gerber after seeing the film, and discovered that he was visiting London. She suggested they go to the launch party of fashion designer Donna Karan's shop in London, and they hit it off. When Kylie went back to Australia for a visit, they got together. The romance amounted to little more than a holiday dalliance. They were seen at various social events around Sydney, including gigs of his rock band Flaming Boa at which Kylie briefly took on the role of enthusiastic rock chick. But their affair foundered when Kylie left Australia to fulfil career commitments. Rarely for her, Kylie commented on their relationship: 'It's a long-distance romance and at the moment my career is at the forefront of everything I do. Any relationship is secondary.' These are thought-provoking words, especially as her birth chart reveals, 'Her strong aspirations blur her idea of love.'

Pauly Shore was a case of 'from the sublime to the ridiculous'. He was very much a product of nineties-style comedy in the US – huge-grossing banana skin. He met Kylie on the set of the film *Bio Dome*, which also starred Stephen Baldwin, and which boasted the same production team as *Dumb and Dumber*. Kylie played an Australian oceanographer called Petra, a role Shore described as a 'baby scientist'. He also referred to her as 'Barbie on the Shrimp'. Until he got together with Kylie, his best-known girlfriend was a porn queen called Savannah, who committed suicide. Kylie does not make a habit of going out with people she works with, but, in Pauly's case, they dated for about four months after filming in the Bahamas had finished. Kylie described their dating as 'hanging out', and ditched him when she fell under the spell of French photographer and video director Stephane Sednaoui, who was probably the second most important relationship she has had – after Michael Hutchence. Pauly got the message after he flew to London to see her, only to discover that their planes crossed in mid-Atlantic as she flew Stateside with Stephane. Pauly Shore was a big name in the US, a regular guest on top-rated shows like David Letterman and Howard Stern. Unfortunately for Kylie, her alignment with Pauly did nothing to improve her status in America. It certainly did not help that *Bio Dome* was a flop.

At last Kylie had now met someone who took her breath away, not because of his looks, but through the raw power of his creative personality. Sednaoui was certainly not traditionally handsome. But, just as Michael Hutchence had done, he made an instant impression on Kylie by behaving outrageously. He did not make a risqué suggestion, but when they met at a party, he did lift Kylie up above his head and whirl her around, which certainly caught her attention. 'I'm attracted,' she said, 'but to what I don't know.' It was the middle of 1995 and Kylie was entering her most creative phase, encouraged by rock poet Nick Cave. Stephane became part of that phase and, with Cave, one of the two key mentors of Kylie's middle period.

Sednaoui was spontaneous and alarming. One newspaper suggested he favoured sexual encounters in public places. His most famous girlfriend before Kylie was the unpredictable and weird Icelandic star Björk. Soon after they met, Kylie decided to take off with him to drive across America. They had been on just two dates, yet here she was emulating Jack Kerouac's *On The Road* journey with a man she hardly knew. By the end of the trip, Kylie was enamoured: 'We were stuck in a car together for three weeks and we really bonded. We're in love.' On the trip Sednaoui took many pictures but one in particular, of Kylie gazing out from their silver convertible during a stop in North Carolina, encapsulated the vulnerable, natural look that she favoured during her time with Stephane. It was a naked look.

Stephane encouraged her to see things differently. He had a growing reputation as an experimental videographer, an image enhanced by his alliance with Madonna. Kylie remains a huge admirer of Madonna, and was impressed with Sednaoui's video for her 1993 top ten hit 'Fever', and with his work on her short film *Justify My Love*. Sednaoui's company Clip-Video was one of the most sought-after in the nineties. He worked with the Red Hot Chili Peppers, The Smashing Pumpkins, Tricky, U2, Tina Turner, Alanis Morissette and, of course, Björk on her classic 'Big Time Sensuality'. He directed Kylie in her 1996 collaboration with Towa Tei entitled 'GBI' ('German Bold Italic') during her least commercial period.

With all due respect to the models she has been out with, the most important men in Kylie's life so far would not be seen dead modelling boxer shorts on a fashion runway – unless it was part of an ironic statement. Intriguingly, with both Michael Hutchence and Stephane Sednaoui there were fears that Kylie's health was suffering. Commentators noticed she was losing weight and looking dreadful.

One picture prompted the *Daily Mail* to observe, 'It wasn't just the mousey hair – cut short and scrunched on top of her head – or the absence of make-up. What really shocked was how painfully thin, even ill, Kylie looked . . . .' In the picture, Sednaoui, wearing combat trousers, tightened his hood close to his face to expose a single, staring eye. He laughed, 'It will be funny. People will think who is that crazy guy that Kylie's going out with?' He was right. They did think that – but they also wondered why.

The couple travelled extensively – to Australia, Hong Kong, Tokyo, Seoul, Los Angeles, and between their respective homes in Paris and London. It was a great adventure for Kylie. But they were also apart a good deal, and Kylie became devoted to her home computer, vainly trying to conduct a relationship via 'chat'. Kylie did take Stephane home to meet her parents in Melbourne, although we will never know what Ron Minogue made of the avant-garde Frenchman, then sporting an interesting mohican haircut.

The end for the couple, in late 1997, came quite suddenly. One moment there was speculation about marriage and babies and the next they were apart. In September, Kylie said, 'Stephane is extremely inspiring. I respect his artistry – he has his own style stamped on what he does.' In November, *Cleo* magazine declared, 'She doesn't want to talk about it, but suffice to say, there is much muttering about men behaving badly and Kylie isn't disagreeing.'

The official line is that the relationship just fizzled out and the couple have remained close friends – a familiar outcome where Kylie and past *amours* are concerned. Perhaps men like Hutchence and Sednaoui are just too exhausting for Kylie. Or perhaps her expectations are too high. She also needed to get her career back on track because at the end of 1997 it was at an all-time low, following the release of an album for which she had made a major writing contribution. Sednaoui remains in demand on the arty music scene and, in October 2001, did become a father when his girlfriend, cover girl Laetitia Casta, gave birth to a baby girl. The beautiful Laetitia, ten years younger than Kylie, is the face of L'Oréal, and has ambitions to be as famous as an actress as she is as a model. Coincidentally, Kylie tried to resurrect her own acting career while she was with Stephane, but with no great success.

November 1997 was a bad month to be Kylie Minogue. She lost the two most important loves of her life. First, she ended her relationship with Stephane – perhaps reluctantly. And then, on 21 November, she heard the dreadful news of the untimely death of Michael Hutchence. Her world collapsed in a very short space of time, but Kylie Minogue has what Rick Sky describes as a 'ferocious inner steel.'

✳

The Caribbean island of Barbados is a perfect setting to ignite a new romance. Kylie had been dating various guys since Stephane but no one too serious. One liaison, with musical director Cassius Coleman, lasted on and off for six months but, as usual, her career came first. Cassius certainly made the effort, and flew out to Barbados to visit Kylie when she was there appearing as Miranda on stage in a production of *The Tempest*. Unfortunately for Cassius, Kylie had already fallen for her leading man Rupert Penry-Jones. He had all the credentials for being a heart-throb, as well as a spark of creativity – a good combination for Kylie.

Like the other blonde hunk in her life, Jason Donovan, Rupert came from a showbusiness background. His mother Angela Thorne was an actress in the British TV series *To The Manor Born* with Penelope Keith, and his father Peter Penry-Jones acted in the popular television drama *Colditz*, as well as the more recent *Longitude*. Rupert was privately educated at Dulwich College in London, and disappointed his parents a little by choosing the same acting profession, mainly because they knew only too well the times of financial strife that might result. Fortunately Rupert, 6′ 1″ tall, blonde with piercing blue eyes, started with a bang by being spotted by model agency Storm, when he was just seventeen, and being whisked off to the Milan catwalk. He therefore had experience of the fashion world of which Kylie is so enamoured. He also revealed an impressive physique in the film *Virtual Sexuality*, which contained so many sex scenes that he had to spend an entire week naked to get them all shot.

Penry-Jones has serious acting ambitions. He achieved his first step when he was understudy to Ralph Fiennes in a production of *Hamlet* in the mid-nineties. His Caribbean odyssey helped pave the way for a lead role with the RSC, as the eponymous hero in Schiller's *Don Carlos*. Kylie did her bit by going up from London to Stratford-upon-Avon to support him. She could be seen perched daintily on the back of his motorbike, something she had a lot of practice of when she rode pillion on Michael Hutchence's Harley. The only difference was the English weather. On Rupert's bike Kylie would wear socks on her hands to keep out the cold.

Rupert was smitten with Kylie and found it very difficult to follow the familiar path of secrecy: 'We're very good friends,' he declared, unconvincingly. 'We're not going out with each other. But if I was going out with someone, it would be her.' In reality, they went out for close on ten months, but he never admitted it, although he told journalist Chrissy Iley: 'Part of me wanted to scream it from the roof tops!' He did take Kylie home to meet his parents, and they liked her. They had Sunday lunch and Kylie chatted away. Her ability to mix easily, even though she is so famous, is something that Michael Hutchence's mother noticed when her son first introduced her to Kylie.

In the end, it was the familiar story of work killing their

relationship. He was in Stratford, and she would be in Los Angeles or Melbourne or London. It is a sad indictment of society that none of the men in Kylie's life have been prepared to sacrifice their careers for her. Not Jason, not Michael Hutchence, Stephane or Rupert. In some unwritten way, it seems to be up to the woman to make the sacrifice. Kylie is prepared to go part of the way but, at the end of the day, why should she give up everything for fleeting love? No wonder so many female pop stars end up getting together with one of their dancers – at least they know they are going to see each other most days. To his credit, Penry-Jones is enthusiastically complimentary about his famous ex-girlfriend: 'I thought I was one of the luckiest men in the world and, to be honest, I can't believe it lasted more than a week.'

Even though Penry-Jones has starred in the television series *North Square*, he is still most famous as one of Kylie's exes, although he does not seem to mind – it is all part of the publicity game to plug your latest role. It is exactly the same for Kylie as she answers the one-millionth question about *Neighbours*, Jason or Michael or Pete Waterman. The person answering that question is the public Kylie, chairman of 'Kylie Minogue Limited'. It is not the person revealed by Rupert Penry-Jones to be a free spirit: 'I don't think she's ever going to belong to anybody.'

A number of Kylie's relationships seem to end just before the turn of the year, as if she is putting her house in order before she returns home for her usual month-long break with her family. Single once more at the beginning of 2000, she met a male model with brooding looks to die for at a pool party in Los Angeles, where she has been spending an increasing amount of time in recent years – on this occasion putting the finishing touches to her comeback album *Light Years*. He was James Gooding, the 'delightful scruff from Essex', who was there with a friend. He was introduced to

Kylie, who went weak at the knees. The party was a bit boring so James, who at the time was living in LA, suggested they should go and get something to eat. But they did not rush into a full-blown passionate affair at once, instead going for a series of getting-to-know-you dates, which was a refreshing change for Kylie. He, endearingly, recalled, 'She was just this little, funny, geeky girl who I thought was really cute.'

Kylie managed to keep her new romance secret for an outstanding length of time, considering her fame. She confessed that there was someone special, but did not name him, although she said she was 'enjoying the romance'. Gooding moved back to London, but did not move into Kylie's millionaire's home. Kylie's cautious approach may have had something to do with his age. He is seven years younger than her, but has been in the world of fashion since he was eighteen, his photogenic looks so much in demand that he has earned the unwanted sobriquet of 'supermodel'. There is something of a role reversal with Kylie and certain of her men. Zane, Mark, Rupert, James – they are trophy boyfriends, great-looking adornments to hang off your arm.

One of the more promising qualities Kylie saw in James Gooding was his domesticity. Kylie has never reacted well to the energy sapping relationships she endured with Hutchence and Sednaoui. Gooding was not hard work. One of his favourite pursuits is making little cardboard boxes. He takes a blank piece of card and then makes a little box from it, into which he puts a gift. He once made a 'really cool box' for Kylie. He likes cooking and the two of them would curl up on the sofa together and watch Pop Idol or they would sip drinks on the balcony of her Chelsea home. Somehow he never seemed exciting enough for Kylie, who described their friendship as a 'nice, simple romance.'

Kylie went to stay with Gooding's mother Jenny Young, who lives in a modest terraced house in the quaintly named

Kirby-le-Soken in Essex, near the seaside resort of Walton-on the-Naze. James split his time as a child between Essex and Scotland where his father David lived and where he originally went to a boarding school in Rannoch. Jenny and Kylie got on well together, as all mums do with her, and then had to run the gauntlet of everyone asking her if Kylie and her son were going to get married. Intriguingly, when Kylie went for her Christmas holiday to Melbourne James did not accompany her.

They did, however, enjoy a break in early November at Puerto Banus, on Spain's Costa Del Sol. They were seen looking in the window of a jewellery store, which prompted a frenzy of engagement speculation.

And he was also on her arm the following February when she arrived at the Brit awards at Earls Court. Kylie exclusively revealed to Dominic Mohan of the Sun that she had enjoyed 'a wonderful weekend with the man she loves.'

But just as they passed the important two-year barrier together the cracks were beginning to appear. James had already bought his own apartment in Shoreditch, East London. There were whispers that he had a roving eye and pictures appeared of him enjoying the company of other glamorous women like Sophie Dahl and Beverly Bloom. Kylie was also seen storming out of a restaurant in tears, after apparently having words with him.

Within three months of the slushy Mohan revelations it was all over and Kylie was once more in tears. The split coincided with the start of her sell-out UK tour which began in Cardiff at the end of April. It put a bit of a dampener on her most ambitious show yet which needed 100 people to take it around the 25 dates. Her sister Dannii revealed that Kylie was 'very upset about splitting up as they had been together a long time'.

Gooding has received a fair amount of flak for being

perceived as a 'rat' – never seen without a beautiful woman by his side – although he maintained that Kylie blamed her career for killing the relationship. He also targeted press and public intrusion into their lives: 'It put a lot of pressure on us and I'm sure it [the relationship] didn't last as long as it could have.'

Meanwhile Gooding's own career has gone from strength to strength, not in the least harmed by his alliance with Kylie. He has starred in a series of high profile advertisements promoting shampoos, peach schnapps, fragrances and Peugeot cars. He was also a guest on Johnny Vaughan's television chat show. The only time he let the side down was when he reportedly became indignant after forgetting his VIP pass to one of Kylie's concerts and was not allowed in. He no longer works as a male model, having turned his hand to photography. His first exhibition entitled 'Game On' was launched at the Barbican in the summer of 2002 and moved on to Edinburgh in October. As well as shots of video games' players the exhibition featured one picture of Kylie naked in the bath.

The couple clearly remain friends – although that does not necessarily make the split any easier to bear for Kylie. He flew over to Australia for the end of her dates in Melbourne in August and they subsequently went on holiday together to Bali which prompted fevered if ill-informed speculation that they might have secretly married and were about to start a family. Despite the great success Kylie has enjoyed in 2002 James Gooding, according to Dannii, has been 'one of her downs'.

Confidentially: 'I really need my own space, and if I don't get it, I just take to my bath.'

kylie
creative

S HE DID NOT LOOK LIKE A SEX GODDESS. She did not even resemble the Girl-Next-Door. This was IndieKylie, as scruffy as an unmade bed, wearing no make-up, green tracksuit pants and a clashing purple T-shirt. She was backstage at the Royal Albert Hall in London with her pal and creative Svengali Nick Cave. On stage, a white-haired old man with a long beard was reading poetry in Braille. Kylie was having second, third and fourth thoughts, and turned to Cave and declared, 'Nick, God's on stage, how can we follow that?' Eventually, it was her turn and Cave literally pushed his protégée on stage. Apprehensively, she stood in front of the microphone and began, 'In my imagination . . .'. It was the start of 'I Should Be So Lucky' and Kylie, with no musical accompaniment whatsoever, spoke the complete lyric to her biggest-selling record to that date.

Kylie's brilliant performance at the closing ceremony of the
2000 Olympic Games in Sydney

'Marilyn' Minogue?

At Sydney's Gay and Lesbian Mardi Gras parade

In her famous gold hot pants

At the *Smash Hits* Poll Winner's party, 2001.

At the *Smash Hits* Poll Winner's party, 2001.

Previous pages: Live at the Hammersmith Apollo, London, in March 2001

It was daring, courageous and took the audience's breath away. It was also a defining moment in Kylie's career because it allowed her to embrace her past, as well as giving her the confidence to push herself forward. Confidence has always been Kylie's drug of choice.

Kylie loves to surprise and shock. She has always had a streak of exhibitionism but, until her association with Cave, she had seemed to accept the boundaries within which she could work. Kylie was unbilled at the Poetry Olympics in 1996, which was a wise precaution as it kept cameras away from what might have been a humiliating experience. She admitted that she had done none of her normal preparation for a live performance that night; she did not put on the 'ego jacket' which Michael Hutchence had told her always to wear. She recalled, 'I broke so many rules.' Kylie remained unsure about the whole thing until she was actually out there, saying the words which she had sung a thousand times. Up until this night, she had distanced herself from her days at The Hit Factory, yet here she was, shouting to the world that this was part of her career and part of her. The extra ingredient of reciting the words in this fashion was that, without the bouncing melody, they took on ironic meaning.

Kylie would not have dared to do this without the support of Nick Cave, a genuine original in the world of contemporary culture. A great friend of the late Michael Hutchence, Cave is a middle-class Australian, the son of a teacher. He went to school in Melbourne, where he founded a band which would later become The Boys Next Door. They released an album in Australia before changing their name to Birthday Party and moving to London in 1980. The band had a raw energy, while Cave had a brand of hip nonconformity which Hutchence, in particular, sought to emulate. Cave was dangerously cool. Intriguingly, it is this charismatic quality that Kylie has found so attractive in two of her most important relationships to date, with Hutchence and with Stephane Sednaoui.

When the band split up, Cave moved to West Berlin, which in the eighties was at the forefront of experimental European culture. By 1984 a new line-up was formed, Nick Cave and The Bad Seeds, which may have been a reference to the gospel of St Matthew. Cave had been influenced by the Bible through his Anglican upbringing. Music author Spencer Bright observed, 'Cave is aptly named, inhabiting a twilight world somewhere between William Faulkner and William Burroughs. He is an intellectual with a grim take on life and death, filling his songs with apocalyptic characters and incidents. There's tons of murder and lust, revenge and retribution in his songs.'

Cave's lyrics were always poetic and, in 1989, he expanded his writing to a novel entitled *And The Ass Saw The Angel*. Of more significance in his appeal to a wider audience was the beautiful 1988 Wim Wenders film *Wings of Desire*, which featured two of Cave's songs. The movie, about an angel who falls in love on earth, remains a favourite of Kylie's since she was first persuaded to see it by Hutchence. A year later, Cave produced his own film *Ghosts . . . of the Civil Dead*, a prison movie starring Cave, written by him and featuring his own soundtrack.

The key ingredient that the gothic-looking Cave – the 'Prince of Darkness' – adds to his art is the challenging aspect, something that both Michael Hutchence and Kylie Minogue found appealing. Kylie has freely acknowledged that she is in awe of him: 'I think Nick Cave is wonderful,' she has simply said. She found him 'mild and gentle', making him sound more like a washing-up liquid than a cutting-edge talent.

Cave is also an example of something else that Kylie

admires – he refuses to be pigeon-holed. His work is a total concept, not just singing or composing, but poetry and prose, photography and film. He, along with Hutchence and Sednaoui, have helped Kylie stretch the boundaries she had set for herself.

After her triumph at the Poetry Olympics, Kylie told *Cleo* magazine in Australia, 'People love to pigeon-hole you, no matter what you do. They place a box over you and you can't get out of it, but I have been able to stretch it a little, to lift up one side and peep out, to shuffle it here and there. I don't know how I've done it. I was supposed to be a one-hit wonder.'

Fate decreed that Kylie and Cave would connect. In the mid-nineties, when he moved back to London, he became one of Hutchence's closest friends. They formed an unlikely business alliance as partners in The Portobello Café, which was one of the most fashionable places to be seen. Kylie was often there and in other Notting Hill spots around this time, even though she still lived in Fulham. When Hutchence had a daughter with Paula Yates in 1996, he asked his mate Nick Cave to be godfather. The following year, Cave joined Kylie at Michael's funeral and sang 'Into My Arms' (The Lemonheads ballad) at Paula's request. It was a moving rendition, made truly bizarre in the best Cave/Hutchence tradition by a man threatening to hurl himself off the balcony while Cave was singing.

Cave first joined up with Kylie professionally when he asked her to sing on his 1995 album *Murder Ballads*, which featured songs dealing exclusively with murder. Kylie sang a duet, 'Where The Wild Roses Grow', which she has often said is her favourite among all her songs, a choice that might amaze her fans. The song is a haunting dialogue between a killer (Cave) and his victim (Kylie). He bludgeons her to death with a rock. Cave had always wanted to do a song with Kylie, finding her basic charm and lack of cynicism fascinating. While the rest of the world thought 'Better The Devil You Know' was a classic pop song, Cave discovered hidden poetic meaning in the combination of a dark lyric, describing a flawed, abusive love, and Kylie's own vocal innocence. He thought it a harrowing portrait of humanity, which could be likened to the Old Testament psalms.

Cave wrote 'Wild Roses' with Kylie specifically in mind, and acknowledged that it 'was a dangerous song for her to sing'. It worked brilliantly, with Cave's Scott Walker-style baritone contrasting powerfully with Kylie's brittle vocal. In the video that accompanied the single, Kylie is seen in the pale repose of a dead Ophelia. To the surprise of many critics, the track reached number two in Australia and a very respectable eleven on the UK chart. It was actually Kylie's biggest UK hit in the five-year period between July 1995 and July 2000, when 'Spinning Around' announced that she was back.

The debt that Kylie owes to her unlikely alliance with Nick Cave is that he made her cool. The coolification of Kylie had begun with Michael Hutchence but, by the mid-nineties, there was an around-the-block queue of credible artists wanting to work with her. Kylie has always chosen collaborations carefully to enhance her image – even 'Especially For You' was timed to perfection. Her most famous collaboration after Nick Cave was with the acclaimed Manic Street Preachers. They had long been admirers of Kylie – bassist Nicky Wire once claimed to have been beaten up for wearing a Kylie T-shirt at school. She met vocalist James Dean Bradfield at an awards ceremony and discovered that, in 1991, he had tried to reach her on several occasions to discuss working together. He had wanted her to sing on the vintage Manics' song 'Little Baby Nothing' – about a starlet used by men – but had eventually enlisted porn star Tracy Lords when he could not get past the 'gates of PWL heaven'.

Kylie and Bradfield decided to meet for tea at his home, and Kylie took along some cherries. She also brought a bunch of lyrics, to try to persuade Bradfield to turn them into a real song for her second deConstruction album *Impossible Princess*. In the best traditions of songwriting, Bradfield strummed a bit and suggested she leave them with him. He played her a track, which she thought sounded like Tamla Motown, that he felt would suit her. She thought he was trying to discover what her own tastes were. 'It was a pop moment,' she recalled. This was the album that would unveil the truly creative Kylie. As soon as the outside world heard of the collaboration between Kylie and Bradfield, she was dubbed IndieKylie. The result of that first meeting was that Bradfield sent her a demo of 'I Don't Need Anyone', which Kylie loved, finding it refreshing and so different from what she had been working on before. Bradfield asked for some more lyrics and he then amalgamated two sets into one for 'Some Kind Of Bliss', a rocky pop classic. Both tracks were unmistakably Manics, guitars exploding like squibs around an anthemic melody.

The track was released as a single in September 1997 and was a flop. Kylie had favoured releasing 'Limbo', a more overt dance cut with an incessant beat, which sounded a bit like Republica. It was her first release since the 'Wild Roses' collaboration two years earlier, so the results were very disappointing – not least for her record company deConstruction. Bradfield was apologetic, blaming himself: 'I loved her voice, got on with her and I am embarrassed that I failed her.' The track peaked at number twenty-two on the UK charts, the only consolation being that it reached a higher position than the re-issue the same month of 'Little Baby Nothing'. It fared even worse in Australia, where the heartland of Kylie's fan-base seemed to have deserted her – it only managed a pitiful number twenty-seven.

Some critics walloped 'Some Kind Of Bliss'. *NME* called it 'supremely irritating' and declared, 'Kylie belts out the lyrics like she's reading from an autocue. Any soul is lost in a slurry of bought-in brass and a ropey guitar solo that'd be more at home on a Shakin' Stevens record.' The difficulty for Kylie was that, despite the credibility she gained by her collaborations, she was still being perceived as a girl who launched a thousand tragic outfits. Or, even worse, as a girl-next-door which, in some unfair way, suggested IndieKylie was a fraud. It seemed like a return to the bad old days of Stock, Aitken and Waterman, when kicking Kylie was a national pastime.

For once, Kylie had no control over the tragic chain of events which scuppered the grand design for the *Impossible Princess* album. She had spent two years working on the project, a labour of love. The gestation period coincided with her relationship with Stephane, which proved a fertile base for the most creative period of Kylie's life so far. The challenging aspect of her relationship triggered a challenging period in Kylie's career. The trash cans are littered with the careers of successful pop stars who suddenly think they can do it all, and inflict their dreadful songs and sentiments on a public which promptly goes off them. It was a brave career move for Kylie. The chasm between the Kylie of *Impossible Princess* and the Kylie of the Hit Factory is so wide, it is hard to believe they are the same person. It clearly showed that Kylie was prepared to take a chance on her own talent.

Both Kylie and her record company deConstruction – which was much more a dance label than an indie label – were dismayed at the poor sales of 'Some Kind Of Bliss'. By an unkind twist of fate, Princess Diana was killed the same week as its release and, despite extensive airplay, everyone was much more inclined to buy Elton John's tribute 'Candle In The Wind 1997', which accounted for 80 per cent of record sales that week. The whole marketing strategy was thrown – a hit single setting up the release of an album. Kylie took the bold step of agreeing to pull the plug – not least because an album entitled *Impossible Princess* did not seem tactful at this time. Kylie gamely said that it would have been insensitive to put the album out, so it was postponed for three months until after Christmas. 'There's no way you can prepare for something like the Princess of the country dying. It's thrown everybody,' she explained.

While it is very true that the death of Diana caused a thoroughly weird few weeks in the record industry – 'Candle In The Wind 1997' sold thirty-three million copies worldwide in three months – it still does not account for why 'Some Kind Of Bliss' failed to make the top twenty. There were still twenty-one better selling singles in the UK that week, and only one of them was a tribute to the Princess of Wales. The following week Kylie's single dropped out of the chart altogether, hardly a good advertisement for the album. The public did not buy into this new Kylie. Spencer Bright thought the record struck an attitude and a pose, rather than truly reflecting where Kylie was moving as an individual, and so was doomed to failure. He explained, 'The chemistry was not right. And most of the material was inferior to Stock, Aitken and Waterman.' Postponing the release of the album was an interesting commercial decision, as it meant no sales at Christmas, the time of the year when the most records are bought.

The new strategy was to release another single in the New Year when more exposure and a higher chart position could be achieved with lower sales. Alas, 'Did It Again' did little better than 'Some Kind Of Bliss', reaching number fourteen in the UK chart. The album was put back yet again, while a third single was put out. 'Breathe' had a more commercial, faster remix than the album version, but this too only reached number fourteen. Eventually, the album (now uninspiringly entitled *Kylie Minogue in Europe*), Kylie's pride and joy, found its way on to the shelves in March 1998, and tottered to number ten in the album charts, before sinking without trace. The whole sorry saga smacked of desperation on deConstruction's part. Kylie remained professionally polite about the whole thing, but it was profoundly disappointing.

Impossible Princess is, by some measure, the most challenging Kylie Minogue album. It remains the one where she had most personal input, especially in the lyrics, which reveal the vulnerable, melancholy and poetic Kylie, far removed from the glossy image of 'Kylie Minogue Limited'. Although the title can be considered an ironic nod to Kylie's reputation – 'the girl on the show pony at the circus' – it does, in fact, come from a book of poetry, *Impossible Poems to Break the Harts (sic) of Impossible Princesses*, which was given to her by the cult poet and children's author Billy Childish, another hip fan who found Kylie cool.

Nick Cave had a profound influence on *Impossible Princess*, teaching her, as Kylie put it, to be totally truthful in her music, to unleash 'the core of myself.' Much of the writing was conceived during her three-week drive across the US with Stephane Sednaoui. For once, the most important item of Kylie's luggage was not assorted outfits by Dolce & Gabbana, but an old notebook, into which she scribbled down all the thoughts and feelings about her life, which might make a lyric later. It was cathartic and cleansing. She confided, 'I got drunk on the process.'

The original concept for *Impossible Princess* was that it would be a collaboration between Kylie and the ultra-fashionable producers Brothers In Rhythm (Steve

Anderson and Dave Seaman). But Kylie, seeking a wider musical base, decided on a number of other 'stoned cool' alliances – Rob D, aka Clubbed To Death, Dave Ball, ex Soft Cell and now The Grid, Rob Dougan of Mo' Wax. Some of the collaboration was rock-style spontaneity. 'I have a friend called Skinny who was playing Clubbed To Death around the house. I loved it and, out of the blue, he said he knew the guy. . . .' And there were the two tracks with the Manics. With twenty-twenty hindsight this may have been a mistake, because the publicity generated by this unlikely mixture tended to overshadow the rest of the work. Anderson, forthrightly, believed the release of 'Some Kind Of Bliss' was a cop-out to satisfy the demands of the media, who wanted it to be the single. He felt 'Too Far' and 'Jump' were more representative of the album.

Kylie's connection with Brothers In Rhythm had been forged four years earlier, during an uncertain period of her career after she finally broke the chains of Stock, Aitken and Waterman. She signed with deConstruction, an independent dance-orientated label which had cracked the mainstream market with the Manchester group M People, led by Heather Small, who resembled a black Carmen Miranda and boasted a unique voice which launched a thousand karaoke impressions. Kylie was a fan, and M People actually produced and arranged the final track on *Kylie Minogue*, her first deConstruction album.

Brothers In Rhythm fell over themselves to work with Kylie, and invited her to a studio session. This saw the birth of 'Confide In Me' and 'Dangerous Game', which would feature a smoother, more mature sound. Steve Anderson paid Kylie a tribute, one which she has been paid throughout her career – he declared her to be the most professional person he had ever worked with, and their mutual respect grew into a close friendship. He gave her confidence in her musical abilities, and she grew as an artist through this transitional period. Like her better publicized collaborations with Nick Cave and the Manic Street Preachers, Brothers In Rhythm played their part in making Kylie cool. They also provided a serving of confidence. 'Confide In Me' was the first time people sat up and took notice of Kylie's lyrical contribution. When it was released as a single, the string-laden arrangement, the hint of Madonna, and the sophistication met with encouraging noises from the critics and the tills. It reached number two on the UK charts, kept off the top by the dire 'Saturday Night' by Whigfield, a one-hit wonder if ever there was one. Even 'The Loco-Motion Girl' would have turned her nose up at 'Saturday Night'. As a consolation, 'Confide In Me' made number one in Australia, New Zealand, Turkey, Croatia and Finland (as usual).

Anderson and Seaman were two of the most innovative producers in the music industry, so it is a tribute to Kylie that they scrapped their own ideas for her second deConstruction album, and allowed Kylie to supply the creative impetus. Anderson recalled, 'As soon as she started writing, it became clear that she was developing as an artist, so we scrapped our original plan and let most of the ideas come from her.'

The result is a darkly autobiographical lyric sheet, which reveals far more about Kylie than any interview in a glossy magazine or a newspaper. Her standard replies to the same old questions never rise above the mildly interesting. Here, though, there was no twee 'Your Arms Are In My Heart' candyfloss. They were complex, serious, introspective and challenging to the listener, none more so than 'Dreams', which chronicled the dreams of an impossible princess, wishing to 'taste every moment and try everything.'

The stand-out track on *Impossible Princess* is by common

consent 'Too Far', which featured Kylie speed-whispering over an intense drum'n' bass beat.

There was a loud lobby to release it as a single, owing to a huge club following for the Brothers In Rhythm unofficial remix. It was unofficial, in that deConstruction originally knew nothing about it, although Kylie, always up for something new, took time to re-sing vocals and add some ad libs. There is literally just a handful of promo copies, which would fetch a fortune if they ever came up for sale.

*

Kylie's next collaboration was altogether less successful. The Japanese-born experimentalist Towa Tei had a massive reputation on the New York Club scene, thanks to his work with Dee-Lite and their dance anthem 'Groove Is In The Heart'. His solo work was considerably less successful but Kylie, ever eager to explore new avenues, left a message on his answer machine saying, 'I'd like to work with you.' Towa called her back, and they worked on a song together called 'GBI', which stood for an invented printing font, German Bold Italic. It was a diverting conceit, which might have seemed amusing at the time. Kylie visited Towa's home studio and listened to the instrumental demo. He recalled, 'She could instantly understand my ideas and direction and, in a very relaxed mood, we started working on the lyrics.' The very abstract concept had Kylie sounding coquettish, while pretending to be a typeface. It proved a little too off-the-wall for Kylie fans, and was her all-time least successful single release in the UK. It went straight in at number sixty-three and then went straight out the following week, never to be heard of again, despite Kylie appearing as a geisha in the video. From this nadir, there was only one way for Kylie to go, and that was back up. 'Spinning Around', however, was nearly two years away.

Before then, there was the little matter of a Duran Duran tribute album. For this, Kylie teamed up with another Australian. After the unlikely duet with Nick Cave, she partnered Ben Lee, a big star in Australia throughout the nineties, but virtually unknown in the UK. First of all, the duo were invited to record 'Girls On Film', and then the brilliant track 'Skin Trade'. Neither of these were good enough for Lee, who claimed he rang the boss of EMI Australia and told him that if he wanted 'the current prince and princess of Australian pop music to be involved in this, they were going to need a more substantial track. For a collaboration of this size, this is something that will capture the imagination of people for generations to come.' They eventually settled on 'The Reflex'. In the event, the collaboration captured the imagination for a nano-second. It was, however, a hint that Kylie was trying to re-establish a more mainstream footing by reclaiming her fan base in Australia, which had been her kicking-off point ever since her very first record 'The Loco-Motion'.

Although *Impossible Princess* represents the pinnacle of Kylie's musical creativity so far, she has continued to push herself in other ways. She had parted from deConstruction, after the release of a new mixes greatest hits album *Hits+* in the summer of 1998. She had released only two albums of new material in five years, so could hardly be said to be a money-spinner. DeConstruction is now defunct, so Kylie probably jumped ship at the right time. Officially, the split was completely amicable.

In March 1999, Kylie could be found on the beautiful island of Barbados – not on a beach, but on stage. It was acting, but it was a long way from *Neighbours*. She had been persuaded by Johnny Kidd, father of model Jodie Kidd, to appear in a production of *The Tempest*, at a cultural festival he organized annually in the hibiscus and palm tree-lined gardens of his plantation estate. It was a musical version of the play – loosely called *The Caribbean Tempest* – but it was still Shakespeare, and not too many of the Bard's verses involved the Aussie pastimes of partaking of a 'smoothie' or behaving like a 'dag'. The mastermind behind the extravaganza was Kit Hesketh-Harvey, best known for his UK fringe-act Kit and the Widow. He adapted the Shakespearean verse to use as lyrics for fifteen new songs. His only disappointment was that Kylie, who played Miranda, refused to sing. She was determined to play the role completely straight and not turn it into a kitsch classic. Hesketh-Harvey observed that she was a model cast member, and even helped carry the props.

Kylie was surrounded by Shakespearean actors, like David Calder and her soon-to-be boyfriend Rupert Penry-Jones. After Kylie, the best known face belonged to Roger Lloyd Pack, familiar on British television in *Only Fools and Horses* and *The Vicar of Dibley*. Kylie's reward for her dedication to the role was an honourable, if slightly patronising, mention in a review in *The Times*: 'The casting of Kylie Minogue as Miranda may have raised the odd knowing smile in anticipation, but she conducted herself more than adequately.' The following spring the production made its way to Sydney, sadly without Kylie who, by this time, was hard at work on her comeback album.

*

Kylie remains a film star waiting to happen. It is not easy to make it in the movies, even if you are enjoying maximum exposure as a pop icon. Even Madonna has failed to excite as a movie actress. Other female artists have had a go, with varying success: Diana Ross, Whitney Houston, Mariah Carey, Jennifer Lopez, Britney Spears and, perhaps most noteworthy, Cher. But, considering she was an actress first, Kylie's efforts have been less than inspiring. She has had a bigger effect as the star of some surprising and eye-catching pop videos. The accompanying video to 'Some Kind Of Bliss', for instance, revealed Kylie as a curvy, scarlet-haired vamp on the arm of a small-time crook.

Her first bid for movie stardom came in *The Delinquents*, a Christmas release in 1989. She had filmed the movie in the spring, in Queensland, in between promoting her first million-selling album and recording her second *Enjoy Yourself*. She went straight into filming after leaving *Neighbours*, thereby mirroring her character Charlene, who also left Ramsay Street for a new life in Queensland. Her new role, as rebellious teenager Lola Lovell, was unlikely to have pitched up in Erinsborough. It was a rites-of-passage movie, set in a small, provincial town in the mid-1950s. The story centred on her love for a young drifter, Brownie Hansen, who was played by the American brat pack actor Charlie Schlatter, then one of a number of young Hollywood actors who appeared to be on the verge of major stardom, but who never quite achieved it. The film, based on a popular Australian novel, was generally thought to have suffered from the influence of its American financial backers (Warner), who diluted the homespun, ethnic feel of the original book.

Kylie had to remove her clothes on a number of occasions, thrash around in the sheets and, more controversially, be taken by her overbearing mother for an abortion when she was fifteen. Kylie was at pains to point out that the book was much more depressing and gritty than the film: 'If we had left it the way it was, it was so depressing you would have wanted to slash your wrists.' This was a totally different project for Kylie who, unlike her Stock, Aitken and Waterman incarnation, was allowed plenty of freedom to express her own ideas on set. It was a refreshing change to be taking part in something grown-up, at the same time as 'Hand On Your Heart' was topping the UK charts. Kylie was being introduced to a world where her opinion counted.

Perhaps inevitably, *The Delinquents* was condemned by the critics. The *Daily Mirror*, who, these days, loves all things Kylie, declared, 'Kylie has as much acting charisma as cold porridge', which was unnecessarily cruel. Although the film did well commercially in both the UK and Australia, it was a flop in the US which, again, spoiled any prospects at this time of Kylie becoming a star there. Because of Kylie's involvement, the film remains a curio on the shelves of local video stores. Much more interesting than the film itself is the change it portrayed in Kylie's image. Lola Lovell was no 'girl-next-door' character. When the film premièred at the end of the year, Kylie was an item with Michael Hutchence, and that relationship garnered many more headlines than the film itself. Everyone was obsessed by Kylie's perceived change under the influence of the rock star, and *The Delinquents* became part and parcel of that. But Kylie filmed *The Delinquents* before she became involved with Hutchence. She was still with Jason Donovan, who would fly up to the location to visit her when his own schedule allowed. Kylie had taken the decision to distance herself from the public image of her as 'girl-next-door' Charlene, without Hutchence's influence.

One of the barriers to Kylie building on her starring role in *The Delinquents*, was the media obsession with focusing on her new 'rock chick' look, and her perceived corruption by Michael Hutchence, rather than on the film itself. It would be another four years before Kylie put her toe in the water of movie stardom again with her first 'Hollywood' film, opposite Jean-Claude Van Damme in the martial arts film *Street Fighter*, which was based on a popular video game. The director, Steven de Souza, had seen Kylie on a magazine cover displaying 'The 30 Most Beautiful People In The World.' She played a character called Cammy, a British Intelligence officer, master of surveillance and lieutenant to Van Damme's Colonel Guile. It was a curious choice of film for Kylie, hardly a major role at a time when she was embarking on a period of much greater personal creativity. This was starlet stuff, although it did have the advantage of being filmed in Australia and Thailand. Kylie had to take martial arts lessons, in particular kick boxing, in order to make believable the notion of her petite frame as a lethal weapon. She also had to pump iron, resulting in a temporary inflation of her upper torso.

Kylie and Van Damme, who is not much taller than her, did not really spark in the film, although it did reasonably well at the box office, thanks to the actor's loyal fans. In the US, it took $70 million. One thing that Van Damme did do for Kylie was to teach her an exercise for maintaining a pert bottom, by squeezing the butt cheeks together. Kylie was very much in awe of the Belgian's backside, which she thought defied gravity – as her own quite obviously still does, even though Kylie always maintains that she does not work out. The most paradoxical thing about *Street Fighter* is that it coincided with the release of 'Confide In Me', which boasted a super sexy video and was an original, sophisticated sound for Kylie. Seeing her dressed up in battle fatigues shooting a bazooka was a strange parallel, to say the least.

Kylie went straight into her next movie, allegedly a comedy, *Bio Dome*, with Pauly Shore and Stephen Baldwin. Critic John Lavin, in *Movie Magazine International*, dismissed it as the 'biggest waste of celluloid space I have ever witnessed'. Kylie, who played a scientist, described it as *Bill & Ted* in an agricultural dome. She played one of the straight roles, while the two male leads played two 'goofy guys', who mistake a bio dome for a mall. And the fun starts there. By coincidence, the video for the single release 'Put Yourself In My Place' depicted Kylie in a weightless bubble, gradually shedding all her clothes, much more memorable than *Bio Dome*. During this period of the mid-nineties, Kylie's career was like a scatter gun, shooting her all over the place in the hope that some of the pellets might hit the target. Sadly, her movie choices did not even make the outer ring. At least Kylie realized it was time to take a break from a very bumpy Yellow Brick Road. She was disappointed and disillusioned with the way that in films women are shoved into tight, short skirts and paraded from one scene to another, with very little point to their existence. This might work successfully in a Kylie video, but becomes threadbare when stretched to an hour and a half. Kylie had wanted American exposure and, once again, had been left in the dark room.

Instead of trying for a third 'nothing' part, Kylie accepted a role more in keeping with this creative mid-period. At least this time she was the star. It was a short, strange, eleven-minute Australian film *Hayride To Hell*, in which Kylie played 'The Girl', who begs a salesman called George Table to help her. One advantage for Kylie was that it involved a week's intensive filming in Sydney, and would allow her to take an extended three-month break in Australia at the beginning of 1995, spending time with her family and friends, as well as her then boyfriend Mark Gerber. In some ways, *Hayride To Hell* was an extended video. Kylie Chameleon, darkly brunette, tells Table she is a diabetic and insists that he give her a lift to her apartment. She goes inside but faints in the elevator, where she is found by Table. She wakes up and hits him with a teddy bear, shouting, 'What the f*** have you done with my things?' It is challengingly arty, which was just the attraction for Kylie. The important thing is that it promoted a different Kylie at a time when she was diversifying. This was no starlet fodder. Kylie achieved a much greater sense of professional pride from this eleven-minute short than from both of her 'Hollywood' films combined.

In retrospect, the films *Street Fighter* and *Bio Dome* were the least cool projects Kylie became involved in during the nineties. A much more fruitful collaboration came about in 1997, when she appeared naked in a video for the contemporary artist and photographer Sam Taylor-Wood. Again, *Misfit* was a short art film for the BBC, more an exhibit than a cinematographic concept; it featured a naked Kylie miming to a piece of castrato opera. Taylor-Wood, who would be nominated for the Turner Prize the following year, was inspired by Kylie's beautiful androgyny. Taylor-Wood portrayed Kylie as a street urchin, and teased the audience by having her sing not with her own voice but that of a nineteenth-century castrato. Taylor-Wood was very influential in the London art scene, not least because of her marriage in the same year to artists' agent Jay Jopling. Jopling owns the White Cube galleries, and represents a Who's Who of the most talked-about modern artists, including Taylor-Wood herself, Tracey Emin and Damien Hirst. It did Kylie no harm at all to be associated with so celebrated a circle.

Kylie's secret for attracting the most original artists of a generation to work with her is her ability to change, like the shape-shifter from the *X Files*. As such, she is a blank canvas, waiting to spring into colourful life at the touch of a paintbrush. That does not mean that Kylie brings nothing to the party – on the contrary, her own creative juices are encouraged by those around her. Taylor-Wood once described her as a 'multi-faceted chameleon woman'. Creative people give Kylie the confidence to be creative herself.

The death of Princess Diana cast a shadow over Kylie's album *Impossible Princess*. By an amazing and rather ghastly coincidence, that year she also completed a cameo role in a film *Diana & Me*, about an Australian tourist called Diana Spencer, who travels to London to meet her famous namesake. Kylie played herself, a celebrity hounded by a paparazzo – a plot line which, in the light of the controversy over Diana's pursuit by photographers, only made the whole thing ten times worse. The timing of the film was quite exquisite in its awfulness and, understandably, never saw the light of day.

Kylie never gives up. Just as she still expects to break through in the American market, she still wants to attain credence as a movie actress. As with her music, Australia remains her starting point for regrouping. And so she made two films in Australia for release in 2000, which reinforced her musical comeback. In the first *Cut*, she doesn't last very long. Poor Kylie is a horror film director, who is butchered with a pair of gardening shears by a masked killer early in the action. It was something like *Friday the 13th* meets *Scream*. Kylie was doing a favour for *Hayride To Hell* director Kimble Rendall, who was making his first full-length feature, and to Mushroom Records boss Michael Gudinski, who was involved in his first major film project. The star of the film was former Hollywood brat packer Molly Ringwald, who had met Kylie over dinner in LA some six months before. Ringwald had been a teenage star just like Kylie, and had suffered some similar difficulties through not really being allowed to grow up. Although Kylie was only on set for a few days, Ringwald really liked her and tried to give her advice on how to 'crack' America, Kylie's greatest unfulfilled ambition.

Kylie also signed up for the lead in an Australian film. *Sample People* was a brash, low-budget, indie thriller, in which Kylie played a nightclub owner, who becomes entangled in various scams involving a lot of cash and drugs. The unknown director Clinton Smith had sent Kylie a script two years earlier and had been astonished to receive a call from Terry Blamey, saying that she had chosen to appear in his film. Kylie liked it because her character was quite cunning and resourceful, not a bit like Charlene from *Neighbours*. For the film, Kylie joined the Pet Shop Boys to sing a version of the pop classic 'The Real Thing', which many viewers thought the highlight of the movie.

Kylie's film career is distinctly weird. Perhaps she has suffered from being a big fish in a small pond as Charlene Mitchell. She may have won awards, but has never professed to have any confidence in her acting abilities. Kylie is always complaining about nerves, insecurities and lack of confidence but, unlike her music career, her movie path seems to lack any overall strategy or purpose. The original idea seems to have been to make her even more famous, and to turn the television star into an international movie star. But it did not work. Ironically, considering she was by far the biggest star of *Neighbours*, two other much more minor actors in the soap have gone on to make it big on the world stage – Russell Crowe and Guy Pearce. There is plenty of time for Kylie to make a half-decent film. More encouraging for the future was her tiny cameo in *Moulin Rouge*, where she played The Green Fairy. We see Kylie twinkling in the night sky, and then she is gone. The director Baz Luhrmann is Hollywood flavour-of-the-moment and, more importantly, a great fan of Miss Minogue.

Confidentially: 'I'm working with people who have given me a lot more confidence and encouraged me to express myself.'

kylie
personal

KYLIE WAS REALLY GETTING ANNOYED. He was more of a drag queen than the usual sort of pest, but he would not stop making snide remarks. All Kylie wanted to do was to relax with her friends after another gruelling day on her Australian tour. She knew that she was good at pool, but he was bitching on about her style, making crude suggestions about where she could stick her cue, and thinking he was absolutely hilarious. Suddenly Kylie snapped, and knew exactly where she was going to stick her cue – right in this guy's face. With the point of the cue an inch from his nose, she told him in Anglo-Saxon terms to leave the establishment. William Baker, who was there at the time, confirmed, 'She does have a breaking point. She's a lot harder than she used to be.'

For the most part, Kylie is easygoing and easy to get along with, but she has been a performer, out there for the public, for more than twenty years and she does need quality time to herself when she is not on show and when she can enjoy the company of her friends without unwelcome intrusion. Rudeness, as displayed by the annoying drag queen, is the one thing guaranteed to get Kylie into a strop. 'It really winds me up,' she admitted. Right Said Fred's singer Richard Fairbrass recalled sharing a car with Kylie after a show on her British tour of 1992: 'There were people trying to get in and she went mad. She hated it, shouting, "how dare they?" I thought "they dare because you are Kylie Minogue and you should remember where you came from."'

Kylie is also not averse to turning the air blue with a few well-chosen expletives when the need arises, and you would not want to be on the receiving end of that. She had a total tantrum at the Party in the Park concert in London in July 2000. Her stage monitors stopped working because of the rain, so that all she could hear in her earpiece was the delayed music from the speakers. As a result, she was singing in all the wrong places and appearing unprofessional, which is the one thing she will not tolerate at any price. Kylie had rehearsed so much for the gig that when it all went wrong, she 'blew off a lot of steam'.

She likes to be in control of the situation and, while not a control freak to the extent of a star like Madonna, she is apt to lose her temper, as certain of her boyfriends have discovered. James Gooding was treated to the Kylie temper at a restaurant before Christmas 2001. She confessed, 'We had a little tiff', which is a bit of an understatement if their faces as they marched out were anything to go by. She was later seen in the street near her home, tears streaming down her face, shouting at him. Kylie maintains that arguments are good in a relationship because they defuse tension that can build up through little disagreements. She can be very jealous, and stories about her boyfriends and other women do not impress. She admitted, 'I'm not superhuman. I can get jealous sometimes. It's a very natural emotion.'

Kylie does not do drugs. She had a taste when she was with Michael Hutchence, but that was ten years ago and although, once in a very long while she might be offered something, she does not partake. At all. She does, however, have a weakness for good liquor, perhaps a bottle of fine wine, champagne or, on a girls' night, tequila slammers, which have, on occasion, given her murderous hangovers. Kylie once admitted to *heat* magazine that she has phases of going out drinking. In Los Angeles, for instance, she toured all the clubs, knocking back exotic shorts. But she is not the clubber she was in the late eighties and early nineties. Nowadays, she would rather have friends round to crack open a bottle of champagne before adjourning to one of the exclusive restaurants near her home in Chelsea. Champagne has always been a particular weakness for Kylie. Her great friend Katerina Jebb tells the story of when they met at the photographer's Paris apartment. Kylie and an assistant appeared on the doorstep bearing champagne. Soon after, Kylie arrived with a sleeping bag and moved in. It was a difficult time, because Katerina suffered a serious car accident shortly afterwards and was hospitalized. But Kylie was there to help when she was allowed to go home. She even managed to persuade Katerina to take her picture even though she could not hold the camera herself and had to have it placed on a stand. The two women remain the closest of friends. They are soul mates.

Kylie likes nothing better than the company of her closest female friends, and meeting for lunch or dinner and having a good old 'girlie' chat is a great normalizing boost for her. The principal difference between Kylie and the rest of her friends is her considerable fortune. She is a multi-millionairess, with a fortune estimated at £12 million and rising fast. She told journalist Jane Oddy, 'I don't remember the moment I became a millionaire, but it must have been in my early twenties.' Kylie and her friends were having dinner one evening when the conversation turned to winning the National Lottery and what they would all do if they had the money. Kylie suddenly realized, 'But I *have* got the money.' Kylie's good sense in all things financial comes from her father Ron. She may have more than twenty pairs of Manolo Blahnik shoes but she will seek out the best bargain in any supermarket. 'The only money I care about is the money I have in my back pocket,' she declared.

Here is a typical Kylie day, if she is not working but just relaxing at home by herself: 9.00 alarm goes off; 9.15 prepare breakfast by blending sundried seeds and pieces of fruit into an energizing drink; 9.45 read newspaper; 10.30 personal training; 12.30 change for lunch; 13.15 lunch with a girlfriend near her home; 14.30 shopping for clothes, maybe furniture – she is always making her flat over, throwing away, ripping something out, replacing; 16.00 massage and beauty treatment; 17.30 taxi home and a chance to check texts and messages; 18.00 arrange to meet friends for dinner, e-mail Ron and Carol, listen to music while choosing outfit; 20.30 dinner at one of favourite restaurants – Nobu, La Famiglia, Vingt-Quatre are popular; 00.00 herb tea and a chat or a good book; 02.00 sleep

*

Casting off the shackles of humdrum suburbia has been a long drawn-out process for Kylie. She was born in the

Bethlehem Hospital in Melbourne on 28 May 1968 on a cool winter day. That's a cool day by Australian standards – at fifty-four degrees it would almost be summer in the UK. Rather aptly, considering her future persona as a woman-child, the UK number-one single was the haunting 'Young Girl' by Gary Puckett and the Union Gap. They would be replaced after a few weeks by the Rolling Stones ('Jumpin' Jack Flash'), probably the only pop act that Kylie will fail to match in the longevity stakes. The Stones, as well as The Beatles, were favourites of Ron Minogue and his young wife Carol, but, to a large extent, the swinging sixties passed suburban Melbourne by. Ron and Carol had moved down from Townsville, Queensland, where Ron had grown up a fifth-generation Australian, and to where Carol and her parents had moved from Wales.

Carol Jones was from Maesteg, a small town not far from Swansea, in South Wales, and lived there until she was ten. Kylie has not forgotten her Welsh roots. Her great uncle Dennis Riddiford still lives near the town and is delighted whenever Kylie can pop down from London in her chauffeur-driven limo. Dennis, a carpenter by trade, is proud of his successful relative, but tries to be discreet about the association, mainly to stop kids singing 'I Should Be So Lucky' outside his front gate. He, too, had emigrated to Australia, but returned more than forty years ago to live in Wales after he contracted malaria. His sister Millie – whom Kylie calls 'nain', Welsh for grandmother – still lives in Melbourne. Kylie is exactly the same height and a similar shape to her mother Carol, whom Dennis can remember as a little girl taking ballet and dancing lessons in a local hotel. Away from her glamorous urban life, Kylie is more than happy to put on an old anorak and wellie boots, and join Dennis for rambles around the hills and woodland overlooking the town. Kylie is a great fan of the outdoors and loves camping: 'Getting out in the middle of nowhere and pitching a tent is my idea of heaven.'

She is very conscientious about her family, taking time to find out all the news and to send them copies of her CDs and autographs. Kylie is officially half-Welsh, which more than qualified her for an entry in a book *One Hundred Great Welsh Women*, by Cardiff academic Terry Breverton. He placed Kylie at number one, proclaiming, 'It's my list and she deserves to be on it.'

By the time she was twenty-five, Carol Minogue had three children and was a full-time housewife. Kylie was the eldest, followed at an interval of two years by her brother Brendan, and then Danielle the next year. Although a talented dancer, the slender and petite Carol gave up any professional ambitions to devote herself to raising her family. She is an unassuming woman, who lacked personal drive, but was very supportive of her two daughters when it became clear that they possessed more than enough of that quality. She had done enough work as a dancer, albeit at a minor level, to understand the problems of performing. Although she made sure the girls had dancing lessons – not just ballet, but jazz and tap as well – she was not at all keen for them to pursue a professional career in dance because she knew it to be such a hard life. Singing would be another matter, even though she herself could not sing a note, not even in church where nobody can really hear you.

The family moved around various suburbs of Melbourne in the 1970s. Kylie's primary school, Studfield Primary in Wantirna South, recently closed despite a campaign by local parents, who contacted Kylie's management in London to ask for support. Unfortunately, Kylie was unable to help because she was recording at the time. Kylie enjoyed her early school days, even though being so small meant she rarely spoke up in class. Despite this early reticence, the image of Kylie as a shy little flower is well wide of the mark. Just ask her mother Carol, who revealed that her eldest daughter was a bit of a poser even when she was a tiny girl. Even Kylie herself thought she was a shy kid until her mother put her right.

The family eventually settled in the Camberwell district of the Melbourne suburb of Canterbury, handy for Ron's job in the finance department of a local council. Named after Viscount Canterbury, a nineteenth-century Governor of Victoria, the suburb lies about six miles (ten kilometres) east of the city and is staunchly middle-class, with spacious houses and plenty of green areas. The easiest way of getting into the city is by tram, a half-hour journey from Camberwell Station. Kylie was enrolled in Camberwell High School, which was co-educational but had more boys than girls by a ratio of two to one. Kylie had to wear a uniform and a proper school blazer and do her Maths homework like every other student.

Melbourne is often considered to be the sporting capital of Australia, and Camberwell High was geared towards sport, which did not interest Kylie one bit. She always hated sport because her 'little legs could not go fast enough.' More importantly for Kylie, there was a progressive music department. She learned violin and then piano – in a competition she once finished runner-up to a Chinese keyboard whizz kid. Her mother Carol was convinced her daughter won the prize for her ability to smile winningly at the judges, and not for any piano-playing ability.

The Melbourne suburbs were a relaxed and easygoing environment in which to grow up. The most upsetting thing that happened to Kylie in her early days was when her pet terrapin ate the family goldfish. She also had Gabby, a large black 'Bitsa' dog (bitsa this, bitsa that), which she missed terribly when she came to London. The

Minogue household was like one of those families from an American sitcom, very normal on the outside, with pets and barbecues, domestic chores and sibling squabbling, and yet Kylie, and particularly Dannii, led extraordinary lives as child stars. Picture the scene at the breakfast table: over a bowl of cornflakes, or vegemite on toast, Ron Minogue inquires what his daughters are doing today, before he sets off for a day's auditing of the housing department. The reply: 'We're going to be singing "Sisters Are Doing It For Themselves" on national television.' Showbusiness became such a normal part of their lives that nobody realized what an unusual thing it was to have two daughters under the age of eleven 'on the stage'.

Ron Minogue has always had a reputation for being a very level-headed, both-feet-on-the-ground sort of man. He has coped with his mercurial offspring in a very capable manner, making sure right from the start that they would use their money wisely. Not much gets under his skin, although he did get cranky at Kylie's annoying childhood habit of raising the inflection at the end of sentences. It is a common trait among Australians, particularly women, to rise to a higher pitch when speaking, so that everything sounds like a question. Mr Minogue realized that it would not aid his daughter's acting career to have a pronounced 'Strine Twang', as it is called.

Kylie's brother Brendan has coped manfully with being the sibling of famous sisters. He has had to suffer the embarrassment of his elder sister revealing that he was once a fan of the American eighties rock group Kiss and used to borrow his mother's high-heeled boots and paint stars around his eyes in homage to his heroes. Mind you, Kylie can talk – she used to think Leif Garrett was cute. When Kylie was well-known, Brendan, a good-looking, dark-haired boy, would go along with her to parties, and generally have the girls swooning in his direction. It was perfect for him, really – reflected adulation and none of the aggravation of being a star. One admirer from the days of *Neighbours* recalled wistfully, 'He was gorgeous, quiet and just a really nice guy.' Over the years, Kylie has answered many questions about Dannii. Her younger sister is in the business and willingly plays the fame game. Kylie remains protective of Brendan, who is very much part of her private life. By profession he is a cameraman for an Australian television company, and has travelled extensively throughout the world. Being away from public scrutiny has allowed him to take time out to go with friends on a backpacking trip around the world. But, for the most part, he has shared Kylie's home in London. When Kylie filmed *An Audience With...* in 2001, she acknowledged Brendan in public and he could be seen grinning uncomfortably next to his sister Dannii as the spotlight settled on him.

When Kylie went to Camberwell High, she was starting off on her acting career but then, when things went quiet, she led a relatively undisrupted school life until *The Henderson Kids* put her on the road to stardom at the age of sixteen. She had to cope with Dannii's fame, learning to forge her sister's signature for fan photos, but she was able to go wild as an adolescent, without the world watching her. As a fourteen and fifteen-year-old she would spend a lot of time at the local bowling alley and became a very good player. She once entered a ladies' competition and won a first prize of Aus $15. 'I was pretty stoked,' she recalled. Although she hates sport, Kylie is expert at pursuits like bowling and pool, which are normally associated with bars and having a good old sociable time. By chance, James Gooding invited her bowling when he met her for the first time, little realizing that it was a quick and easy way to her heart.

The other teenage hang-out was the municipal pool, where she met the first boy she ever kissed, at the age of thirteen. Kylie had built up to the big moment by practising on the back of her hand. The boy's name was David and he was darkly handsome – not a bit like Leif Garrett. Kylie had fancied him for ages and, when he was put on 'trash duty' as a reprimand for being a nuisance to others by 'bombing', she saw her opportunity. She went round with him picking up the rubbish. It was very romantic and, finally, they kissed and it was not a disappointment.

Ron and Carol Minogue were understanding parents, in that they let Kylie make her own mistakes and learn from them. She, of course, thought all her friends had much more freedom than she did – she was sixteen before she was allowed to have her ears pierced. But one area where they did let their daughter make up her own mind was on the question of boys. She explained, 'If you meet a boy, you know pretty soon if he's any good for you or not.'

Kylie's wild stage of fighting with her parents, smoking because she thought it made her tough, and generally playing the difficult teenager did not last past *The Henderson Kids*, which took her away from home for the first time. She had on-set teachers and had to put in a lot of work to pass the English exam she needed to get her Year Eleven, as it is called in Australia. Kylie eventually passed the Australian equivalent of two A-levels, in art and graphics. She described herself as of average intelligence, preferring the arts to sciences, which she loathed almost as much as sport. Her school considered her 'sensible' about juggling acting and studying.

On her last day at school, she joined two other girls on the second floor of the main building where they found a hose, turned the taps full on, and proceeded to drench everybody walking below. When a teacher arrived to sort things out, Kylie ducked and hid, while her two friends took the rap and were ignominiously expelled. On leaving school, Kylie temporarily flirted with the idea of going to business school or working in a handicraft shop – she was very good at sewing and embroidery – but, in reality, she was always going to be a performer. So she signed on the dole and auditioned for *Neighbours*. One of the great benefits of her parents' attitude to their children is that they have never let their offsprings' fame go to their head. Kylie observed that they were not the least bit precious about her, and were 'never gushing' over everything she did. Instead, her family have always been her rock. When, for instance, she was struggling with stress and tiredness in the mid-nineties, she rang up and asked if her parents would come for a visit. They dropped everything and flew straight over to England to spend two weeks with their daughter.

Kylie travels back to Melbourne for an extended visit twice a year. Sadly for Ron and Carol, all three of their children live abroad, but Carol is always on board if Kylie is touring. It was just the same when Dannii was touring around on the *Young Talent Time* bus; her mother would be there to support her. At the end of 2001, everybody had a scare when Ron, at sixty, had to have an operation for prostate cancer. He has always been the power behind the Minogue family, so it came as a shock to Kylie, stuck 12,000 miles away while her father was in hospital. For once, her manager Terry Blamey was positively garrulous: 'Thankfully the news is good,' he said. 'Kylie was very concerned, but the operation was 100 per cent successful and Ron has been cleared by the doctors. He is fully recovered and is resting at home with his family.'

When Kylie went back to visit, she promptly bought her parents a new home in Canterbury with a heated swimming pool and tennis court. Although in need of a little refurbishment, the two-storey house is in one of the most prestigious residential streets in the whole of Melbourne. Kylie bought the house at auction for Aus $2.43 million, which is the equivalent of about £890,000 – a very expensive property by Australian standards. Their old single-storey family home in Alexandra Avenue was sold at auction on 23 February 2002 and made Aus $1,300,000. A few days earlier, at the Brit awards, Kylie paid tribute to her father: 'He will be so proud of me. He'll be the first person I call when I come off stage.'

*

Kylie's parents have been happily married for thirty-five years. It is rather ironic, and more than a little puzzling, that neither Kylie nor Dannii have managed more than five minutes in the relationship stakes. Instead, the lives of the two sisters are beginning to resemble a Bette Davis and Joan Crawford movie, inter-connecting and twisting in and out, as all the time they get older and begin to resemble each other more and more. There was a time, when they were younger, when Dannii was darker and plumper – not any more. They are both slim to the bone and if they wore their hair in exactly the same style and colour, it would be virtually impossible to tell them apart. *Whatever Happened To Baby Dannii* – coming to a cinema near you – would be a horror movie to send a shiver down the spine.

One of the great myths of Kylie's life is that there is an irreconcilable rift between her and her equally ambitious younger sister. They have been spurred on by sibling rivalry and by the inevitable comparisons between them. Kylie admitted that they both have feelings precariously balanced between jealousy and admiration. In a cynical sort of way, it is easy to see how Dannii has been good for Kylie's career. Poor Dannii gets rotten press, portrayed as the pushier, less talented version of her elder sister. Dannii was the one whose changing body shape, to a more voluptuous 'Baywatch' physique, derailed any suggestion that Kylie too might have quietly gone up a bra size. It is considered vulgar when Dannii takes her clothes off for *Australian Playboy*, but tasteful or arty when Kylie does the same thing for *Sky* or *GQ* magazine. Dannii's perceived shortcomings have helped to define Kylie's good qualities.

Like all the best movie scripts, the true situation is not so cut and dried. Dannii was the first to be famous, first to be married and first to be divorced. She was also the first to have her own line of designer clothing and to star in a hit stage musical. And she's been out with a grand prix racing driver, something which Kylie has yet to do. Friends of both girls believe Dannii to be the warmer, more compassionate sister, ruled more by her heart than her head. She was always thought to be the more feisty, but, in fact, is probably more maternal and likely to be the first to send flowers if a friend has a baby. She is also a compulsive shopaholic, who spends money like it is going out of fashion, does not understand the meaning of the phrase 'clothes budget' and has always needed her father to keep a firm eye on her finances.

Since her initial success in *Young Talent Time*, Dannii has followed professionally in her big sister's footsteps. Kylie was a star in *Neighbours*; Dannii landed the part of rebel Emma Jackson in rival Aussie soap *Home and Away*. Kylie's first UK record in 1988 went to number one. Two years later Dannii followed her, but her debut 'Love And Kisses' only reached number eight. Dannii also has Terry Blamey as her manager, but there is just a hint that this is more to keep an eye on little sister than anything else. Dannii did not join the Stock, Aitken and Waterman Hit Factory.

Waterman has said that they could have signed Dannii but Kylie preferred them to pass. Instead, the younger Minogue joined MCA.

Dannii's wedding in 1994 was a glittering affair – in Australian terms, a wedding of showbiz royalty. The groom was Julian McMahon, a co-star in *Home and Away* and the son of a former Australian prime minister. Kylie was a bridesmaid and played the role of the unattached spinster sister. She was alleged to have designed Dannii's wedding dress, which was a bit of a surprise to the New York couturier who supplied it. At the wedding reception the two girls sang an impromptu rendition of 'We Are Family', the last time they sang together in public. Practically every time they give an interview they are asked when they are going to do a duet. As kids, they once sang 'Sisters Are Doing It For Themselves' on *Young Talent Time* and subsequently performed the same song at a charity gala. There was talk of a duet on *An Audience With...* but they did not have time to rehearse a number properly. The rumours surfaced again at the 2002 Brit Awards, but were strongly denied, as usual. The truth is that Kylie has absolutely nothing to gain from a duet with Dannii, who would almost certainly have her first number one from such a venture.

Dannii's marriage to McMahon lasted no more than fifteen months before collapsing acrimoniously amid rumours that he was playing less at home and more away. McMahon was portrayed as a cad, especially as he had professed undying devotion to Dannii on their wedding day. 'She is my world,' he cried. After the break-up, Kylie was a considerable comfort to her sister, a divorcee at twenty-three, who found herself now back living in London. In the early days, the sisters had lived together but, latterly, Dannii has preferred her independence. However, they talk most days on the telephone, particularly if they want to moan about the men in their lives – which is most days. They are rarely seen together in public, preferring to catch up and have a gossip with a take-away pizza, a bottle of wine and something good on the telly.

Dannii found love again two years later, in a whirlwind romance with ex-Formula One World Champion Jacques Villeneuve. They met at the 1999 Spanish Grand Prix, became engaged, and Dannii moved away from London and the shadow of her elder sister to share Villeneuve's two-million-pound penthouse apartment in Monaco. Up until now, Kylie has not made any ostensible sacrifices for love; that is not the case with Dannii, who immediately dropped out of sight to be with her millionaire. Alas, the engagement did not last and, after eighteen months in Monaco, Dannii returned to London once more to focus on her career. Neither girl would appear to be able to crack the two-year barrier and either one of the sisters could have made the following statement: 'I don't regard them [past relationships] as failures. You aren't going to find Mr Right by sitting at home. You have got to go out and try a few.' It was, in fact, Kylie speaking.

When Dannii split up with Jacques, she had her hair cut short for her part as Esmerelda in the West End musical *Notre Dame de Paris*. She was thrilled to be at last doing something that Kylie had never done. There is a suspicion that Dannii's eagerness to plunge into marriage and engagements is because they, too, are something Kylie has never done.

Dannii continues to be disarmingly frank about herself in interviews: 'I was the most crap singer and crap dancer and crap everything, but I worked my bollocks off, because that's what I wanted to do.' At least she has the consolation – if it is one – of being the Minogue sister preferred by *Pop Idol* judge Simon Cowell, who called Kylie a 'one-trick pony'. In Cowell's defence, Dannii was often considered to be the prettier of the two sisters until the past five years or so, during which Kylie has really blossomed.

Kylie is asked time and again about marriage and, now that she is approaching her mid-thirties, whether she is feeling broody and wants to have children. A woman cannot reach a certain age without having to answer that fatuous question. When Kylie was asked, at the beginning of her chart career, where she thought she would be in ten years' time, she had absolutely no idea that she would by then be even more popular, having staged one of the greatest comebacks in pop history. Instead, she used to answer glibly that she would definitely be married with two children. In 1989, she declared that she wanted a church wedding plus two girls and a boy. In 2002, with her career at a height she has never before attained, she had to deny reports that she was getting married to James Gooding.

It is a celebrity thing. You are seen having a second cappuccino with someone, and a glossy magazine is bidding for the wedding pictures – Dannii's were in *Hello!* Sometimes Kylie feels broody, sometimes she doesn't. She told Dominic Mohan of the *Sun*, 'I don't know when I'd squeeze them [children] in.' After her appearance on *Parkinson*, she was obliged to put the record straight by saying that she and James were not getting married. She had only implied that she might get married at some time in the future. The truth of the matter is that marriage is not something Kylie is much bothered about. She may marry, she may not.

Confidentially: 'If my life is complete in other ways then I don't mind being a sixty-five-year-old spinster.'

kylie

successful

ROBBIE HAD A BIG CRUSH ON KYLIE. He may have been the biggest solo star in Britain, but this was Kylie Minogue and he had been just an ordinary fourteen year-old, football-obsessed boy from Stoke-on-Trent when she had taken the charts by storm with 'I Should Be So Lucky'. Kylie, the older woman, knew exactly how to play it with Robbie. A record company insider observed, 'He would follow her around and she was like, "Robbie, you stink", but I think she ended up quite liking him really.' Robbie himself admitted he was slightly nervous of Kylie. There was never any romance, despite attempts by the media to link the two of them together. It would have been a wonderful story if they had become an item, but Kylie had a steady boyfriend and Robbie adopted his usual, outrageous, naughty-boy persona, asking publicly, 'Do you reckon she'd shag me?'

Kylie got her own back when they shared a stage in Manchester to perform their duet 'Kids'. Robbie had not seen the dress Kylie was going to wear. If he had blinked he would have missed the tiny silver slip of a costume. Kylie loved the moment when Robbie's usual serene on-stage confidence dipped when he first glimpsed his barely clad duet partner: 'For a second he completely lost it. He was sweating and I loved it.' She had actually always had a soft spot for Robbie, nominating him on more than one occasion as her favourite member of Take That. She is not a fan of boy bands, but thought Robbie stood out: 'I always knew he was going to be a star. He's such a natural.' Robbie and Kylie were put together by their management teams. Robbie was on Chrysalis which, like Kylie's new record label Parlophone, is a subsidiary of EMI. They were keen to reposition Kylie in the mainstream after her few years in the independent wilderness. Robbie jumped at the chance to write some songs for her new album *Light Years*. He told her she had everything going for her but just needed a good song to turn things around – just as 'Angels' had for him a couple of years before. With his songwriting partner Guy Chambers, he contributed three songs: the mellow lounge-track 'Loveboat', the high camp 'Your Disco Needs You' and the anthemic 'Kids'. Kylie shared the songwriting credit on the first two. She actually asked Robbie for a song called 'Loveboat' because she liked it as a title. It was Robbie who thought up the phrase 'Your Disco Needs You'. He also wrote the lyrics to 'Kids', which were quite mischievous, to say the least, with their tongue-in-cheek references to anal sex. Only Robbie could rhyme 'sodomy' with 'Billy Connolly'.

Although Kylie might prefer to disagree, Robbie made her appear hip at a vital time. 'Spinning Around' went straight to number one on a wave of support from Kylie's gay fan base, but that achievement would have been wasted if her comeback had begun and ended there. An alliance with Robbie was guaranteed to cement her position in the mainstream marketplace. Not only would the great man not alienate her gay fans, he would introduce Kylie to a whole new generation of young girls, who would see her next to Robbie and want to be just like her. He had just had a big selling number one with 'Rock DJ', so between them Kylie and Robbie monopolized the charts for a few months. She was the guest star on his *Top Of The Pops* Special in August 2000. The other reason why Robbie was such a perfect musical partner for Kylie is that he augmented her camp image. Robbie may not yet be a gay icon of Kylie's stature – although Take That found popularity appearing live in gay clubs before they became chart stars – but he is a showman *par excellence*, who can move effortlessly between brooding sexuality and naughtiness, just a step away from being a drag queen. His 'Rock DJ' became a great favourite among the transvestite ladyboys of Bangkok when Robbie toured the Far East. They loved it when Robbie bared his bottom and simulated sex with a cardboard cut-out of Kylie.

This initial phase of Kylie's great comeback has been labelled by some as CampKylie. But it was nothing new for Kylie to be the darling of the gay community. From the very beginnings of 'The Loco-Motion' and 'I Should Be So Lucky', Kylie was adopted by the gay culture of Melbourne and, particularly, Sydney. 'Kylie Nights', where drag queens would dress up and perform as Kylie, became hugely popular. The first she says she knew about these events was on a trip back to Australia, when she was driving past The Albury, the most famous gay club in Sydney. It was a Sunday night and one of her friends mentioned that it was 'Kylie Night'. She had absolutely no idea that such a thing existed, and was all for going in and amazing everyone: 'I was almost the last to know about it.' Kylie had this fantasy picture of herself leaping on to the bar and doing a routine from *South Pacific*. Unfortunately, she was not allowed in that night, because the club would have needed special security measures to handle the pandemonium that would certainly have ensued. Kylie did get to see a 'Kylie Show' at The Three Faces club in Melbourne, on her Christmas visit home in 1993. It was the first time Kylie had seen anyone impersonating her. She loved two performers in particular – one who wore ostrich-feather pink hot pants, like those she had worn in the video for 'Shocked' and another who donned the noughts and crosses dress, with which she had amazed her fans at *The Delinquents* première. Kylie was not an innocent where gay culture was concerned. She had been an actress since the age of eleven and inevitably came across the usual blend of luvvies and camp thespians that make up the profession. Kylie once mentioned that on *Neighbours*, for instance, both her make-up artist and hair-dresser were gay, so homosexuality was hardly a shock. It might have been a shock to an innocent girl-next-door – but then Kylie was never that innocent.

It was not just gay men in Australia who adopted Kylie. She became a downtrodden heroine for the gay community throughout the world. She herself cited 1989 as the crucial year when a gay audience started supporting her and react-ing against the accusations that she was both 'popular and uncool'. These attacks made her appear a victim, a key ingredient in becoming a gay icon. In most cases, there must be tragedy in the diva's life. Madonna, for instance, lost her mother at the age of five and was brought up by her father Silvio. Kylie noted this anomaly in her status when she proclaimed, 'I am not a traditional gay icon. There's been no tragedy in my life, just my tragic outfits.'

Kylie has achieved her status more through her battle to find a true identity and her own voice in a pop world determined not to take seriously a suburban girl from Melbourne, than through any tragic history. Paul Watson explored this in his 1999 paper about gay icons in pop. He explained, 'Gay men embrace those who represent embodied conflicts similar to their own and whose oppression explodes into a torrent of sensuality that is sublimated through their sound.' As Kylie herself has said, she changed her image because it was the only thing she had control over. Gay men could identify with her various incarnations and her search for a true self, especially as she was an appealing mixture of vulnerability and fragility. Watson believed Kylie became such a powerful image for gay men because she, like them, had fled to the city to escape 'blind suburbia'. Kylie's career has been a personal voyage of discovery, from soap star, to servile singer of Stock, Aitken and Waterman songs, to raunchier Kylie, and on to IndieKylie and beyond. The struggle for self-awareness, the willingness to reinvent herself and break the chains of pop subservience are all aspects of Kylie's career that are attractive to gay society. Watson argued, 'The narrative of Minogue's life could have been an adaptation from the diaries of dejection of a gay man, who felt instant empathy with her plight of pop subordination.'

Unintentionally, and much to Pete Waterman's surprise, the music he was producing in the late 1980s hit exactly the right note with the gay market. He now acknowledges that he was making money out of the 'pink pound', but just did not realize it at the time. From their earliest number one in 1985, 'You Spin Me Round' by Dead Or Alive, Stock, Aitken and Waterman employed a formula of incessantly catchy melodies and very good-looking singers, which was manna from heaven to the gay clubs of the time. It was no accident that Kylie's great revival began with the almost identically titled 'Spinning Around', which also had a tight disco tune – an archetypal gay sound. Waterman told *BBC Radio One*, 'Kylie is a strange amalgam of pop and gay. We wrote songs about normal feelings – "I still love you, I don't know why". Of course she became a gay icon. She was saying things that, if you are emotionally sensitive, you feel every day of your life.' Paul Watson elaborated on this theory by recognizing that her gay audience could empathise with Kylie as they 'shared and reflected on the betrayal and indignation that they collectively experienced by men'. This could not be better illustrated than by the sentiments of 'Better The Devil You Know', arguably the all-time gay favourite among Kylie's songs. She cemented her position as a leading gay icon in February 1994, when she appeared in front of 20,000 adoring fans at Sydney's annual Gay and Lesbian Mardi Gras parade, the only artist to perform. Wearing a pink tutu, and surrounded by a thirty-strong legion of admiring, similarly-dressed drag queens, Kylie performed 'What Do I Have To Do?' She had wanted to sing 'Better The Devil', but that number had already been commandeered by something like forty other 'Kylies'.

Kylie's persona as a *survivor* in the pop world has been absolutely vital in her maintaining the loyalty of her gay audience. Paradoxically, she has needed that audience to survive, but those fans have stuck with her because of their admiration for her perseverance. Not for nothing is Gloria Gaynor's 'I Will Survive' an all-time classic song for both gay men and gay women. Kylie is slightly bemused by her appeal to a gay audience of both sexes. When she was asked by *Boyz* magazine if she got 'hit on by girls', she replied ambiguously, 'Not really, no.'

She is really chuffed to be a gay icon. She confessed, 'They are incredibly loyal. I'm flattered that they pretty much adopted me before I even knew about it.' At a charity show at the Royal Albert Hall, she reprised her duet of

'Sisters Are Doing It For Themselves'. Her partner on this occasion was not her sister Dannii, but a man dressed up as Donatella Versace. The man was Elton John at his most flamboyant. Kylie was back at the Sydney Mardi Gras in 1998 and, this time, she performed 'Better The Devil You Know' ('BTDYK' as it is familiarly known at gay events), with dancers and fireworks and a crowd that went ballistic with pleasure. 'BTDYK' featured again, two years later, when she showcased numbers from *Light Years* at G.A.Y. at the London Astoria. She only did seven songs, but changed costumes four times, including the ever-popular red, spangly dress and a pair of devil's horns. Her gay fans have always appreciated Kylie's outfits, and William Baker seldom disappoints them. The designer Patrick Cox observed, 'She's a living Barbie doll. All gay men want to play with her, dress her up and comb her hair.' One of the more amusing reviews of a Kylie concert pointed out that the majority of men there were more interested in the embroidered stitching on her hot pants than what lies beneath. They are not interested in learning anything about the real woman behind their image of her as a cute little sister. Theirs is unconditional adoration and anything that upsets this is liable to be labelled filth or sacrilege. They want to take Kylie home and keep her in a box in the bedroom. To a certain extent, that is what all Kylie fans want to do: men who lust after her would want to take her out and re-enact the sexual experiences of Michael Hutchence, while young girls would want to swap clothes and compare lipsticks with her.

Crucially, Kylie has never shunned or alienated her gay audience. Ironically, that was exactly the mistake that Jason Donovan made, and his career has been in decline ever since. In the Stock, Aitken and Waterman days, Jason, too, was adopted by a gay audience. He was a good-looking, muscular blond, who sang prettily of his broken heart. He was also the number-one teen idol. It was the spring of 1992 and Jason was appearing in the Lloyd Webber musical *Joseph and the Amazing Technicolor Dreamcoat* when posters of him started appearing outside the Palladium Theatre in London with the logo, 'Queer as F***'. As fast as they could be pulled down, another would be put up. There was absolutely no evidence to support the assertion, but Jason was a victim of a whispering campaign that was trying to force gay celebrities out into the open and admit their true sexuality.

The Face magazine which, at the time, was seriously cool – Kylie aspired to feature in its pages – wrote about the campaign. They acknowledged that Jason was not gay, but reprinted the poster and also called him 'bleached-blond'. Jason decided to sue for defamation and immediately put himself in an absolutely 'no win' situation; sure enough, he won the case but was, ultimately, the loser. If he had ignored the magazine with its relatively small readership (relative to national newspapers), he might have sailed on with nothing more to face than the sort of whispers which affect a number of artists. Mel C and Ricky Martin are just two modern stars who ignore repeated innuendo. But, by fighting the case, Jason made the original poster headline national news. His gay audience ostracized him because he seemed to be disowning them, as if to be called gay was positively the worst thing that could happen to a man. And his heterosexual audience thought there could be no smoke without fire. Even today, when he has a steady girlfriend and two young children, mention of his name is still likely to provoke a debate on whether he is actually gay or not.

Jason Donovan has not had a top ten record in the UK since *The Face* débâcle. After the court case, he sunk deeper into drugs. *The Face* extended his agony by starting a fighting fund to raise money to pay his damages, even though he agreed to waive most of them. He admitted that he was 'going crazy with drugs', and the newspapers took great delight in stories of Jason falling over in clubs and generally behaving badly. The lowest point came in January 1995 – his drug problems became public knowledge when he was found slumped on the pavement outside the fashionable Viper Room in Los Angeles, and had to be rushed to hospital. Even his father Terry Donovan made public his concerns over Jason's welfare and drug use. Jason revealed, 'The drugs thing started getting big for me after the court case. I had wanted to make the move from *Smash Hits* to *The Face* but I couldn't move there. I was snookered and I couldn't come to terms with that.' He could not reinvent himself.

Kylie made the transition that eluded Jason, although he did have some cause for optimism in 2002. On the night that Kylie received two Brit awards, a now drug-free Jason was revealed to be playing a small venue in Grimsby for £2,000. His boyish looks may have gone, but he is still a good-natured, good-humoured interviewee. The *Sun* newspaper even launched a campaign entitled 'Let's Get Donovan On Again' which revived interest and had Jason dreaming that he, too, might one day win a Brit.

*

The Brit Awards, the *Top of the Pops* Awards and the Carling *NME* Awards, to name but three of the accolades thrust upon Kylie in 2001 and 2002, represent the height of her critical acclaim. They applaud her music in the same way that *GQ* magazine's Services for Mankind and *Elle's* Style Icon of the Year awards reveal the role of Kylie, sex kitten. But if one event can reflect her global standing, it is the performance of a lifetime at the closing ceremony of the Sydney Olympic Games. This spectacle fused together all the key elements of Kylie, and 3.7 billion people in 185 countries watched it – a few more even than watched Charlene marry Scott.

What an entrance Kylie made! A bevy of muscled Bondi Beach life savers carried her on a surf board to the centre of the main stadium, where a live audience of 100,000 people had gathered, all in party mood. She was dressed in the identical costume worn by Nikki Webster, the child who had starred in the opening ceremony. It was some slightly tortuous symbolism, typical of the Olympics, of a girl maturing to a woman – rather ironic considering it was Kylie, the most famous of all child-women, that Nikki had matured into.

The beach boys hoisted Kylie on to the stage where her dancers, a vision in pink, obscured her while they began their athletic movements to the strains of Abba's 'Dancing Queen'. Suddenly, the announcer's voice rang out above the audience: 'Mesdames et Messieurs . . . Miss (the music pauses for a split second and the dancers are frozen in time) Kylie Minogue.' And there she was, miraculously changed into the costume of a Busby Berkeley showgirl, complete with a magnificent head-dress. She performed 'Dancing Queen', the alternative national anthem of Australia, and her own 'On A Night Like This' and was, by common consent, magnificent. As if to crown her status as the world's number one gay icon, she was encircled by an enormous representation of Sydney's drag queens in all their finery, their devotion to Kylie absolutely constant and unaffected through the years. Her performance was the ultimate in camp and, as such, is unlikely to be topped. Many of Australia's most popular figures performed or appeared at either the opening or closing ceremonies, but it was Kylie not Greg Norman, nor even Olivia Newton-John, Kylie's own childhood heroine, who stole the show. Hers was the performance that stuck in the memory.

The Olympic Games did more than confirm Kylie's position as the number one gay icon, it established her as the world's all-Australian heroine. Even though she had deserted her homeland for London a decade earlier, hers would be the first Australian's name inked in during a game of 'name five famous Australians'. Kylie remains proud of her heritage and, ten months before her Olympic triumph, she had been the forces' pin-up entertaining the Aussie troops in East Timor, Indonesia, where they had been sent to keep the peace after the bloody civil war there. This was much more Marilyn Monroe than Vera Lynn. Kylie, in a tight-fitting, wet-through white shirt, skin-tight olive pants and boots, handed out Christmas cards which she had specially signed for the boys. She flew by helicopter to areas of mud, monsoon rains and mosquitoes – hardly the King's Road – to try to cheer up the men who would not be travelling back home for Christmas, which was five days away.

Kylie was profoundly affected by what she witnessed, especially when those not lucky enough to be singing Christmas carols with Kylie found a mass grave of butchered civilians, just a few miles away. She declared, 'I am fiercely proud of being Australian and to be part of all this is among the most rewarding things I have done.' To paraphrase an old cliché – you can take Kylie out of Australia, but you cannot take Australia out of Kylie. She admitted, 'In my heart I am so Australian. I am ridiculously patriotic. I can tell Aussies a mile away and I am always chatting to them in the street.'

Wales has tried to adopt Kylie as one of their own because of her mother's roots in the principality. The UK has also tried to affect ownership of Kylie. She has lived here so long, she is probably qualified to play for the England cricket team. She has thrived in London and understands that she is an honorary Brit. Everybody wants a piece of Kylie, recognizing some quality they can claim as their own but, in reality, she is an Australian and will remain so, wherever she ends up. And she may yet move to Los Angeles or New York.

*

At the end of the Olympic closing ceremony, Kylie returned to the stage to sing along to the Australian favourite 'Waltzing Matilda'. Poignantly, the surviving members of INXS were among those on stage with her. Kylie's position as a performer of fame and stature was assured throughout the world. Or nearly. One place remained unconquered: the United States of America. Kylie's very first hit, 'The Loco-Motion' remained her biggest success there and the unwanted sobriquet 'The Loco-Motion Girl' lingered on. The famous and much-lauded Australian film *Priscilla Queen of the Desert*, about drag queens crossing Australia in a battered old bus, was originally going to be about acts from the 'Kylie Show'. This would have been colossal international exposure for Kylie. Alas, it was decided that Kylie's name would not sell the film to the US public, so the plot was changed to make them Abba impersonators. The promoters obviously felt that the 'Loco-Motion Girl' was not going to sell ten tickets to a barn dance. It was little better for Kylie to be described as the Australian Madonna, which suggested something parochial and imitative. Kylie was not an absolute unknown in the US because her American gay fans still adored her, but she could walk down Rodeo Drive in Los Angeles and be taken for a boutique assistant, rather than one of the world's biggest superstars. The only places in the US where Kylie is likely to be recognized are in traditionally gay areas, like the Chelsea district of Manhattan: 'It can get a little manic there. The boys start to go wild.'

What Kylie needed to go back into battle in the US was a universally acclaimed, big-selling record. *Light Years*, 'Spinning Around' and 'Kids' had re-established her in the UK and other strong Kylie markets, but the follow-up would be crucial. She was with The Beatles' old record label Parlo-

A sudden change of image: Kylie and escort Michael Hutchence
at the Sydney première of her film *The Delinquents*, December 1989

Kylie loveable...

Above: With Jason Donovan. Their three-year affair was already over when Kylie and Michael Hutchence became lovers (**opposite**), perhaps the single greatest influence on her life. **Opposite inset**: At Micheal Hutchence's funeral at St Andrew's Cathedral, Sydney, November 1997. They had split early in 1991

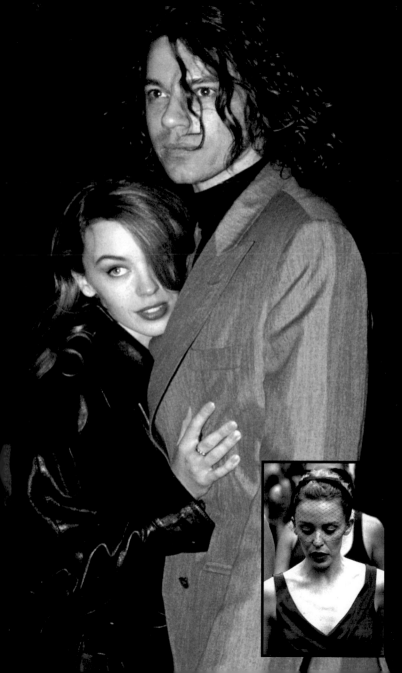

Kylie loveable, again...

Opposite page, top left: With Lenny Kravitz at a *Vogue* party.

Top right: With Tim Jeffries.

Bottom left: With photographer Stephane Sednaoui – their relationship lasted from 1995 to 1997.

Bottom right: With British actor Rupert Penry-Jones.

Above: With her ex 'scruff from Essex', British model James Gooding, at the NRJ music awards ceremony in Cannes, January 2002.

Left: With Gooding again, this time at the Royal Première of *Charlie's Angels*, London, November 2000.

Left: Little black number and red hair — almost unrecognizable at the première of *Muriel's Wedding* in 1995.

Opposite page

Top left: Presenting the Outstanding Contribution to Music award to Sting during the Brits at Earls Court, London, February 2002.

Middle left: At the Ivor Novello Awards in May 1999.

Bottom left: Posing in front of the cover photo of her latest album, *Kylie Minogue*, in October 1994.

Right: Arriving at the Brit Awards, where she picked up awards for 'Best International Female' and 'Best International Album' (*Fever*).

Following page: Arriving for the première of Moulin Rouge in September 2001. There's nothing 'Green Fairy' about this outfit, though.

phone, who had a commercial tie-up in the States with Capitol records, so the framework would be in place just so long as there was a half-decent record to promote. *Light Years* was a very pink album. The next release needed to be more mainstream. Kylie herself was heavily involved in producing and writing the new album, to be called *Fever*, but one song was destined to change the perception of Kylie worldwide. Finally, despite all the hits in between, she would have a record bigger than 'I Should Be So Lucky'.

When the demo for 'Can't Get You Out Of My Head' arrived at the offices of Parlophone in West London, it was almost perfect. The voice sounded familiar. It was former dance darling Cathy Dennis, who had five top ten records in the 1990s, and a much-copied bob haircut, but was a bigger name in Europe and the US than in the UK. Her biggest solo hits were '(Touch Me) All Night Long' and a version of The Kinks' classic 'Waterloo Sunset'. The melody for 'Better the Devil You Know' was actually inspired by 'Come On And Get My Love' by D Mob on which Cathy sang the vocal in 1989. Cathy has a similar self-deprecatory style to Kylie: 'It never even crossed my mind that I could be a pop star, because I came from Norwich. Pop stars don't come from Norwich.' She has a healthy contempt for many singers, Kylie excepted, of course: 'They're celebrities, not pop artists – if you asked them about music they wouldn't have a Scooby-doo.' Ironically, she was probably a bigger name Stateside than Kylie but, by the end of the nineties, she had tired of performing and become a full-time writer for other artists. She has written most of the S Club 7 hits. Her collaborator on the song with the most infectious hook of 2001 was Rob Davis, guitarist with the seventies chart act Mud and one of the campest figures of the glam rock age. Davis was also responsible for the catchiest dance record of 2000, Spiller's 'Groovejet', which featured Sophie Ellis-Bextor on vocals.

Dennis was not convinced that 'Can't Get You Out Of My Head' was number-one material. But when Kylie first heard the demo, she leaped around, saying, 'When can I do it?'

The song was an obvious choice for first single from the new album. It had all the ingredients of a Stock, Aitken and Waterman hit, but in a more sophisticated package. The first line sounded eerily similar to Dead or Alive's chorus: 'You Spin Me Right Round'.

To whip up some publicity, and thus increase record sales, there were stories of great rivalry between Kylie and Victoria Beckham. This was a cynical marketing trick to try to persuade more people to buy the record they preferred – thereby increasing sales of both tracks. The media generally colluded with this mock battle. The outcome was complete victory for Kylie, when her record went straight in at number one in the UK charts on 23 September 2001. Kylie sold 306,000 copies in the first week of release, compared with 35,000 of Victoria's 'Not Such An Innocent Girl', which only made number six. As a recording artist 'Posh Spice' is just not taken seriously by media or the public, a state of affairs which Kylie knows all about from her own career. Victoria Beckham is also disadvantaged because she is so happily married, with two children she adores. Kylie is single, available and can be a little dangerous. There's nothing dangerous about sitting around in your mansion watching television with your hubby. The public is not that stupid. Kylie's single proceeded to top the charts in twenty countries worldwide. Ironically in Finland, which has traditionally adored Kylie, it only reached number two. To make up for that Finnish disappointment, the single topped the chart in both the United Arab Emirates and Israel. Kylie unites the world!

In the months since the release of the 'la-la-la' song, scarcely a day has gone by without Kylie featuring on a newspaper front page, a magazine cover, on television or radio. Suddenly Kylie has become a British national institution, like *Dad's Army* or Del Boy. Yes, she is a sexy and stylish survivor making the best music of her career, but she is also a reassuring presence, especially after the shock of 11 September. Bryan Appleyard of the *Sunday Times* observed, 'God's in his heaven, Kylie's at number one, surely nothing really bad can happen now.'

Not all the news has been welcome. A suspect package arrived at the EMI offices. It allegedly contained soil and a note warning the record company that owns Parlophone to drop Kylie, or else staff would be infected with anthrax. The perpetrator apparently loathed *Neighbours*. On a jollier note, Kylie featured in *An Audience With Kylie Minogue* on British television. Brendan and Dannii were there. The cameras also picked out Pete Waterman, looking every inch the proud father watching his daughter in a school nativity play. A tremor of expectation filtered through the audience when the band played the opening bars of 'Especially For You'. Kylie and Jason together again? Poor Jason – he had been replaced by Kermit the Frog, who said to Kylie, 'If you kiss me, I might turn into Jason Donovan.' Kylie replied, 'I like you just the way you are.' Everyone had a good laugh at Jason's expense.

When *Fever* was released in October 2001, it debuted at number one in the UK album charts. Awards began to pile up from all over the world. In Germany, Kylie won the 'Bambi' award for best comeback of the year. Tickets for four UK dates in 2002 sold out within one hour. Already, plans were well advanced to promote Kylie as a star in the US. The single was released and Kylie was promoting it everywhere, including on the *Tonight Show* with Jay Leno. She reached number one in the dance charts and climbed into the top twenty of the Billboard Hot 100 chart. *Fever* was released just after it won best international album at the

2002 Brit awards at the end of February. The reviews were good, although the description of Kylie as a pop vixen was cringe-making. *Billboard* said, '*Fever* harks back to a more innocent time when sex and dance floors merged to create one carefree nation under a groove.' The album entered the charts at number three, a wonderful result. The same week the single finally made the top ten.

Kylie's unparalleled desire for success makes it unlikely that she will ever give up on America. She has admitted that if an album took off she might follow it up. Of course she will! Until *Fever*, America represented one of two career failures in her life that needed addressing. The other is her movies. They have been worse than average. Perhaps her alliance with Baz Luhrmann may hold some promise for the future, with rumours that she may appear in his version of the acclaimed musical *Rent*. Madonna is showing signs of moving back into acting in her forties, and Kylie may well go down that route, as flashing her bottom into middle age would be a little sad. Will she give it all up for love and a family? The high from the drugs of fame and adulation would be so hard to give up, that any domesticity would have to fit around the public Kylie. She has never been more popular than she is now, she has never sung so well or performed a song so expertly. Her professional life is at a peak. And she has never looked so good, or been so admired for the way she looks. Who would want to give all that up?

Confidentially: 'There were always a lot of Kylie fans in the closet and now they've come out.'

kylie

desirable

A MINUSCULE PAIR of gold bondage hot pants slid teasingly up and down a pole, while their wearer sang a modern disco classic. 'Spinning Around' was the track which took Kylie back to the top of the UK charts for the first time since 1990. It had been ten long years. The video for 'Spinning Around' was even more important than the song itself. For those who had not been paying attention, it provocatively displayed the allure of a woman who had reached her sexual peak and was not afraid of shouting it to the world. Even Kylie was in awe of those hot pants, asserting that they had 'a mind of their own'. They plucked the strings of sexual fantasy for the millions of men who could not believe that they were being worn by the girl with the bubble haircut and the anaemic eighties hit list. More importantly, it brought this new sexy image to a younger audience, which had no preconceptions as to the kind of artist Kylie was.

The video also launched Kylie's bottom on an unsuspecting world – as if that part of her body had not really existed before. In reality, her bottom was nothing new to the readers of lads' mags. It had notoriously been revealed on the front cover of *GQ* magazine, as a re-enactment of the famous Athena poster. Under the banner 'Kylie at your Service', she was pictured dressed in white tennis clothing and wearing no knickers. Afterwards, Kylie insisted her G-string had been air-brushed out, which is neither here nor there. Celebrities are forever bleating about magazines using technology to change photographs, usually protesting that they were not actually naked. Kylie and her management, however, have always maintained a stranglehold on photo shoots, anxious to protect and project the exact image they want at any given time. In her defence, Kylie took a very light-hearted approach to the whole thing: 'I thought it would be fun to show a bit of cheek,' she said. The only truly bogus thing was Kylie pretending to play tennis – as if she would! Kylie's favourite sport is pool, preferably played in a bar with her friends. She is a very good player, which is not surprising, considering how much time performers have to kill waiting to sing, have their picture taken or be interviewed.

The pinnacle for Kylie's rear end, to date, occurred in the aftermath of the 2001 MTV Music Awards, when her immaculate behind was the runaway winner of a Best Arse competition, voted for by the public on MTV's interactive service. Entire photo galleries on the web are now devoted to pictures of her bottom. Brian Appleyard, of the *Sunday Times* no less, described it as a 'wonder of nature'. As the MTV site eulogized, 'We believe that, if used properly, it [Kylie's arse] could help the world come together in peace and harmony, rebuild cities and probably crack a nut the size of a continent.'

Kylie's spectacularly pert behind shows absolutely no desire to head south as she creeps towards her mid-thirties. It is a remarkable achievement in a woman of her age to have the world's most photographed and applauded rear. There has never been such a fixation on a bottom. In anyone other than Kylie it might be considered 'pervy' but, somehow, in Kylie's case, it is considered good clean, family fun – a latter day equivalent of Barbara Windsor's boobs. Kylie herself has likened her sexuality to a *Carry On* film, which is not exactly accurate. The fascination with her fanny, as Americans would call it, is rather pervy if you consider part of sexual allure to be her persona of a child-woman.

Kylie exploits her new desirability to the full and flaunts her body at every tasteful opportunity, including on the videos for 'Can't Get You Out Of My Head' and the follow-up 'In Your Eyes'. Never was this more in evidence than in her performance at the 2002 Brit Awards, where she dominated the next day's pictures in her Dolce & Gabbana costume, a skimpy white dress, with criss-cross lacing down one side, boned to accentuate her breasts, silver over-the-knee boots and silver Agent Provocateur knickers flashing teasingly. She resembled something Captain Kirk would have told Scotty to beam up speedily to the *Starship Enterprise*.

Kylie can be a little touchy about her bottom. She has even had people asking her to turn around so they can get a closer look. When one interviewer asked if he could talk about her arse, she replied firmly, 'I've put it away for a while now.' Inevitably there was a backlash over Kylie's bottom, with newspaper suggestions after her breathtaking Brits performance that all was not as natural as it seemed. It was described as a 'bumlash'. Kylie was mortified by the stories, especially as they undermined her perfectly natural image. A rearguard action in friendly magazines and newspapers strongly refuted the very idea of cosmetic enhancement. Having used her bottom as a pertinent weapon in her re-emergence, it may be time for Kylie to play down this particular feature in the future if it has a counter-productive effect. She had actually worn hot pants in a video before 'Spinning Around'. For 'Some Kind of Bliss', she wore a skimpy denim pair, which gave her the germ of the idea that this might be something to exploit in the future. When she asked Johnny Douglas, one of her producers, why he liked that particular video, he confided that it all came down to those hot pants. Kylie filed away that information for use on the next available occasion. The famous gold hot pants were actually passed on to Kylie by William Baker, who found them on a market stall for 50 pence. Who on earth other than Kylie could ever wear them? – there is hardly enough material to cover an oyster shell.

There was absolutely no point to the 'Spinning Around' video other than as a showcase for the gold hot pants. In some ways, it harked back to something saucy from the Pan's People or Hot Gossip television dance troupes. The video which, according to Kylie, was just about 'having fun in a club' was filmed in two days in a freezing cold studio at Pinewood, north of London. It was especially cold in hot pants. The most difficult part for Kylie was having to dance on a slippery bar in her stiletto heels. If there was little point to the 'Spinning Around' video other than Kylie's bottom, the observation is even truer when applied to the *GQ* magazine cover. Charlotte Raven in the *Guardian* rumbled it: 'This is no stolen moment, but the product of the model's wish to show the world her butt.' In other words, this was Kylie manipulating her public image in a calculating and, ulti-mately, very successful manner. Kylie's overtly sexual display is saucy-erotic, not smutty soft porn.

*

The transformation of Kylie, from Charlene Mitchell to the most desirable woman on the planet, did not happen overnight, despite the claims of a pair of gold hot pants. The reality is that Kylie had been striving to be considered sexy for more than a decade, but nobody would take her seriously. In the early days, no red-blooded male would have voted Kylie as the number-one doll with whom they would want to spend the night. She might have won a poll for which celebrity would be your preferred babysitter. It was a case of 'look at Charlene flaunting those long eyelashes – what does she think she's doing?' They even stuck a label on this incarnation – SexKylie – just as she became IndieKylie during her collaboration with the Manic Street Preachers and ArtyKylie when she performed with Nick Cave. SexKylie was considered fraudulent. The implication was that all the hair lacquer and bare flesh in the world was not going to transform this middle-class, suburban Miss Nice into a sex symbol.

In 1988, one magazine even featured Kim Wilde versus Kylie Minogue and gave the British singer eight out of ten for looks, while assessing Kylie as a six, claiming she was a 'bit on the skinny side'. Kim also won the style stakes, scoring another eight for her 'natural grace', whereas Kylie looked like 'she should be modelling digital watches', and was allotted a feeble four. It has been a huge effort, but today Kylie would assuredly score ten out of ten in both sections. Kim is now an old married lady with children, happily participating in eighties revival concerts when not designing gardens. Kylie is winning prestigious awards and is unlikely ever to be seen fronting a Stock, Aitken and Waterman tribute tour.

It is not Kim Wilde who has stood between Kylie and the position of number-one female icon. Kim is far too nice, homely and English for that. Instead, it is the spectre of

Madonna, already the most famous female pop star of all time. While Kylie was still climbing into her mechanic's overalls for another Charlene scene in *Neighbours*, Madonna had chalked up five number ones and eighteen top ten hits in the UK before 'I Should Be So Lucky' kick-started Kylie's chart career. By a strange coincidence, the only year since 1984 in which Madonna did not have a top ten single was 1988, the year Kylie under the Stock, Aitken and Waterman banner had her first five. Unsurprisingly, Madonna was someone Kylie looked up to as a musical icon long before anybody thought of using the same word to describe her. Pete Waterman could never understand it: 'I found it amazing that she was outselling Madonna four to one, but still wanted to be her. Everyone wanted to be Kylie Minogue except Kylie Minogue, who wanted to be Madonna.'

Making comparisons is part of human nature. When Prince William is seen in public with a girlfriend, she will inevitably be compared to his mother – the mother of all icons – Diana, Princess of Wales. It will be dreadful for the poor girl in question. In the early days, when Kylie tried to adopt a raunchier image during her time with Michael Hutchence, she lapped up the comparisons to Madonna, because of her aspirations to match her iconic image. By 1992, Kylie wished she had never heard of the Madonna comparisons, complaining that Madonna herself had borrowed the images of other stars, from Marilyn Monroe to Greta Garbo. 'I'm sick of people saying I am ripping off Madonna,' she moaned. The now defunct *Sky* magazine launched a withering attack on poor Kylie, undermining her sex appeal in the bitchiest of manners: 'When Kylie bares all, she shows us merely that she has nothing to show. Kylie is trying to follow Madonna – she bared all, thus Kylie must. But where Madonna understands the game, Kylie doesn't. Madonna's a tough egg, a control freak who manipulates her own image in order to manipulate us. Basically, Kylie isn't sex.' Just what twenty-six-year-old Kylie had done to provoke such unkind observations is a mystery, but post-1998 they would appear absolutely absurd.

MADONNA	KYLIE
Suburban middle-class background in Detroit, Michigan	Suburban middle-class background in Melbourne
An ambitious, precocious child	An ambitious, precocious child
Very small, 5 feet 4 inches on a good day	Even smaller, 5 feet plus a hair
Known only by her first name	Now officially known only by her first name, since the release of *Light Years*
Icon for a gay audience	Icon for a gay audience
Much publicized sex, erotica and S&M stage	Bondage-lite
Single and childless at thirty-three	Single and childless at thirty-three
Has made London her home	Has made London her home
Released single called 'Fever' – video directed by Stephane Sednaoui	Released album called *Fever* – went out with Stephane Sednaoui
Queen of reinvention: Has been geisha girl, cowgirl, angel/whore, earth mother	Queen of reinvention: Has been geisha girl, cowgirl, angel/whore and sees herself going back to nature in future as 'glitter hippy'
Explores French electro pop	Uses French electro pop
Reworked early pop song 'Like A Virgin' for live tour	Reworked early pop song 'I Should Be So Lucky' for live tour
Never habitual drug user, despite the company she has kept	Never habitual drug user, despite the company she has kept
Very thrifty and financially astute	Very thrifty and financially astute
Tours with group of gay male dancers	Tours with group of gay male dancers
Loves Dolce & Gabbana	Loves Dolce & Gabbana
Rediscovers disco with 'Music', summer 2000	Rediscovers disco with 'Spinning Around', summer 2000
Wore suicide blonde hair for Blonde Ambition tour 1990	Wore suicide blonde wigs in 1990
Supports Aids causes	Supports Aids causes
Most Fashionable Woman of the Year 1994	Style Icon of the Year 2001

MADONNA	KYLIE
Gave birth to daughter in Good Samaritan Hospital, LA	Born in Bethlehem Hospital, Melbourne
Book of photographs of herself	Book of photographs of herself
Strong use of Catholic imagery	Photographed as kitsch nun by Pierre et Gilles
Early acting success (film)	Early acting success (TV)
Subsequent film career a flop	Subsequent film career a flop
Rode a bucking bull on 2001 Drowned World Tour	Rode a bucking bronco for Agent Provocateur ads 2001
Always seeks best music producer	Always seeks best music producer
Did an ad for Pepsi	Did an ad for Pepsi
Wanted to be in a musical (*Evita*)	Wants to be in a musical
Vegetarian	Vegetarian for seven years
Imitated Marilyn Monroe for her *Material Girl* video	Has performed as Marilyn Monroe
Has been seen out with Prince	Has been seen out with Prince
Number Ones in 1980s, 90s and oos	Number Ones in 1980s, 90s and oos
Very close to younger brother Christopher	Very close to younger brother Brendan
Dallied with lesbian image, rumoured affair with stand-up Sandra Bernhard	Snogged Geri Halliwell on *TFI Friday*
Husband Guy is ten years her junior	Ex-boyfriend James is seven years her junior
Voted No 1 in VH1 poll of greatest women in music history	Voted No 2 in VH1 poll of greatest women in music history
Survivor	Survivor

Madonna had one important edge over Kylie for many years – a sense of irony. She once said, 'I love irony. I like the way things can be taken on different levels.' She was talking about one of her first hits, 'Like A Virgin', and the fact that it was considered provocative at the time. Kylie did not reach an understanding with irony until after her collaboration with Nick Cave in the mid-nineties. It is all about age and worldliness. 'I'm tough, I'm ambitious and I know exactly what I want.' That is a quote from Madonna, but it could just as easily have come from Kylie, who has shown these qualities in abundance in making such a triumphant comeback. While it is diverting to list the similarities of the two women, it is through their differences that they are more readily defined.

Kylie is forever putting herself down; it is a self-deprecating style she has perfected over the years. She frequently declares herself to be nervous, and laughs at her various incarnations. Madonna would never do that. She considers herself to be an artist and not a commodity, like 'Kylie Minogue Limited'. She is also never afraid to have an opinion, or to shock. When she was advised not to swear when presenting the 2001 Turner Prize, it was like a red rag to a bull. She quite deliberately said 'motherf***er' and the moral majority of curtain twitchers promptly rang in to complain. One could not conceive of a situation when Kylie would say 'motherf***er' before the watershed on national television. Or after the watershed, for that matter. Her swearing is strictly behind closed doors. Madonna is an object of desirability in a down and dirty way. A Madonna fantasy is what she might do to you. Kylie is desirable in a white, cotton knickers sort of way. A Kylie fantasy is what you might do to her. Irvine Welsh, the author of *Trainspotting*, wrote a short story *Where The Debris Meets The Sea*, about four celebrity women who lounge around in a Santa Monica beach-house and lust after unattainable Edinburgh manual workers ('schemies' as he called them). They are Kylie, Madonna, Victoria Principal and Kim Basinger. At one point, his Kylie fantasizes about replacing the beloved dog of a Scottish removal man, wishing that she was the animal wearing a collar, tied to his arm. Welsh, who is proud to reveal himself as one of Kylie's original fans, was more than impressed that she did not attempt to sue him.

These days Madonna is a housewife-superstar, has two young children and is married to Guy Ritchie. Her two children are said to be mad on Kylie, especially 'Can't Get You

Out Of My Head'. Little one-year-old Rocco puts his hands together to the 'la la la' bits. Kylie and Madonna had never actually met until the night of the MTV Awards in November 2000, when the American famously wore a T-shirt with 'Kylie Minogue' written across the front. William Baker knew Madonna and simply asked Kylie if she wanted to meet her: Kylie recalled, 'The first thing I said to her was, "Finally nice to meet you", because I would have thought I would have met her before.'

*

In reality, Kylie was never the girl-next-door. That image was invented by smart television publicists, and accepted by the media. How many girls living next door are on television at the age of eleven, and major stars while still in their teens? It is a rarefied atmosphere, an unreal existence. The problem for Kylie was that, for quite a while, it stopped her claiming a place as a real woman. Eventually, she succeeded through perseverance, self-awareness and a change in popular culture, in which everybody wanted to be less threatened and less challenged. Kylie is now the acceptable face of eroticism. Becoming the world's most desirable woman has been a long journey.

1987/88

Kylie is a hugely popular television star but has an irritatingly wholesome image, based around the character of Charlene Mitchell – part tomboy, part big sister.

Neighbours is addictive, but everyone makes fun of it. There is a hint of kitsch, which will serve Kylie well when she becomes a gay icon.

When she arrives in London, she has terrible, frizzy hair which was assumed to be a bad perm. It turns out to be naturally curly and she has struggled to straighten it ever since.

The mischievous media adopt the phrase 'pint-sized' to describe the petite Kylie, which immediately undermines her credibility.

In interviews, she is eager to please but comes across as suburban without a ready sense of humour. In particular, she has no sense of irony.

She has absolutely no sex appeal, a state of affairs exacerbated by press descriptions of her as the 'singing budgie' and 'little gonk'.

Her fashion sense is tragic. She favours hats with the top cut out to show the frizzy hair, and huge loop earrings.

She appears uneasy in photographs, either looking too much like Smiley Kylie, or as if she has been caught in headlights.

Stock, Aitken and Waterman are the antithesis of 'cool', and so Kylie is uncool by association.

Kylie does not appear to be having sex with anyone. Her duet with Jason Donovan is a strange, anaemic affair, strictly for the under-twelves.

Topless photos of her on a Bali beach reveal a teenage gamine waif, with a lack of any discernable curves.

Kylie lacks confidence in her image.

1989/90

Kylie makes her first feature film, *The Delinquents*, and, while the film is uninspiring, she does have better hair. She also has sex on screen – quite a lot.

Her celebrity status is assured by achieving the biggest selling first album by a female artist.

She stuns her public by appearing on the arm of rock star Michael Hutchence. He oozes sex appeal but, at first, none of it seems to rub off on Kylie.

At the Australian première of *The Delinquents*, she looks stunning in a micro-skirt and a seriously blonde wig. Kylie is a rock chick!

Overnight – and probably unintentionally – Kylie creates an angel/whore persona which remains with her to this day.

Kylie is photographed wearing short skirts, riding pillion on Hutchence's Harley-Davidson.

The public perception of Kylie as Girl-Next-Door gradually changes, amid lurid tales of sex on an airplane and handcuffs in her luggage.

Being in love gives Kylie confidence in her looks and the self-belief to follow her instincts.

Kylie takes responsibility for her own videos and, thereby, takes control of her image. 'Better The Devil You Know' reveals a sexier, more grown-up Kylie.

1991/92

Kylie's relationship with Michael Hutchence ends before they become a boring celebrity couple. He gave her the hint of sex appeal but he did not make her convincingly cool.

She is embraced by the gay scene and, along with Madonna, becomes a favourite role model for drag queens.

The video for 'Shocked' reveals Kylie the Vamp. Gay favourite 'What Do I Have To Do?' had already assured her a place as Kylie the Camp.

Kylie begins to distance herself from The Hit Factory and decides she will leave PWL at the end of her contract.

She begins to realize that there are people out there who would like to work with her, regardless of her status as the star act of Stock, Aitken and Waterman.

Kylie is now a London girl, leaving behind the suburbs of Melbourne.

Post-Hutchence Kylie discovers a new 'set' of friends in the world of art and fashion.

Kylie is going through a confident stage, but there is one hindrance in her bid for recognition as a bona fida sex goddess: she is deemed to be a bargain basement copy of Madonna.

1993/94

Kylie joins the deConstruction record label and, musically, begins to become a more credible artist.

Her parting from Stock, Aitken and Waterman is the final nail in Charlene the Girl-Next-Door's coffin.

She releases 'Confide In Me' which is not only a memorable song but allowed an opportunity for a new look Kylie – very Barbarella.

Kylie becomes a cover girl for trendy magazines like *Sky* – pictured minus any clothes – and *The Face*, which have a readership young enough to have totally missed Kylie in *Neighbours*.

She continues to be compared to Madonna at every opportunity, but it is Kylie's own fault: Madonna brings out a sex book, Kylie brings out a sex book. 'Confide In Me' is Kylie's answer to Madonna's 'Justify My Love'.

She is the token crumpet in a lacklustre film, *Street Fighter*, opposite Jean-Claude Van Damme. It does nothing for her image.

Kylie is no longer a teen idol, but has yet to establish a positive new identity. Once more, she needs confidence to move forward.

Her video strip for 'Put Yourself In My Place' becomes an MTV classic.

1995/97

Labelled unwisely Kylie's 'indie years', Kylie grows up, matures like a fine wine but, commercially, almost sinks.

Kylie begins a process of coolification, beginning with her collaboration with underground hero, Nick Cave, with whom she duets on the sombre song of murder 'Where The Wild Roses Grow'.

In the video for 'Wild Roses' Kylie appears dead, floating face-up in water with a rose between her teeth.

Nick Cave persuades Kylie to recite the lyrics of 'I Should Be So Lucky' at the Poetry Olympics. At last Kylie finds irony and, soon, the confidence to embrace her past in all its cheesy glory will be a strength rather than a weakness.

Kylie falls in love with acclaimed photographer and videographer, Stephane Sednaoui, who encourages her to believe in her own creativity and try new things.

Collaboration with Indie favourites, the Manic Street Preachers, enhances new, cool Kylie.

She cuts her hair and adopts the look of waif/street urchin, a role for which she has always had the figure.

Kylie appears naked in a short film for trendy British artist Sam Taylor-Wood. She demonstrates a complete lack of inhibition.

The benefit of these years is that they would enable Kylie to become a sex symbol in the future. It had not been credible for her to jump from uncool to sexy, but it would be believable to make that transition from being considered cool.

Michael Hutchence dies at the end of 1997 and her relationship with Sednaoui ends. Is this the end for Kylie, too?

1998/99

The *Impossible Princess* is a commercial flop. Kylie's desire to be popular is greater than her need to be innovative.

Kylie leaves deConstruction and her career in music appears to be over.

Kylie comes under the influence of 'gay husband' William Baker, who sets about repositioning Kylie in the marketplace.

Baker restyles Kylie as a gay icon, a winning mixture of outrageous and high camp.

With Baker's encouragement, she releases a pink book of photographs of Kylie in all her manifestations, together with textual appreciation from the seriously cool, including Baz Luhrmann, and Irvine Welsh, as well as old favourite, Pete Waterman.

One of the photos in the 1999 publication – entitled *Kylie* – is from 1994, and has Kylie dressed as a schoolgirl, five years before Britney Spears copied the look.

Another photo has Kylie dressed as a nun on a rocking horse.

William Baker's own photo of Kylie from 1997 depicts her naked, kneeling on a velvet sofa, a naughty, yet innocently happy grin on her face, and her curvaceous bottom much in evidence.

The book reveals the fun side of Kylie, a sense of humour being absolutely essential to a true sex symbol. It didn't hurt that the camera now adored her.

Kylie turns thirty, and the media begin to realize she is now more woman than child. 'Pint-sized' is rejected in favour of 'petite' or 'perfectly proportioned'.

For the first time in her career, Kylie goes more than a year with no single release. Instead, she is keeping a low profile, acting in a version of *The Tempest* in the Caribbean. It is almost time for the 'comeback'.

2000/2002

Madonna wears a T-shirt with 'Kylie Minogue' emblazoned across her chest. It is like she is passing the baton.

Kylie's appearance at the closing ceremony of the Sydney Olympics is a camp triumph. Wearing a creation of pink feathers, she performs Abba's 'Dancing Queen' and her own 'On A Night Like This' to rapturous applause. It is the perfect platform for Kylie's re-emergence.

She releases an album *Light Years*, which is a return to the disco diva sound of the eighties.

An alliance with Robbie Williams on the hit 'Kids' introduces Kylie to a new generation, for whom past styles and pigeon-holing mean absolutely nothing.

Everybody realizes that Kylie's best feature is her bottom; it gets an honourable mention in almost every article, as well as a starring role in all her videos and photo shoots.

Kylie recreates the famous Athena poster of a tennis player and flashes her bare bottom for the front cover of *GQ* magazine.

'Spinning Around', the first single from *Light Years*, goes straight into the UK charts at number one, her first for a decade. But all attention is focused on the gold hot pants she wears for the video.

Kylie's new boyfriend is revealed as male supermodel James Gooding. He is referred to as her toy boy, which gives her a gloss of domination. For the first time, there is no suggestion that she is being defined by her boyfriends.

She trounces Posh Spice in a hyped chart battle.

She is voted Style Icon of the Year 2001. It is now officially OK for both sexes to adore Kylie. And she is still the number one gay icon. Kylie's music is acceptable at the trendiest club or at an auntie's wedding.

The ultimate accolade – Kylie wins two Brit Awards in 2002 and her picture, wearing the sexiest of Dolce & Gabbana outfits, adorns the front page of all the newspapers. Kylie's waxwork in Madame Tussaud's creates controversy with its too revealing bottom which is over-groped by tourists and admirers. Kylie was a little surprised at the 'lack of wardrobe judgement'.

She wins Woman of the Year at 2002 Elle Style Awards. The competition has been blown away (Madonna may be voted the greatest woman in music history but she turned forty in 1998 and could now be considered a middle-aged 'mom').

✳

The ultimate accolade for Kylie as the 'world's most desirable woman' came in 2001, when she was chosen to front an advertising campaign for Agent Provocateur underwear. She agreed to do it for nothing because the designer of the range, Joe Corre, the son of Vivienne Westwood, is a close friend of both herself and William Baker. The lacy, frilly, sexy range of bras, basques and briefs come with a government health warning that they could seriously damage your wallet – £200 for a pair of skimpy knickers. In the cinema advertisement for the range, Kylie is first seen in a pink Westwood-designed nurse-style uniform (Nurse Kylie) and then strips off to reveal matching see-through black bra and briefs. The outfit is completed by stockings, suspenders and high-heeled shoes. The Provocative Kylie then acts out several fantasies, including one where she is seen writhing on a mechanical bucking bronco. Turning towards the camera, Kylie breathlessly informs the, by now, sweating viewer that, 'It's the most erotic lingerie in the world. Would all the men in the audience now stand up. . . .' It left little to the imagination, and was too much for television watchdogs who banned it from the small screen, which was, of course, great publicity for the products. The ninety-second commercial was condemned to be seen on cinema screens only, although it did not take long for it to pop up on the Internet.

Back in Australia (and the worldwide web), Kylie already has her own range of 'Love Kylie x' products, including a knuckle-duster ring with the word Kylie on it, a leather wrist band with the word Kylie on it, a Kylie neon light and a pair of long, dangly earrings with a 'K' on them. Pride of place in the range, though, is a pair of white knickers, bearing the logo 'Lucky' on the crotch.

Confidentially: 'I'm like safe sex.'

Kylie Minogue

discography

and videos

1987 The Loco-Motion (7-inch Version) / Glad To Be Alive: Australia 7-inch single

1987 The Loco-Motion (Chugga-Motion Mix) / The Loco-Motion (Girl Meets Boy Mix) / Glad To Be Alive: Australia 12-inch single

1987 The Loco-Motion (7-inch Version) / The Loco-Motion (Chugga-Motion Mix) / The Loco-Motion (Girl Meets Boy Mix) / Glad To Be Alive: Australia cassette maxi-single; included pop pinup.

1987 I Should Be So Lucky / I Should Be So Lucky (Instrumental): Australia, UK, US 7-inch single; US cassingle.

1987 I Should Be So Lucky (Extended) / I Should Be So Lucky (Instrumental): Australia & UK 12-inch single.

1987 I Should Be So Lucky (Original Dance Mix/Extended Version) / I Should Be So Lucky (Dance Remix/Bicentennial Remix) / I Should Be So Lucky (Instrumental): US 12-inch single; The Bicentennial Mix was a limited edition remix released for Australia's 200th Birthday, but in Australia it was called the Special UK Remix.

1988 I Should Be So Lucky (Bicentennial Remix) / I Should Be So Lucky (Instrumental): UK 12-inch single.

1987 I Should Be So Lucky (Special UK Remix) / I Should Be So Lucky (Instrumental): Australia 12-inch single.

1987 I Should Be So Lucky (Special UK Remix) / I Should Be So Lucky (7-inch Version) / I Should Be So Lucky (Instrumental): Australia cassette maxi-single; with pop pinup.

1987 I Should Be So Lucky (Single Version) / I Should Be So Lucky (Instrumental Version) / I Should Be So Lucky (Extended Version): Australia cassingle.

1988 Got To Be Certain / Got To Be Certain (Out For A Duck, Bill, Platter Plus Dub Mix): Australia & UK 7-inch single; in UK second track is listed as instrumental.

1988 Got To Be Certain (Extended) / Got To Be Certain (Out For A Duck, Bill, Platter Plus Dub Mix) / Got To Be Certain (7-inch Version): Australia cassingle; Australia & UK 12-inch single.

1988 Got To Be Certain (Ashes To Ashes) (The Extra Beat Boys Remix) / Got To Be Certain (Out For A Duck, Bill, Platter Plus Dub Mix) / Got To Be Certain (7-inch Version): Australia & UK 12-inch single.

1988 Got To Be Certain (Extended) / I Should Be So Lucky (Extended) / Got To Be Certain (Out For A Duck, Bill, Platter Plus Dub Mix): UK CD single.

1988 The Loco-Motion (LP Version) / I'll Still Be Loving You: US 7-inch single & cassingle.

1988 The Loco-Motion (7-inch Version) / I'll Still Be Loving You: UK 7-inch single.

1988 The Loco-Motion / I Should Be So Lucky: US 7-inch single.

1988 The Loco-Motion (Kohaku Mix) / I'll Still Be Loving You: UK 12-inch single.

1988 The Loco-Motion (Sankic Mix) / I'll Still Be Loving You: UK 12-inch single.

1988 The Loco-Motion (Kohaku Mix) / The Loco-Motion (Sankie Mix) / The Loco-Motion (LP Version) / I'll Still Be Loving You: US 12-inch single.

1988 The Loco-Motion (Album Version): US CD single.

1988 Je Ne Sais Pas Pourquoi / Made In Heaven: Australia 7-inch single & cassingle; 2 x UK 7-inch singles (one had a poster sleeve); Australia single was called I Still Love You (Je Ne Sais Pas Pourquoi).

1988 I Still Love You (Je Ne Sais Pas Pourquoi) / Made In Heaven: US 7-inch single & cassingle.

1988 Je Ne Sais Pas Pourquoi (Moi Non Plus Mix) / Made In Heaven (Maid In Australia Mix): Australia 12-inch single; the Maid in Australia Mix was retitled Made in England Mix in UK release.

1988 Je Ne Sais Pas Pourquoi (Moi Non Plus Mix) / Made In Heaven (Made In England Mix): UK 12-inch single; the Made in England Mix was called Maid in Australia Mix in Australia.

1988 Je Ne Sais Pas Pourquoi (The Revolutionary Mix) / Made In Heaven (Made In England Mix): UK 12-inch single.

1988 Je Ne Sais Pas Pourquoi (The Revolutionary Mix) / Je Ne Sais Pas Pourquoi (7-inch Version): US 12-inch single.

1988 Je Ne Sais Pas Pourquoi (12-inch single Mix) (Moi Non Plus Mix) / Je Ne Sais Pas Pourquoi (The Revolutionary Mix) / Made In Heaven (Made In England Mix): US 12-inch single.

1988 Je Ne Sais Pas Pourquoi (Moi Non Plus Mix) / Made In Heaven (Made In England Mix) / The Loco-Motion (Sankic Mix) (Long): UK CD single.

1988 Especially For You / All I Wanna Do Is Make You Mine: Australia 7-inch single, cassingle & CD single; UK 7-inch single; both tracks with Jason Donovan.

1988 Especially For You (Extended) / All I Wanna Do Is Make You Mine (Extended): Australia & UK 12-inch single; both tracks with Jason Donovan.

1988 Especially For You (Single Version) / Especially For You (Extended Version) / All I Wanna Do Is Make You Mine (Extended): UK CD single.

1988 It's No Secret (12-inch Version) / Made In Heaven (Made In England Mix): US 12-inch single.

1989 It's No Secret / Made In Heaven: US 7-inch single & cassingle.

1989 Hand On Your Heart / Just Wanna Love You: Australia 7-inch single & cassingle (also with poster pack); UK 7-inch single.

1989 Hand On Your Heart (The Great Aorta Mix) / Just Wanna Love You / Hand On Your Heart (Dub): Australia & UK 12-inch single.

1989 Hand On Your Heart (The Heartache Mix) / Just Wanna Love

You / Hand On Your Heart (Dub):
UK 12-inch single.

1989 Hand On Your Heart / Hand On
Your Heart (The Great Aorta
Mix) / Just Wanna Love You / It's
No Secret: Australia CD single.

1989 Hand On Your Heart (The Great
Aorta Mix) / Just Wanna Love
You / It's No Secret: UK CD single.

1989 Hand On Your Heart (The Great
Aorta Mix) / Hand On Your
Heart / Just Wanna Love You: UK
cassingle.

1989 Wouldn't Change A Thing / It's No
Secret: Australia & UK 7-inch single
& cassingle; limited quantities of
Australia 7-inch had a poster.

1989 Wouldn't Change A Thing (Your
Thang Mix) / It's No Secret
(Extended) / Wouldn't Change A
Thing (Instrumental): Australia
12-inch single.

1989 Wouldn't Change A Thing (Your
Thang Mix) / It's No Secret
(Extended): UK 12-inch single.

1989 Wouldn't Change A Thing
(Espagna Mix) / Wouldn't Change
A Thing / It's No Secret
(Extended): UK 12-inch single.

1989 Wouldn't Change A Thing (Your
Thang Mix) / Wouldn't Change A
Thing / Turn It Into Love: Australia
CD single.

1989 Wouldn't Change A Thing /
Wouldn't Change A Thing (Your
Thang Mix) / Je Ne Sais Pas
Pourquoi (Revolutionary Mix): UK
CD single.

1989 Wouldn't Change a Thing (Espagna
Mix) / Wouldn't Change a Thing
(Your Thang Mix) / It's No Secret
(Extended) (Shorter Extended) /
Wouldn't Change a Thing
(Instrumental): US 12-inch single.

1989 Never Too Late / Made In Heaven
(Heaven Scent Mix): Australia
7-inch single & cassingle.

1989 Never Too Late / Kylie's Smiley
Mix: UK 7-inch single & cassingle;
Smiley Mix contains: Je Ne Sais Pas
Pourquoi, Turn It Into Love, I
Should Be So Lucky, Got To Be
Certain.

1989 Never Too Late (Extended) / Made
In Heaven (Heaven Scent Mix):
Australia 12-inch single.

1989 Never Too Late (Extended) /
Kylie's Smiley Mix (Extended): UK
12-inch single; Smiley Mix
(Extended) contains: I'll Still Be
Loving You, It's No Secret, Je Ne
Sais Pas Pourquoi, Turn It Into
Love, I Should Be So Lucky, Got To
Be Certain.

1989 Never Too Late / Never Too Late
(Extended) / Kylie's Smiley Mix
(Extended): UK CD single.

1989 Tears On My Pillow / We Know The
Meaning Of Love: Australia 7-inch
single & cassingle; UK 7-inch single.

1989 Tears On My Pillow / Nothing To
Lose: US cassingle.

1989 Tears On My Pillow (More Tears
Mix) / Wouldn't Change A Thing
(Espagna Mix): Australia 12-inch
single.

1989 Tears On My Pillow (More Tears
Mix) / We Know The Meaning Of
Love (Extended): UK 12-inch
single.

1989 Tears On My Pillow / We Know The
Meaning Of Love / Tears On My
Pillow (More Tears Mix) / Wouldn't
Change A Thing (Espagna Mix):
Australia CD single.

1990 Better The Devil You Know / I'm
Over Dreaming (Over You)
(Remix): Australia 7-inch single &
cassingle; UK cassingle; first
Australia copies were shrink-
wrapped with Tears On My Pillow
7-inch single.

1990 Better The Devil You Know (Mad
March Hare Mix) / I'm Over

Dreaming (Over You) (Extended Remix): Australia & UK 12-inch single; Australia cassette maxi-single.

1990 Better The Devil You Know / Better The Devil You Know (Mad March Hare Mix) / I'm Over Dreaming (Over You) (Remix): Australia & UK CD single.

1990 Step Back In Time / Step Back In Time (Instrumental): Australia & UK 7-inch single & cassingle.

1990 Step Back In Time (Walkin' Rhythm Mix) / Step Back In Time (Instrumental): Australia & UK 12-inch single; Australia cassette maxi-single.

1990 Step Back In Time / Step Back In Time (Walkin' Rhythm Mix) / Step Back In Time (Instrumental): Australia & UK CD single.

1990 Step Back In Time (The Big Shock Mix): UK 12-inch single.

1991 What Do I Have To Do? / What Do I Have To Do? (Instrumental): Australia & UK 7-inch single & cassingle; limited edition of UK 7-inch with two postcards.

1991 What Do I Have To Do? (Pumpin' Mix) / What Do I Have To Do? (Instrumental): Australia & UK 12-inch single.

1991 What Do I Have To Do? (The Pump & Polly Mix) / What Do I Have To Do? (Instrumental) / Shocked / What Do I Have To Do? (UK Remix): Australia CD single & cassette maxi-single; the Pumpin' Mix & the Pump & Polly Mix are the same track.

1991 What Do I Have To Do? / What Do I Have To Do? (The Pump & Polly Mix) / What Do I Have To Do? (Instrumental): UK CD single.

1991 Shocked (DNA Mix) / Shocked (Harding/Curnow 7-inch Mix): Australia & UK 7-inch single &

cassingle; UK limited edition of 7-inch picture disc.

1991 Shocked (DNA 12-inch Mix) / Shocked (Harding/Curnow Mix): Australia & UK 12-inch single.

1991 Shocked (DNA Mix) / Shocked (DNA 12-inch Mix) / Shocked (Harding/Curnow Mix): Australia & UK CD single; Australia version was a picture disc.

1991 Word Is Out (7-inch Version) / Say The Word – I'll BeThere: UK 7-inch single & cassingle.

1991 Word Is Out / Say The Word – I'll Be There/ Word Is Out (Summer Breeze 12-inch Version): Australia CD single & cassingle; CD was a picture disc.

1991 Word Is Out (Summer Breeze 12-inch Version) / Word Is Out (Instrumental) / Word Is Out (12-inch Version) / Say The Word – I'll Be There: Australia 12-inch single.

1991 Word Is Out (12-inch Version) / Say The Word – I'll Be There/ Word Is Out (Instrumental): UK 12-inch single.

1991 Word Is Out (Summer Breeze 12-inch Version): UK 12-inch single; Kylie's autograph engraved on B-side.

1991 Word Is Out (7-inch Version) / Word Is Out (12-inch Version) / Say The Word – I'll Be There: UK CD single.

1992 If You Were With Me Now (with Keith Washington) / I Guess I Like It Like That: Australia & UK cassingle; UK 7-inch single.

1992 If You Were With Me Now (7-inch Version) / I Guess I Like It Like That (7-inch Version) / I Guess I Like It Like That (Extended Version): Australia & UK 12-inch single.

1992 If You Were With Me Now / I Guess

I Like It Like That / I Guess I Like It Like That (Extended Version): Australia picture disc CD single.

1992 If You Were With Me Now / I Guess I Like It Like That / If You Were With Me Now (Extended Version) (with Keith Washington): UK CD single.

1992 Give Me Just A Little More Time / Do You Dare? (NRG Edit): Australia & UK cassingle; UK 7-inch single.

1992 Give Me Just A Little More Time (12-inch Version) / Do You Dare? (NRG Mix) / Do You Dare? (New Rave Mix): Australia & UK 12-inch single.

1992 Give Me Just A Little More Time / Give Me Just A Little More Time (12-inch Version) / Do You Dare? (NRG Mix) / Do You Dare? (New Rave Mix): Australia & UK CD single.

1992 Finer Feelings (Brothers In Rhythm 7-inch Mix) / Closer (The Pleasure Mix Edit): Australia & UK cassingle; UK 7-inch single.

1992 Finer Feelings (Brothers In Rhythm 12-inch Mix) / Finer Feelings (Original Mix) / Closer (The Pleasure Mix): Australia & UK 12-inch single.

1992 Finer Feelings (Brothers In Rhythm 7-inch Mix) / Finer Feelings (Brothers In Rhythm 12-inch Mix) / Finer Feelings (Original Mix) / Closer (The Pleasure Mix): Australia & UK picture-disc CD single.

1992 What Kind Of Fool (Heard All That Before) / Things Can Only Get Better (Remix): Australia & UK cassingle; UK 7-inch single.

1992 What Kind Of Fool (Heard All That Before) (No Tech No Logical Mix) / What Kind Of Fool (Heard All That Before) (No Tech No Logical Mix) / Things Can Only

Get Better (Remix): Australia & UK 12-inch single.

1992 What Kind Of Fool (Heard All That Before) / What Kind Of Fool (Heard All That Before) (No Tech No Logical Mix) / What Kind Of Fool (Heard All That Before) (No Tech No Logical Mix) / Things Can Only Get Better (Remix): Australia & UK CD single.

1992 Celebration / Let's Get To It (7-inch Mix): UK 7-inch single & cassette.

1992 Celebration / Too Much Of a Good Thing: Australia cassingle.

1992 Celebration (Have a Party Mix) / Let's Get To It (12-inch Mix): Australia & UK 12-inch single.

1992 Celebration / Celebration (Have A Party Mix) / Too Much Of A Good Thing: Australia CD single.

1992 Celebration (7-inch Version) / Celebration (Have a Party Mix) / Let's Get To It (12-inch Mix): UK CD single.

1994 Confide In Me (Radio Edit) / Confide In Me (Truth Mix): UK cassingle; also issued as 7-inch single for jukeboxes.

1994 Confide In Me (Radio Mix) / Where Has The Love Gone? (Fire Island 12-inch Mix): US cassingle.

1994 Confide In Me (Master Mix) / Confide In Me (Truth Mix) / Confide In Me (Big Brother Mix): UK 12-inch single.

1994 Confide In Me (Master Mix) / Confide In Me (Truth Mix) / Confide In Me (Big Brother Mix): US 12-inch single.

1994 Confide In Me (Master Mix) / Confide In Me (Big Brother Mix) / Confide In Me (Truth Mix): UK CD single.

1994 Confide In Me (Master Mix) / Nothing Can Stop Us Now (Single Mix) / If You Don't Love Me

(Single Mix): Australia & UK CD single; Australia cassingle.

1994 Confide In Me (Master Mix) / Confide In Me (Big Brother Mix) / Confide In Me (Truth Mix) / Where Has The Love Gone? (Fire Island Mix) / Where Has The Love Gone? (Roach Motel Mix): Australia cassingle & CD single.

1994 Confide In Me (Radio Edit) / Confide In Me (Master Mix) / Confide In Me (Truth Mix) / Where Has The Love Gone? (Fire Island Mix): US CD single.

1994 Put Yourself In My Place (Radio Edit) / Put Yourself In My Place (Dan's Quiet Storm Extended Mix): UK cassingle.

1994 Put Yourself In My Place (Dan's Quiet Storm Extended Mix) / Put Yourself In My Place (Dan's Quiet Storm Club Mix) / Put Yourself In My Place (Driza-Bone Mix) /Put Yourself In My Place (All-Star Mix): UK 12-inch single.

1994 Put Yourself In My Place (Radio Mix) / Put Yourself In My Place (Dan's Quiet Storm Extended Mix) / Put Yourself In My Place (Dan's Quiet Storm Club Mix) / Confide In Me (Phillip Damien Mix): Australia cassingle; Australia & UK CD single.

1994 Put Yourself In My Place (Radio Mix) / Put Yourself In My Place (Driza-Bone Mix) / Put Yourself In My Place (All-Star Mix) / Where Is The Feeling? (Morales Mix): Australia cassingle; Australia & UK CD single.

1995 Where Is The Feeling? (BIR Dolphin Mix) / Where Is The Feeling? (BIR Bish Bosh Mix): UK cassingle.

1995 Where Is The Feeling? (BIR Dolphin Mix) / Where Is The Feeling? (BIR Soundtrack Mix) / Where Is The Feeling? (Da Klubb Feelin Mix) / Where Is The Feeling? (Short Morales Mix) / Where Is The Feeling? (BIR Bish Bosh Mix): Australia cassingle; Australia & UK CD single.

1995 Where The Wild Roses Grow (with Nick Cave) / Ballad Of Robert Moore & Betty Coltrane (Album Mix): UK 7-inch single & cassingle.

1995 Where The Wild Roses Grow (with Nick Cave) (Album Mix) / Ballad Of Robert Moore & Betty Coltrane (Album Mix) / Willow Garden (Album Mix): Australia cassingle; Australia & UK CD single; Kylie only appears on the first track.

1997 Some Kind Of Bliss / Love Takes Over Me: UK 7-inch single.

1997 Some Kind Of Bliss / Limbo: UK cassingle.

1997 Some Kind Of Bliss / Limbo / Some Kind Of Bliss (Quivver Mix): Australia & UK CD single.

1997 Did It Again / Tears: Australia & UK cassingle.

1997 Did It Again / Tears / Did It Again (Did It Four Times Mix) / Some Kind Of Bliss (video): Australia & UK CD single.

1997 Did It Again / Did It Again (Trouser Enthusiasts Goddess Of Contortion Mix) / Did It Again (Razor'n'Go Mix): Australia & UK CD single.

1998 Breathe (Radio Edit) / Breathe (Sash! Club Mix Edit): UK cassingle.

1998 Breathe (Radio Edit Mix) / Breathe (Tee's Freeze Mix) / Breathe (Nalin & Kane Mix) / Breathe (Album Mix): Australia & UK CD single.

1998 Breathe (Radio Edit Mix) / Breathe (Sash! Club Mix) / Breathe (Tee's Radio Edit Mix) / Did It Again (video): Australia & UK CD single.

1998 GBI (with Towa Tei) (Radio Edit) / GBI (Album Mix): UK cassingle.

1998 German Bold Italic (with Towa Tei) (Intro) / German Bold Italic (Radio Edit Mix) / German Bold Italic (Ebony Boogie Down Mix) / BMT (SP-1200 Mix) / German Bold Italic (Rekut Mix) / German Bold Italic (German Bold Light Mix): Australia CD single.

1998 German Bold Italic (with Towa Tei) / GBI (The Sharp Boys Deee-Liteful Dub) / Boldline: UK CD single; Boldline does not feature Kylie.

1998 German Bold Italic (with Towa Tei) / GBI (Rekut) / GBI (Ebony Boogie Down Mix) / BMT (SP-1200 Remix) / Boldline / GBI (Ebony Boogie Down Mix) / GBI (Rekut): UK CD single; BMT does not feature Kylie.

1998 Cowboy Style (Single Mix) / Love Takes Over Me / Cowboy Style (video): UK CD single.

1998 Better The Devil You Know / Better The Devil You Know (Movers & Shakers 12-inch Mix): Australia CD single; issued as part of Mushroom's 25-years celebrations.

2000 Spinning Around / Spinning Around (Sharp Double Dub Mix): UK cassingle.

2000 Spinning Around (Sharp Double Dub Mix) / Spinning Around (Sharp Vocal Mix): UK 12-inch single.

2000 Spinning Around (7th District Club-Mental Mix) / Spinning Around (7th District Dub Like This Mix): UK 12-inch single.

2000 Spinning Around (Sharp Vocal Mix) / Spinning Around (Sharp Double Dub) / Spinning Around (7th Spinnin' Dizzy Dub) / Spinning Around (7th District Club Mix): UK double 12-inch single.

2000 Spinning Around (7th District Exclusive Vocal Remix) / Spinning Around (7th District Exclusive Vocal Dub): UK 12-inch single; limited edition with white label; unique remixes.

2000 Spinning Around / Spinning Around (Sharp Vocal Mix) / Spinning Around (7th Spinnin' Dizzy Dub) / Spinning Around (enhanced video): Australia & UK CD single.

2000 Spinning Around / Cover Me With Kisses / Paper Dolls: Australia & UK CD single.

2000 On A Night Like This / On A Night Like This (Bini & Martini Club Mix) / On A Night Like This (Motiv8 Nocturnal Vocal Mix): UK cassingle.

2000 On A Night Like This (Rob Searle Mix) / On A Night Like This (Bini & Martini Vocal Club Mix) / On A Night Like This (Halo Mix): UK 12-inch single.

2000 On A Night Like This (Rob Searle Mix) / Your Disco Needs You (Almighty Mix) / On A Night Like This (Motiv8 Nocturnal Vocal Mix) / On A Night Like This (Bini & Martini Vocal Mix): UK double 12-inch single.

2000 On A Night Like This (Bini & Martini Vocal Mix) / On A Night Like This (Bini & Martini Dub Mix): UK 12-inch single.

2000 On A Night Like This / On A Night Like This (Rob Searle Mix) / On A Night Like This (Bini & Martini Club Mix) / On A Night Like This (Motiv8 Nocturnal Vocal Mix) / On A Night Like This (enhanced video): Australia CD single.

2000 On A Night Like This / On A Night Like This (Halo Mix) / Ocean Blue / Your Disco Needs You (Almighty Mix): Australia CD single.

2000 On A Night Like This / Ocean Blue / On A Night Like This (enhanced video): UK CD single.

2000 On A Night Like This (Single Version) / Ocean Blue / Your Disco Needs You (Almighty Mix) / On A Night Like This (enhanced video): UK CD single.

2000 On A Night Like This / On A Night Like This (Rob Searle Mix) / On A Night Like This (Motiv8 Vocal Club Mix): UK CD single.

2000 Kids / John's Gay / Often: UK cassingle.

2000 Kids / John's Gay / Often / Rock DJ (video): UK CD single.

2000 Kids / Karaoke Star / Kill Me Or Cure Me / Kids (video): UK CD single.

2000 Please Stay (Metro Mix) / Please Stay (7th District Club Flava Mix) / Please Stay (7th District Club Dub): UK 12-inch single.

2000 Please Stay (7th District Club Dub) / Please Stay (Hatiras Dreamy Dub) / Please Stay (7th District Club Flava Mix): UK 12-inch single.

2000 Please Stay (Hatiras Dreamy Dub): UK 12-inch single.

2000 Please Stay / Santa Baby / Please Stay (video): UK CD single.

2000 Please Stay / Santa Baby / Good Life: Australia & UK CD single; included a Kylie calendar/poster.

2000 Please Stay / Santa Baby / Good Life / Please Stay (video): UK CD single.

2000 Please Stay / Please Stay (7th District Club Flava Mix) / Please Stay (Hatiras Dreamy Dub) / Please Stay (enhanced video): Australia & UK CD single.

2000 Your Disco Needs You (Album Version) / Your Disco Needs You (German Almighty Radio Edit) / Your Disco Needs You (UK Almighty Mix) / Your Disco Needs You (Casino Radio & Club Mix) / Your Disco Needs You (German Album Version): Australia CD single.

2000 Can't Get You Out Of My Head / Boy: UK cassingle.

2000 Can't Get You Out Of My Head (Deluxe's Dirty Dub) / Can't Get You Out Of My Head (Deluxe's Dirty Dub Instrumental) / Can't Get You Out Of My Head (Plastika Mix) / Can't Get You Out Of My Head (Superchumbo Todo Mamado Mix) / Can't Get You Out Of My Head (K & M Mindprint Mix): UK double 12-inch single.

2000 *Get Out Of My Head Artist: Special K:* Can't Get You Out Of My Head (Superchumbo Todo Mamado Mix) / Can't Get You Out Of My Head (Superchumbo Leadhead Dub) / Can't Get You Out Of My Head (Superchumbo Voltapella Mix): UK 12-inch single.

2001 Can't Get You Out Of My Head (K&M Mindprint Mix) / Can't Get You Out Of My Head (Nick Faber Mix): UK 12-inch single.

2001 *Get Into My Head Artist: Special K:* Can't Get You Out Of My Head (Deluxe's Dirty Dub) / Can't Get You Out Of My Head (Deluxe's Dirty Dub Instrumental) / Can't Get You Out Of My Head (Plastika Mix): UK 12-inch single.

2001 Can't Get You Out Of My Head / Boy / Rendezvous At Sunset (with enhanced video section): Australia CD single.

2001 *Can't Get You Out Of My Head Mixes:* Can't Get You Out Of My Head / Can't Get You Out Of My Head (K & M's Mindprint Mix) / Can't Get You Out Of My Head (Plastika Mix): UK CD single.

2001 Can't Get You Out Of My Head / Can't Get You Out Of My Head (K&M's Mindprint Mix) / Can't Get You Out Of My Head (Plastika Mix) / Can't Get You Out Of My Head (Superchumbo Todo

Mamado Mix): Australia CD single; limited edition.

2001 In Your Eyes (Saeed & Palesh Main Mix) / In Your Eyes (Powder's Spaced Dub) / In Your Eyes (Roger Sanchez Release The Dub Mix): UK 12-inch single.

2002 In Your Eyes (Album Version) / In Your Eyes (Mr Bishi Mix) / In Your Eyes (Jean Jacques Smoothie Dub) / In Your Eyes (Saeed & Palesh Main Mix): Australia CD single.

2002 In Your Eyes / Spoken (Non-LP) / Harmon (Non-LP) / In Your Eyes (The S Man's Release Mix): Australia CD single.

2002 In Your Eyes / Tightrope / Good Like That: UK CD single.

2002 In Your Eyes / In Your Eyes (The S Man's Release Mix) / In Your Eyes (Jean Jaques Smoothie Mix): UK CD single.

Vinyl, cassette and CD albums chronologically

1988 *Kylie*: LP, DAT; cassette issued in a long box; CD issued as picture disc. I Should Be So Lucky; The Loco-Motion; Je Ne Sais Pas Pourquoi; It's No Secret; Got To Be Certain; Turn It Into Love; I Miss You; I'll Still Be Loving You; Look My Way; Love At First Sight.

1988 *The Kylie Collection*: Issued in Australia only as double LP with poster, and on cassette. As in *Kylie*, but including: I Should Be So Lucky (Extended); The Loco-Motion (The Kohaku Mix); Je Ne Sais Pas Pourquoi (Moi Non Plus Mix); Got To Be Certain (Extended); Made In Heaven (Maid in Australia Mix).

1989 *Kylie's Remixes*: Australia CD. I Should Be So Lucky (The Bicentennial/UK Remix); Got to Be Certain (Ashes To Ashes) (Remix/ The Extra Beat Boys Remix); The Loco-Motion (The Sankie Remix); Je Ne Sais Pas Pourquoi (Moi Non Plus Mix); Turn It Into Love (Album Version); It's No Secret (Extended Version); Je Ne Sais Pas Pourquoi (The Revolutionary Mix); I Should Be So Lucky (New Remix); Made in Heaven (Made in England/Maid In Australia Mix).

1989 *Enjoy Yourself*: LP, cassette and CD; UK LP included free poster and 'Meet Kylie' competition. Hand On Your Heart; Wouldn't Change A Thing; Never Too Late; Nothing To Lose; Tell Tale Signs; My Secret Heart; I'm Over Dreaming (Over You); Tears On My Pillow; Heaven And Earth; Enjoy Yourself.

1990 *Enjoy Yourself*: US CD issued in long box; also on cassette and LP. Extra track: Especially For You (with Jason Donovan).

1990 *Rhythm of Love*: LP, cassette and CD; UK LP in two editions: with poster or with picture sleeve and 'Kylie' in gold leaf; Australia CD issued as picture disc. Better The Devil You Know; Step Back In Time; What Do I Have To Do?; Secrets; Always Find The Time; The World Still Turns; Shocked; One Boy Girl; Things Can Only Get Better; Count The Days; Rhythm Of Love.

1991 *Let's Get to It*: cassette and CD; LP in UK; also as picture disc CD in Australia. Word Is Out; Give Me Just A Little More Time; Too Much Of A Good Thing; Finer Feelings; If You Were With Me Now (with Keith Washington); Let's Get To It; Right Here, Right Now; Live And Learn; No World Without You; I Guess I Like It Like That.

1991 **Rhythm of Love**: Australia reissue on double cassette.
Extra tracks: Better The Devil You Know (US Remix); Step Back In Time (Walkin' Rhythm Mix); What Do I Have To Do? (UK Remix); Shocked (DNA Mix); Shocked (Harding/Curnow Mix).

1991 **Rhythm of Love**: Australia reissue on double CD.
Extra tracks: Better The Devil You Know (US Remix); Step Back In Time (Walkin' Rhythm Mix); What Do I Have To Do? (UK Remix); Shocked (DNA Mix); Shocked (DNA 12-inch Mix); Shocked (Harding/Curnow Mix).

1991 **Rhythm of Love**: Australia reissue on double LP, boxed cassette and boxed picture disc CD.
Extra tracks: Better The Devil You Know (US Remix); Step Back In Time (Walkin' Rhythm Mix); What Do I Have To Do? (UK Remix).

1991 **Rhythm of Love**: UK reissue on limited-edition gold CD or boxed.
Extra tracks: Step Back In Time (Walkin' Rhythm Mix); What Do I Have To Do? (Between The Sheets Mix); Shocked (DNA 12-inch Mix, also called UK Remix).

1992 **Enjoy Yourself**: Australia budget re-release on CD and LP only.

1992 **Kylie's Remixes Vol. 2**: CD (Festival). Better The Devil You Know (US Mix); Step Back In Time (Walkin' Rhythm Mix); What Do I Have To Do? (Remix); Shocked (DNA Mix); Word Is Out (12-inch Version); If You Were With Me Now (Extended Version); Keep On Pumpin' It (12-inch Version); Give Just A Little More Time (12-inch Version); Finer Feelings (Brothers In Rhythm 12-inch Remix); Do You Dare? (NRG Mix); Closer.

1992 **Greatest Hits**: LP, cassette and CD;

Australia limited edition CD with fold-out digipack, including 5 pictures from booklet; also as picture disc; UK LP with double vinyl gatefold.
I Should Be So Lucky; Got To Be Certain; The Loco-Motion; Je Ne Sais Pas Pourquoi; Especially For You (with Jason Donovan); Turn It Into Love; It's No Secret; Hand On Your Heart; Wouldn't Change A Thing; Never Too Late; Tears On My Pillow; Better The Devil You Know; Step Back In Time; What Do I Have To Do?; Shocked (DNA Mix); Word Is Out (UK Remix); If You Were With Me Now (with Keith Washington); Give Me Just A Little More Time; Finer Feelings; What Kind Of Fool (Heard All That Before); Where In The World?; Celebration.

1992 **Kylie**: Australia budget re-release on cassette and CD only.

1992 **The Kylie Collection**: Reissued in Australia as double LP (no poster) and on cassette.

1993 **Kylie's Non-Stop History 50+1 (Megamix)**: Australia CD.
Do You Dare?; I Guess I Like It Like That; Closer; Shocked; Things Can Only Get Better; What Do I Have To Do?; Better The Devil You Know; What Kind Of Fool (Heard All That Before); Secrets; Where In The World?; Give Me Just A Little More Time; I Miss You; Step Back In Time; Celebration; Right Here, Right Now; Always Find The Time; Look My Way; Count The Days; One Boy Girl; Rhythm Of Love; Word Is Out; Just Wanna Love You; It's No Secret; I'll Still Be Loving You; Let's Get To It; Too Much Of A Good Thing; Live And Learn; Finer Feelings; World Still Turns; My Secret Heart; No World Without

You; Especially For You (with Jason Donovan); Say The Word I'll Be There; Tears On My Pillow; Tell Tale Signs; If You Were With Me Now (with Keith Washington); Heaven And Earth; Nothing To Lose; Wouldn't Change A Thing; Je Ne Sais Pas Pourquoi; Made In Heaven; Hand On Your Heart; Enjoy Yourself; I'm Over Dreaming (Over You); Never Too Late; Love At First Sight; Got To Be Certain; Turn It Into Love; I Should Be So Lucky; The Loco-Motion; Celebration (Techno Rave Remix).

1993 *Greatest Remix Hits Vol. 1*: Australia CD.
I Should Be So Lucky (Bicentennial Remix); Got To Be Certain (Ashes To Ashes); Locomotion (Sankie Remix); Je Ne Sais Pas Pourquoi (Moi Non Plux Mix); Made In Heaven; All I Wanna Do; It's No Secret (Extended); Hand On Your Heart (Dub); Just Wanna Love You; Never Too Late (Extended); We Know The Meaning Of Love; Step Back In Time (Walkin' Rhythm Mix); What Do I Have To Do? (Remix); Shocked (DNA Mix); Word Is Out; Keep On Pumpin' It Up (Astral Flight Mix); If You Were With Me Now (with Keith Washington); Do You Dare? (New Rave Mix); Finer Feelings (Brothers In Rhythm 7-inch Mix); Closer (Edit); What Kind Of Fool (No Tech No Logical Mix); Celebration (Have A Party Mix).

1993 *Greatest Remix Hits Vol. 2*: Australia CD, previously only available from Japan.
Got To Be Certain (Extended); Kylie's Smiley Mix (Extended); Getting Closer; Je Ne Sais Pas Pourquoi (Revolutionary Mix); Made In Heaven (Made In England

Mix); Especially For You (with Jason Donovan); Hand On Your Heart (The Great Aorta Mix); Wouldn't Change A Thing (Your Thang Mix); Tears On My Pillow; Better The Devil You Know (Mad March Hare Mix); I'm Over Dreaming (Over You); The Loco-Motion; What Do I Have To Do? (Pump & Polly Mix); Shocked (Harding/Curnow Mix); Say The Word I'll Be There; Keep On Pumpin' It Up (Angelic Remix); Give Me Just A Little More Time (12-inch Version); Do You Dare? (NRG Mix); Finer Feelings (Brothers In Rhythm 12-inch Mix); Closer (The Pleasure Mix); What Kind Of Fool (No Tech No Logical Mix); Got To Be Certain (Out For A Duck, Bill, Platter Plus Dub Mix).

1994 *Kylie Minogue*: cassette and CD; LP in UK; UK CD with gatefold in lilac slipcase with silver lettering.
Confide In Me; Surrender; If I Was Your Lover; Where Is The Feeling?; Put Yourself In My Place; Dangerous Game; Automatic Love; Where Has The Love Gone?; Falling; Time Will Pass You By.

1997 *Greatest Hits/50 + 1*: Australia re-release double-CD, comprising *Greatest Hits* plus *Kylie's Non-Stop History 50+1 (Megamix)*.

1998 *Impossible Princess /* (in UK & Japan) *Kylie Minogue in Europe*: cassette and CD.
Too Far; Cowboy Style; Some Kind Of Bliss; Did It Again; Breathe; Say Hey; Drunk; I Don't Need Anyone; Jump; Limbo; Through The Years; Dreams.

1998 *Impossible Remixes*: Australia CD, with various remixes from *Impossible Princess*.
Too Far (Brothers In Rhythm House Mix); Breathe (TNT Club Mix); Did It Again (Trouser

Enthusiasts Goddess Of Contortion Mix); Breathe (Tee's Freeze Mix); Some Kind Of Bliss (Quivver Mix); Too Far (Junior Vasquez Remix); Did It Again (Razor 'n' Go Mix); Breathe (Sash Club Mix); Too Far (Brothers In Rhythm Dub Mix); Breathe (Nalin & Kane Remix).

1998 *Greatest Remix Hits Vol. 3*: Australia double-CD.
Disc 1. Better the Devil You Know (Movers 'n' Shakers 12-inch Mix); The Loco-Motion (Chugga Motion Mix); Glad to Be Alive (7-inch Mix); The Loco-Motion (12-inch Master); Hand on Your Heart (Heartache Mix); Step Back in Time (Harding Curnow Remix); What Do I Have to Do? (Extended LP Mix); Word Is Out (Dub 1); No World Without You (Original 7-inch Mix); Do You Dare? (Itália 12-inch Mix).
Disc 2: 1. Especially for You (with Jason Donovan) (Original 12-inch Mix); Wouldn't Change a Thing (Yo Yo's 12-inch Mix); Never Too Late (Oz Tour Mix); Better the Devil You Know (Dave Ford Remix); Step Back in Time (Original 12-inch Mix); One Boy Girl (12-inch Mix); Word Is Out (Summer Breeze 12-inch Mix); Live and Learn (Original 12-inch Mix); Right Here, Right Now (Tony King 12-inch Mix); Finer Feelings (Brothers in Rhythm Dub); Celebration (Original 7-inch Mix).

1998 *Greatest Remix Hits Vol. 4*: Australia double-CD; most of the remixes are rare or previously unreleased.
Disc 1: What Do I Have to Do? (Movers 'n' Shakers 12-inch Mix); The Loco-Motion (Girl Meets Boy Mix); Made in Heaven (Heaven Scent 12-inch Mix); Wouldn't Change a Thing (Espagna Mix); Better the Devil You Know

(Alternative 7-inch Mix); Things Can Only Get Better (Original 12-inch Mix); The Loco-Motion (Kohaku Mix); Let's Get to It (Tony King 12-inch Mix); What Kind of Fool (Pete Waterman's 12-inch Master Mix).
Disc 2: I Should Be So Lucky (Extended Mix); The Loco-Motion (7-inch Mix); Hand on Your Heart (Smokin' Remix); I Am the One for You; Step Back in Time (Tony King Remix); Too Much of a Good Thing (Original 12-inch Mix); If You Were With Me Now (Orchestral Version); Finer Feelings (Brothers in Rhythm Ambient Reprise); Celebration.

1998 *Intimate & Live*: Australia CD.
Too Far; What Do I Have To Do?; Some Kind Of Bliss; Put Yourself In My Place; Breathe; Take Me With You; I Should Be So Lucky; Dancing Queen; Dangerous Game; Cowboy Style; Step Back In Time; Say Hey; Free; Drunk; Did It Again; Limbo; Shocked; Confide In Me; The Loco-Motion; Should I Stay Or Should I Go?; Better The Devil You Know.

2000 *Light Years*: cassette and CD.
Spinning Around; On A Night Like This; So Now Goodbye; Disco Down; Loveboat; Kookachoo; Your Disco Needs You; Please Stay; Bittersweet Goodbye; Butterfly; Under The Influence Of Love; I'm So High; Kids; Light Years; Password (hidden track).
To find the hidden track, start the CD (so that 'Spinning Around' actually begins to play), then reverse from the first track backwards. Once you've gone back a negative 3:47, 'Password' will begin!

2000 *Hits+*: UK CD.
Confide In Me; Put Yourself In My Place; Where Is The Feeling?; Some

Kind Of Bliss; Did It Again; Breathe; Where The Wild Roses Grow (with Nick Cave); If You Don't Love Me; Tears; Gotta Move On; Difficult By Design; Stay This Way; This Girl; Automatic Love (Acoustic Version); Where Has The Love Gone? ; Take Me With You.

2000 *Hits+*: Australia CD with 12-page book, and sleeve notes by Kylie plus pictures from her 1994 book. Confide In Me (Radio Version); Put Yourself In My Place (Radio Version); Where Is The Feeling? (Dolphin Mix); Some Kind Of Bliss; Did It Again; Breathe (Radio Version); Where The Wild Roses Grow (with Nick Cave); If You Don't Love Me; Tears; Gotta Move On (Produced By Rapino Bros); Difficult By Design (Produced By Rapino Bros); Stay This Way; This Girl (Demo); Automatic Love (Acoustic Version); Where Has The Love Gone? (Roach Motel Mix); Take Me With You (New Version).

2000 *Triple Set*: *Kylie, Enjoy Yourself* and *Rhythm Of Love:* issued in a card slipcase in Australia only.

2001 *Fever*: UK and Australia CD. More More More; Love At First Sight; Can't Get You Out Of My Head; Fever; Give It To Me; Fragile; Come Into My World; In Your Eyes; Dancefloor; Love Affair; Your Love; Burning Up. Extra track (Australia): Tightrope.

2001/2 *Fever*. Australia Limited Edition CD with 2 Bonus Tracks: Boy; Butterfly.

2001 *Light Years*: Australia CD with bonus CD, issued as special tour edition. Extra tracks: Spinning Around (7th District Club-Mental Mix); Spinning Around (Sharp Vocal Mix); On A Night Like This (Rob Searle Mix); On A Night Like This (Bini &

Martini Club Mix); Please Stay (Hatiras Dreamy Dub Mix); Please Stay (7th District Radio Mix); Please Stay (7th District Club Flava Mix); Butterfly (Sandstorm Dub); Your Disco Needs You (Casino Radio & Club Mix).

2001 *Light Years (Australia Tour Edition)*: Australia double-CD. Extra tracks: Physical (Olivia Newton John cover); On A Night Like This (Bini & Martini Dub Mix).

2001 *Light Years*: CD with bonus CD/DVD; only issued in Asia. CD/DVD had three audio tracks: Spinning Around (Sharp Vocal Mix); On A Night Like This (Motiv8 Nocturnal Vocal Mix); Your Disco Needs You (Almighty Mix); and two video tracks: Spinning Around; On A Night Like This.

Music videos and DVDs chronologically

1988 *The Videos*: The Loco-Motion; I Should Be So Lucky (Australia).

1989 *The Kylie Collection*: I Should Be So Lucky; Got To Be Certain; The Loco-Motion; Je Ne Sais Pas Pourquoi; It's No Secret; Made in Heaven (Australia).

1989 *The Kylie Collection*: I Should Be So Lucky; Got To Be Certain; The Loco-Motion; Je Ne Sais Pas Pourquoi (UK, sometimes called *The Videos*).

1989 *Kylie Minogue – The Videos 2*: It's No Secret; Hand On Your Heart; Wouldn't Change a Thing; Never Too Late.

1990 *Kylie On The Go – Live in Japan*: Hand On Your Heart; The Loco-Motion; Made In Heaven; Got To Be Certain; Je Ne Sais Pas Pourquoi; Wouldn't Change A Thing; Tears On My Pillow; I Should Be So Lucky.

1991 ***Jason Donovan: Greatest Video Hits*** (Australia): Especially For You (with Kylie).

1992 ***Let's Get To . . . The Videos***: Better The Devil You Know; Step Back In Time; What Do I Have To Do?; Shocked; Word Is Out; If You Were With Me Now.

1992 ***Kylie (Live) – Live in Dublin***: Step Back In Time; Wouldn't Change a Thing; Got To Be Certain; Let's Get To It; Word Is Out; Finer Feelings; I Should Be So Lucky; Love Train; If You Were With Me Now; Too Much Of A Good Thing; What Do I Have To Do?; I Guess I Like It Like That; Shocked; Better The Devil You Know.

1992 ***Kylie Minogue – Greatest Hits***: I Should Be So Lucky; Got To Be Certain; The Loco-Motion; Je Ne Sais Pas Pourquoi; It's No Secret; Especially For You (with Jason Donovan), Hand On Your Heart; Wouldn't Change A Thing; Never Too Late; Tears On My Pillow; Better The Devil You Know; Step Back In Time; What Do I Have To Do?; Shocked (DNA Mix); Word Is Out; If You Were With Me Now (with Keith Washington); Give Me Just A Little More Time; Finer Feelings; What Kind Of Fool.

1997 ***Did It Again***: Did It Again; Some Kind Of Bliss (Australia).

1998 ***The Kylie Tapes 94–98***: Breathe; Did It Again; Some Kind Of Bliss; Confide In Me; Where Is The Feeling?; Put Yourself In My Place.

1998 ***Nick Cave and The Bad Seeds: The Videos*** (Australia): Where The Wild Roses Grow (with Kylie).

1998 ***Intimate and Live***: Too Far; What Do I Have To Do?; Some Kind Of Bliss; Put Yourself In My Place; Breathe; Take Me With You; I Should Be So Lucky; Dancing Queen; Dangerous Game; Cowboy Style; Step Back In Time; Say Hey; Free; Drunk; Did It Again; Limbo; Shocked; Confide In Me; Locomotion; Should I Stay Or Should I Go?; Better The Devil You Know.

2001 ***Kylie Minogue – Live In Sydney*** (DVD) (Widescreen): this live show was filmed in Sydney on 11 May 2001. Songs included are: Love Boat; Kookachoo; Hand on Your Heart; Put Yourself in My Place; On A Night Like This; Step Back In Time; Never Too Late; I Wouldn't Want to Change a Thing; Turn it into Love; Celebrate; Can't Get You Out of My Head; Your Disco Needs You; I Should Be So Lucky; Better the Devil You Know; So Now Goodbye; Physical; Butterfly; Confide In Me; Kids; Shocked; Light Years; plus twenty minutes of backstage footage.

kylie
chronological

28 May 1968 Kylie Ann Minogue born in Melbourne

1970 Brendan Minogue born

October 1971 Danielle (Dannii) Minogue born

1979 KM Attends her first TV audition and lands role as Dutch girl Carla in the Australian series *The Sullivans*
Dannii appears for the first time on *Young Talent Time*

1980 KM starts at Camberwell High School, Melbourne
Appears as Robin in an episode of the Australian TV series *Skyways;* on set, meets Jason Donovan for the first time
First visit to Britain, with her family to see relatives in Wales and go sightseeing in London

June 1982 Dannii becomes a permanent team member of *Young Talent Time* and is temporarily the more famous of the two sisters

October 1984 KM wins role as Charlotte (Char) Kernow in TV mini-series *The Henderson Kids.* Goes on location for the first time during the five months of filming in New South Wales

May 1985 Aged nearly 17, plays a 12-year-old, 'Yvonne the Terrible', in an episode of children's TV programme *The Zoo Family*
Beats 50 other hopefuls to win female lead as Samantha Collins in 6-part TV mini-series *Fame and Misfortune*
First episode of *The Henderson Kids* shown on Australian TV

January 1986 Leaves Camberwell High School having passed her Year 12

exams in Art and Graphics
Auditions for *Neighbours* and is cast as Charlene Mitchell. Initial contract is for 13 weeks but that is quickly extended to 26 weeks when bosses sense screen chemistry between Charlene and Scott Robinson (Jason Donovan)

April 1986 First episode of *Neighbours* featuring KM shown on Australian TV. She has begun a relationship with Jason which is kept secret from the public

August 1986 Sings in public for the first time at a benefit for an Australian Rules Football team. Performs 'I Got You Babe' and 'The Loco-Motion'

October 1986 First screening of *Neighbours* on British TV

December 1986 Jason and Kylie slip away for a private holiday on Bali

April 1987 Becomes youngest ever artist to be crowned Most Popular Actress in Australia at the annual Logie Awards; Jason is named Best New Talent
Sings a duet with Dannii, 'Sisters Are Doing It For Themselves', at an anti-drugs concert in Melbourne

July 1987 Releases first single in Australia, 'The Loco-Motion', which reaches No. 1 and stays there for 7 weeks
The wedding of Charlene and Scott in *Neighbours* is the TV event of the year
Meets Michael Hutchence for the first time at a party after a music awards ceremony in Sydney
Appoints Terry Blamey as her manager

October 1987 During a break in filming *Neighbours*, flies to London to record with Stock, Aitken and Waterman. They write 'I Should Be So Lucky' while she waits in reception

December 1987 Sings 'I Should Be So Lucky' on Noel Edmonds's BBC TV Christmas Special

January 1988 BBC decides to screen *Neighbours* twice a day; UK viewing figures top 15 million per episode
'I Should Be So Lucky' is KM's first single release in UK, where it reaches No.1. It is also tops charts in Australia, Germany, Finland, Hong Kong, Israel and Switzerland
Meets the Prince and Princess of Wales in Sydney during Australia's Bicentennial celebrations. KM later admits to being tongue-tied in front of the Princess

March 1988 Wins four Logie awards including the top Gold Logie as Most Popular Personality on Australian TV

April 1988 Savaged in print by famous British columnist Jean Rook for arriving at Heathrow looking like a 'slept-in Qantas blanket'. Ms Rook suggests KM should try to emulate the style of Joan Collins

May 1988 'Got To Be Certain', her second single in Britain, reaches No.2 where it stays for 6 weeks. In Australia it is the first ever single to debut at No.1

June 1988 Films her last scenes for *Neighbours*. Cries at a leaving party at a Melbourne restaurant where she is presented with an antique mahogany mirror and a framed montage of her magazine covers

August 1988 Her first album, *Kylie*, released in the UK and Australia. Its success will make her the youngest ever female to top the UK album charts
'The Loco-Motion' released for the first time in UK but just misses the No.1 spot

September 1988 Becomes known as 'The Loco-Motion Girl' after the single

becomes her first hit in the USA. It will remain her biggest hit there until 'Can't Get You Out Of My Head' in 2002

October 1988 'Je Ne Sais Pas Pourquoi', Pete Waterman's favourite Kylie song, is her third consecutive single to reach No.2 in the UK. It was originally intended to be a double A-side with 'Made in Heaven'

November 1988 In response to public demand records a duet, 'Especially For You', with Jason

December 1988 *Kylie* is the biggest-selling album of the year in the UK. The accompanying *Kylie – The Videos* also reaches No.1
'Especially For You' misses the Christmas No. 1, kept off the top by Cliff Richard's 'Mistletoe and Wine'
Becomes the first artist to have four consecutive No.1s in Finland

January 1989 'Especially For You' finally reaches No. 1 in the UK. It will be her biggest-selling record until 'Can't Get You Out Of My Head'
Has three simultaneous worldwide No. 1s when 'Turn It Into Love' reaches the top in Japan and 'The Loco-Motion' matches it in Canada

April 1989 'Hand On Your Heart', the first single from her second album, *Enjoy Yourself*, becomes her third UK No. 1
Begins work on *The Delinquents*, her first movie, playing Lola Lovell

May 1989 Celebrates her 21st birthday with a champagne party for 150 at the trendy Red Eagle Hotel in Sydney. An over-eager bouncer slams the door in Jason's face

July 1989 Her seventh single in the UK, 'Wouldn't Change A Thing', reaches No. 2. Her first seven singles in the UK have gone 1-2-2-2-1-1-2.

September 1989 While in Hong Kong, preparing for her first international tour, has dinner with Michael Hutchence, who has a home in the colony

October 1989 *Enjoy Yourself* is released in the UK and reaches No. 1

November 1989 'Never Too Late', the second single from the album, spoils Kylie's run by only reaching No. 4 in the UK charts. She had wanted to release the track 'Enjoy Yourself' but was overruled by Waterman

December 1989 Switches on the Christmas lights in London's Regent Street
Joins Bob Geldof and other Stock, Aitken and Waterman stars to record Band Aid II's version of 'Do They Know It's Christmas?', which becomes the Christmas No. 1
Enjoy Yourself, complete with free Kylie poster, tops 1 million sales in Britain
At the Australian première of *The Delinquents* KM is barely recognizable in blonde wig and microskirt
Attends the première of *The Delinquents* in Leicester Square and is greeted by a huge crowd of fans. The film is not well received by the critics, however
Voted Best Female Vocalist of 1989 at the Japan Radio Music Awards

January 1990 'Tears On My Pillow', from *The Delinquents* soundtrack, is Kylie's fourth British No. 1 from her first nine singles

February 1990 First concert tour – with, for the first time, a live backing band – in Australia is praised by both critics and fans
Receives the UK Video Industry's Top Music Video of 1989 award for *Kylie – The Videos*

March 1990 First signs of a break from Stock, Aitken and Waterman when KM records four songs in Los Angeles with different producers. She dedicates one, 'Count the Days', to boyfriend Michael Hutchence

April 1990 Takes control of her image for the first time with the video for her next single, 'Better The Devil You Know'; she is seen to writhe

provocatively in the arms of a naked black man almost twice her size

May 1990 'Better The Devil You Know' reaches No. 2 in the UK, and becomes an anthem for a generation of gay fans. It is widely assumed that the song is about her relationship with Hutchence

June 1990 Moves to London with Hutchence, who also buys a farmhouse in the South of France which she helps to furnish

November 1990 Third album, *Rhythm Of Love*, is her least successful so far, peaking at No. 9 in the UK and No.10 in Australia. A single from it, 'Step Back In Time', reaches No. 4 in Britain. The video features Kylie in seventies disco gear cruising the streets in an open-topped car

December 1990 For the first time spends Christmas away from her family in Melbourne, preferring to celebrate with Hutchence at the farmhouse in Roquefort-les-Pins

February 1991 Splits with Hutchence amid rumours of his philandering on tour
'What Do I Have To Do?', another Waterman favourite, reaches No.6 in the UK (Dannii appears in the video) and becomes one of the most popular of all Kylie songs live

May 1991 Wins Bestselling Australian Artist at the World Music Awards in Monte Carlo

June 1991 'Shocked', which boasts a raunchy video, becomes her thirteenth consecutive Top 10 hit, a record. It places her ahead of Elvis Presley, The Beatles and Madonna

August 1991 Her first flop: 'Word Is Out' manages a lowly No. 16, the first time a Kylie release fails to make the UK Top 10. Davina McCall, later the presenter of *Big Brother*, plays one of Kylie's friends in the video

October 1991 Releases her fourth album, *Let's Get To It*. The second single from it,

'If You Were With Me Now', with Keith Washington, is much better received and reaches No. 4 in the UK. The album is also praised in the music press Begins her second sellout tour of the UK

January 1992 Releases her first cover since 'The Loco-Motion': 'Give Me Just A Little More Time', a 1970 hit for Chairmen of the Board, takes her back to her favourite chart position, No. 2

April 1992 Her new video, *Kylie Live*, recorded at a concert in Dublin, is released and enters the UK video chart at No. 2

June 1992 Takes part in the Rhythm of Life charity fashion gala in London, joining models and other celebrities at the Grosvenor House Hotel, recruited by Sting to support his Rainforest Foundation

July 1992 Her name is linked in the British press with superstar Prince after they are seen leaving a London nightclub together

August 1992 Her final Stock, Aitken and Waterman release is a compilation of 20 numbers entitled *Kylie's Greatest Hits*. It is a runaway success, reaching No. 1 in both the album and video charts. Not so her final Pete Waterman single, 'Celebration', which only reaches No.20 in the UK chart

February 1993 Signs to independent British dance label deConstruction, responsible for pop soul favourites M People. The year marks key restyling of KM – she meets William Baker for the first time

October 1993 Invited by Baz Luhrmann to pose at Universal Studios for world-famous photographer Bert Stern. The '60s-style spread' fills 21 pages of Australian *Vogue*

January 1994 Bridesmaid to Dannii at her wedding to Julian McMahon, soap actor and son of a former prime minister of

Australia. The marriage is over within a year

February 1994 Performs 'What Do I Have To Do?' at the gay Mardi Gras in Sydney

June 1994 In Thailand for the start of filming for *Street Fighter*, in which she takes the female lead, Cammy, alongside Jean-Claude Van Damme

August 1994 Releases her first deConstruction single. 'Confide In Me', 5 minutes long, is a radical departure from Stock, Aitken and Waterman but receives a thumbs-up from fans, reaching No. 2 in Britain, kept off the top spot by Whigfield's 'Saturday Night'

October 1994 Her first deConstruction album, *Kylie Minogue*, is released to critical acclaim. It features arrangements and mixes by producers Brothers in Rhythm – one half of that team, Steve Anderson, becomes a long-term friend and collaborator

November 1994 One of her most famous videos accompanies 'Put Yourself In My Place'. She is seen floating in a spacecraft slowly undressing until completely naked. The single, however, only reaches No. 11 in the UK Plays herself in guest appearance on *The Vicar of Dibley*

December 1994 Wins Best Female Solo Singer at the *Smash Hits* awards *Street Fighter* proves to be big Christmas box office, but does nothing for KM's movie career

January 1995 Records 'Where The Wild Roses Grow', a dark and brooding duet with Nick Cave, in Melbourne

February 1995 Films short art-house film *Hayride to Hell* in Sydney. KM plays a psychotic girl who terrorizes a man who gives her a lift home

April 1995 Spends three months making *Bio-Dome*, playing Petra Von Kant, in Los Angeles, during which she has a fling with co-star Pauly Shore. The film is a turkey, however

June 1995 Features on the front cover of *Loaded*, the definitive British lads' magazine

July 1995 Meets photographer Stephane Sednaoui at a party. Shortly afterwards spends three weeks driving across the USA with him
The final single from the *Kylie Minogue* album, 'Where Is The Feeling?', only reaches No. 16 in the UK

August 1995 Performs live at a rock festival for the first time when, backed by a 9-piece band, she performs in front of 30,000 at the 'T in the Park' in Glasgow. Cave joins her on stage to perform 'Where The Wild Roses Grow'

October 1995 'Where The Wild Roses Grow' released; reaches No.11 in UK but does better in Australia, climbing to No. 2. The video features an apparently dead Kylie floating face up in a lake
Appears on stage for an AIDS benefit at the Royal Albert Hall to perform a duet with Elton John (in drag) of 'Sisters Are Doing It For Themselves'

January 1996 KM has no record releases in 1996 but performs live throughout the year, beginning with the 'Big Day Out' concerts in Australia with Nick Cave and his band, The Bad Seeds

July 1996 Kylie reads words to 'I Should Be So Lucky' at the Poetry Olympics at the Royal Albert Hall

August 1996 Hard at work on her next album, taking her most active role to date in the material and writing all the lyrics. In London, performs 'Where The Wild Roses Grow' with Nick Cave at the Brixton Academy

October 1996 'Where The Wild Roses Grow' wins Best Single, Best Pop Release and Best Song of the Year at the Australian Record Industry Awards

December 1996 Appears on stage in London with Manic Street Preachers, performing their song 'Little Baby Nothing'

January 1997 Her second deConstruction album was due for release this month, but is put back. The original plan for exclusive collaboration with Brothers in Rhythm is scrapped in favour of KM working with a number of producers, including Manic Street Preachers

February 1997 Appears on British TV in a special episode of comedy series *Men Behaving Badly* in aid of Comic Relief

May 1997 Makes a special appearance with Ray Charles and Australian rock legend John Farnham at the opening of world's largest casino in Melbourne. Elton John is among 1,500 guests

August 1997 Performs 'Some Kind of Bliss', written by Manic Street Preachers, at the Radio 1 Roadshow in Newquay, Cornwall. Song will be first single released from her new album *Impossible Princess*. However, the death of Diana, Princess of Wales in Paris prompts a radical rethink of album title and marketing

September 1997 'Some Kind of Bliss' flops, only reaching No. 22 in the UK chart. James Dean Bradfield of Manic Street Preachers later says he failed Kylie
Records MTV special *Some Kind of Kylie*
Wins award for Most Stylish Female Pop Star at the *Elle* magazine style awards in London
Release of the new album is put back until after Christmas

October 1997 Goes ahead with filming video for 'Did It Again', the second single from the new album. It features four Kylie 'personas' in battle with each other

November 1997 Relationship with Sednaoui ends
Michael Hutchence found dead in a Sydney hotel room. Kylie attends funeral at St Andrew's Cathedral, Sydney

December 1997 'Did It Again' is another disappointment, only reaching No. 14 in the UK

February 1998 Performs at the Sydney gay Mardi Gras. Sister Dannii does the 2 a.m. show while Kylie goes on at 4 a.m. to perform 'Better The Devil You Know'

March 1998 'Breathe', the third single from the new album, also only reaches No. 14

Album finally released in UK under the title *Kylie Minogue In Europe*. It just scrapes into the album chart at No.10

May 1998 KM turns 30

June 1998 A new-look Kylie starts tour in Australia. The Intimate & Live Show, with its camp, Las Vegas-show atmosphere, is received rapturously

August 1998 Leaves deConstruction by 'amicable agreement'.

London concerts grab rave reviews in the national press

December 1998 Kylie is honoured at the annual Australian Export Awards in Sydney where she receives a special award for selling more than 30 million records up to that point

March 1999 Plays Miranda in a version of Shakespeare's *The Tempest* in Barbados

April 1999 In New York to record 'The Reflex' with Ben Lee for a Duran Duran tribute album

May 1999 In Adelaide, shoots cameo role in teen horror movie *Cut*, in which she suffers a grisly death

Signs for The Beatles' old record label, Parlophone, the start of a carefully planned musical comeback

July 1999 In Vienna for the annual Life Ball, takes to the catwalk in the Imperial Palace to raise money for AIDS charities

October 1999 Publication of acclaimed book *Kylie*, a photographic journey through images of KM and her life

December 1999 Wearing a revealing Santa outfit, entertains 10,000 Australian troops who are part of a peacekeeping force in East Timor and who will not be home for Christmas

January 2000 Meets British model James Gooding at a pool party in Los Angeles

June 2000 Photo of her bottom appears on the front page of the *Sun*

July 2000 'Spinning Around', her first release on Parlophone, becomes the first of her singles to debut at No. 1 on the UK chart

August 2000 Special guest on Robbie Williams's *Top of the Pops* special performing their duet 'Kids'

October 2000 Performs 'Dancing Queen' and 'On A Night Like This' at the closing ceremony of the Olympic Games in Sydney. The global audience is estimated at 3.7 billion. Less than three weeks later she sings at the opening ceremony of the Paralympics

The album *Light Years* reaches No. 2 in the UK album chart, but fills the top spot in Australia

'Kids' reaches No. 2 on the UK chart

November 2000 Kylie and Robbie duet at the MTV Europe Awards in Stockholm before a worldwide TV audience of 1 billion

December 2000 Films her role as The Green Fairy in *Moulin Rouge*

February 2001 Makes Pepsi commercial in Australia

Appears as a guest on *An Audience with Ricky Martin*, sharing a duet on his biggest hit, 'Livin' La Vida Loca'

March 2001 The On A Night Like This world tour opens in Glasgow. KM performs 19 songs, opening with 'Loveboat' and closing with 'Spinning Around'

April 2001 Launches her own brand of lingerie, 'Love Kylie x'

Performs a record 9 sellout nights at the Sydney Entertainment Centre. Ticket sales in Australia alone net $8 million

August 2001 Stars at the V2001 Festival in Weston Park, Staffordshire and Chelmsford, Essex. At the latter she

performs 12 numbers to an audience that had been drenched in the rain
An Australian album called *Corroboration* features a duet between KM and Aussie folk singer Jimmy Little. The song, 'Bury Me Deep In Love', had been the background music in *Neighbours* when Charlene's mother Madge married Harold Bishop

September 2001 'Can't Get You Our Of My Head' races to the top of the Australian charts, displacing 'Bob the Builder'. Her seventh No. 1 in her home country, it sells 140,000 copies in its first week of release. A week later it becomes her sixth UK No. 1, selling 77,000 copies on its first day on sale. KM sells more records (306,000) than the rest of the Top 10 combined, including Victoria Beckham, who languishes at No. 6
Makes her first British TV advertisement as the face of Eurostar. She is seen catching a train from London to Paris
Wins *GQ* magazine's Services to Mankind Award

October 2001 *An Audience with Kylie Minogue* is broadcast in the UK. Kermit the Frog and Adam Garcia appear as guest stars; Brendan, Dannii and Pete Waterman are in the 'audience'
'Can't Get You Out Of My Head' stays as the UK No. 1 for 4 weeks, keeping Michael Jackson's long awaited 'You Rock My World' off the top spot
Tickets for her 2002 British tour sell out in one hour
Sings the theme tune for the new TV soap *Night and Day*
Named Best Female Solo Artist at the Australian Record Industry Awards, the Arias

November 2001 Wins a Bambi, Germany's top pop award, for Best Comeback of the Year
A pair of her knickers raises £4,000 as

part of a fashion package auctioned in aid of BBC *Children In Need*
Kylie tops the list of 100 greatest Welsh women
Fever, Kylie's second Parlophone album, reaches No. 1 in the UK album charts

December 2001 Wins two of the inaugural *Top of the Pops* awards for Best Single and Best Tour
'Can't Get You Out Of My Head' is placed third in the Record of the Year contest on UK TV; the winner is S Club 7's 'Don't Stop Moving'
Her advertisement for underwear firm Agent Provocateur is considered too sexy for a TV audience

February 2002 'Can't Get You Out Of My Head' tops the US dance charts and enters the *Billboard* Top 100
Appears on the *Tonight Show with Jay Leno* as part of US publicity campaign
Fever released in the USA
'In Your Eyes' enters UK chart at No. 3
Wins two Brit awards for Best International Album and Best International Female

March 2002 *Fever* debuts on US chart at No. 3, selling 107,000 copies in first week. It is her highest ever album position in the US
Crowned Bestselling Australian Artist at the World Music Awards in Monaco. She performs at the ceremony wearing a short red dress by Dolce & Gabbana and thigh-high black boots. Allegedly, Prince Albert of Monaco gropes her bottom

April 2002 Kylie begins her most ambitious world tour to date at the Cardiff Arena. 25 UK dates would be followed by a further 13 in Europe leading up to 12 in August in Australia. William Baker and Kylie devised a show borrowing style from Dr Who, Star Trek, David Bowie's Diamond Dogs. Photos of Kylie in a white boiler suit and black bowler hat also revealed a link to the notorious film A Clockwork Orange. Kylie's break-up from James Gooding becomes public.

July 2002 Madame Tussaud's unveils Kylie waxwork which forms centre point of new interactive exhibition. Kylie is on all fours and breathes seductively 'I Can't Get You Out Of My Head' at passers-by. Visitors ignore the 'Do Not Touch' sign. Her DVD/video 'Live In Sydney' is banned in Malaysia where authorities consider it too hot.

She cancels US tour claiming she wants to devote more time to private life. She admits to having 'faint' cellulite.

October 2002 The awards keep coming . . . Kylie is named Woman of the Year at Elle style awards. She is also second in a VH1 poll of the 100 most important women in music history. She is named 29th most powerful person in the music industry – for once ahead of Madonna. She is nominated for four MTV Europe music awards and six Arias's (the Australian Record Industry Awards).

Travels with mother Carol to a remote retreat in Western Australia for complete rest following reported breakdown.

Kylie attends Paris Motor Show as the face of Ford Streetka and is paid £350,000 for a five minute appearance. She signs a special pedal car version for the Great Ormond Street Children's Hospital in London.

about the
author

Sean Smith is a former UK national newspaper columnist who is fast becoming one of the country's leading celebrity biographers. His first biography, Sophie's Kiss, revealed the story of the love affair between Prince Edward and Sophie Rhys Jones. He followed it with Stone Me! a Rolling Stones companion. His latest book J.K. Rowling: A Biography has been praised worldwide and translated into fourteen languages. He lives in West London.